The Sociology of Canadian Mennonites, Hutterites and Amish:
A Bibliography with Annotations

Edited by

Donovan E. Smucker

Canadian Cataloguing in Publication Data

Smucker, Donovan E., 1915-
    The sociology of Canadian Mennonites, Hutterites
and Amish

Includes index.
ISBN 0-88920-052-1 bd.   ISBN 0-88920-051-3 pa.

1. Mennonites in Canada - Bibliography.   2. Hutterite
Brethren - Canada - Bibliography.   3. Amish in
Canada - Bibliography.   I. Title.

Z7845.M4S58   016.2897'71   C77-001545-X

Wilfrid Laurier University Press
Waterloo, Ontario, Canada
N2L 3C5

Cover design by R. B. MacDonald
using illustrations by Peter Etril Snyder

To Barbara

whose recent novel based on Canadian history was the catalyst for this book on Canadian sociology

Table of Contents

IV. Amish, Holdeman, Old Order Mennonites and Old Colony Mennonites

Preface and Acknowledgements

This book emerged from the realization that an enormous expansion of scholarly activity has focused on the Mennonites, Amish and Hutterites of North America; and that Canadian universities from McGill to British Columbia were in the forefront of this expanded interest; and that the social science disciplines, principally sociology, were the centre of the copious research.

Smaller bibliographies without annotation were published in the *Mennonite Quarterly Review* and *Mennonite Life*. Professor A. J. Klassen in the States is completing a massive 25,000-item bibliography without annotations covering every field of interest from the sixteenth century to 1961. Against this background, it seemed wise to develop an annotated bibliography focusing on the recent social and cultural life of the Mennonites, Amish and Hutterites of Canada as a tool for scholars who needed better information concerning the nature of the item cited.

The four categories of books, theses, articles and unpublished manuscripts were chosen as available in the English language with only a few items in German from the pens of scholars in North America. While the choice of subject matter is principally from Canada, some titles from the U.S. and the U.K. were included when these provided reliable context for similar groups here.

In launching the work I was aware that the Mennonites are divided into two main groups because of different origins in Europe (Switzerland and Russia) and different times and styles of migration; that there is different social organization from Hutterite communalism, Old Order Mennonite semi-communalism, and mainline individualism supplemented by enormous cooperation on programs around the world. I was also aware that some are sub-cultures and the Hutterites are a counter-culture. Highly varied patterns of conflict and assimilation, stratification and equality, socialization and dissent, social norms and spontaneity and communal versus individualist responses are present. The reader is urged to read the introductory essay for further clues on these matters.

It is the hope of the editor that this book will underscore the need for communication among the scores of scholars who are at work without much awareness of what is being done in other institutions. The "in-group" research of Mennonites may be an exception to this but the sociological research is now mainly in the hands of the non-Mennonites.

Scholarly activity is cooperative experience in which many persons work with a chairperson like myself. Hence, I am happy to acknowledge the contributions of others.

Without two grants from Canada Council the book could not have been written. A Canada Council research grant permitted me to have two research assistants, Judy Wasylycia Leis and Sharon Mathies, and to finance field trips to the Prairie universities and to duplicate hundreds of items. The book has been published with the help of a grant from the Humanities Research Council of Canada, using funds provided by the Canada Council. This subvention was utilized by Wilfrid Laurier University Press and its excellent director, Norman Wagner. The University of Waterloo provided a small grant permitting a crucial retyping of the manuscript with the help of Karen Bowman. It was, however, Pauline Jahnke Bauman whose long experience with manuscript preparation proved to be most helpful.

The Conrad Grebel College library, now located in a splendid new building, aided considerably with the assistance of Irma Kadela and Mary Kramer. The Arts Library of the University of Waterloo was especially cooperative in procurement of inter-library loans. My colleagues on the faculty have always provided a stimulating environment because of the presence of some of the leading Mennonite scholars of North America.

Four outstanding scholars of Mennonite culture read the manuscript: Leo Driedger of the University of Manitoba; Leland Harder of the Associated Mennonite Biblical Seminaries; and my two colleagues, J. Winfield Fretz and Frank H. Epp.

Peter Etril Snyder, artist-in-residence at Conrad Grebel College during 1977, provided illustrations from Waterloo County Mennonite life.

Conrad Grebel College   *Donovan E. Smucker*
University of Waterloo
Waterloo, Ontario

January, 1977

Introduction*

This 800-item annotated bibliography on the sociology of Canadian
Mennonites, Amish, and Hutterites was developed by the present
writer and research assistants under a Canada Council grant. It includes books, graduate theses, pamphlets, articles and unpublished
sources.

The three groups are considered together because of common
origins in the radical Anabaptist Reformation of sixteenth-century
Europe; and, proximity of residence in Canada and common projects
through the Mennonite Central Committee at the present time. While
the Amish and Hutterites have similar orientations wherever they are
found, the Mennonites are so varied that the single term needs constant qualification. They differ in technology ranging from Old Order
Mennonites, who reject automobiles, to progressives who sell them.
They differ in European origins in Holland and Switzerland with most
of the latter migrating to the United States before coming in the early
1800's to Ontario in covered wagons. Again, community structures are
present in large variety from communal to ethnic villages in large cities.
Moreover, schism has created fourteen different ecclesiastical bodies
of Mennonites in Ontario alone.

As Canadian sociologists have practiced empirical research the 182,000
Mennonites from Halifax to Vancouver have provided excellent possibilities for many studies. The universities of Toronto, Waterloo,
Manitoba, Saskatchewan, Alberta and British Columbia are the major
centers of research with Manitoba the most active under Professor Leo
Driedger. In addition to the centers of research in Canada there is
genuine interaction with sociologists in the States, particularly among
scholars with Mennonite background in Indiana and Pennsylvania.

---

* Original version of Introduction presented to annual meetings of Canadian Sociology and Anthropology Association, University of Toronto, 1974.

John Hostetler, the leading scholar of Amish and Hutterite studies, started his career at Alberta and is now teaching at Temple. In 1973-74 James Urry of Oxford spent half of the year in Canada studying the Russian Mennonites in connection with a doctoral dissertation.

Moving from general to empirical research, the methods include questionnaire, observer and participant observer. The initial focus on the cultural is being replaced by the cross-cultural as, for example, Alan Anderson's dissertation at Saskatchewan focusing on the area around Rosthern. Categories in current research include demography, family, education, community organization, social aspects of church organization, cultural patterns such as leisure and mass media, migration and urbanization, technology and economic activities, competition and conflict including race, ethnicity and nationality; acculturation and assimilation, mutual aid and the sociology of evangelism. Key categories are acculturation and assimilation. Or, both under the rubric of social change.

Models of the change process from social theorists include Troeltsch and the sect-church typology; the refinement of Troeltsch by Park and Burgess in the sect-cycle; Yinger's restatement of Troeltsch; Redfield's folk-urban dichotomy; Toennie's Gemeinschaft and Gesellschaft typology; Littell's conception of free church voluntaryism; Weber's distinction between charismatic and bureaucratic, and Gordon's analysis of assimilation.

It was Troeltsch who provided the first model for the study of Mennonites, Amish and Hutterites in his great book of 1911. In 1931 Edmund George Kaufman used a version of this typology in a Chicago dissertation on North American Mennonites.[1] To this day sociological studies of Mennonites are applying various versions of Troeltsch's model with its emphasis on dynamic, prophetic, anti-hierarchical, primary fellowships over against institutionalized structures of religion at peace with the culture.

Leland Harder has accepted Yinger's elaboration of Troeltsch in his study of North American Mennonites as an established sect which is not a denomination but a sect which has undergone social change due to the training of its offspring, the admitting of new members and the stablizing of its structures.[2] Harder has argued that social change in sects, established or youthful, is not primarily due to outside stimulation but structural disequilibrium, a concept he found in Godfrey and

---

[1] *The Development of the Missionary and Philanthropic Interest Among the Mennonites of North America* (Berne: The Mennonite Book Concern, 1931).

[2] Leland Harder, "The Quest for Equilibrium in an Established Sect, A Study of Social Change in the General Conference Mennonite Church" (unpublished Ph.D. dissertation, Northwestern University, 1962).

Monica Wilson's *The Analysis of Social Change* (Cambridge, 1954). This structural inconsistency in Mennonites is the conflict between voluntaryism and separatism. The voluntary aspect impels the sect to a conversionist character which is incompatible with the separatist, hence, the tendency to pursue one at the expense of the other.

In passing we may note that Harder is the premier demographer of North American Mennonites, making an intensive analysis of Steinbach, Manitoba and a comparative demographic analysis of two associations or conferences of Mennonites in the U.S. and Canada.[3] He has also utilized the work of Lenski, Glock and Stark to refine his research instruments.

As co-author of *Anabaptists Four Centuries Later. A Profile of Five Mennonite and Brethren in Christ Denominations*, (Kitchener, 1975) Harder has completed the first sociological study of Canadian and American Mennonites utilizing a sophisticated, computerized statistical methodology. This book presents evidence that contemporary Mennonites are in continuity with the normative sixteenth century. The new revisionist scholars disagree with this conclusion.

Calvin Redekop is best known for his study of the Old Colony Mennonites who came to Canada from Russia in 1874 and then migrated to Mexico in the twenties.[4] The move to Mexico was prompted by the pressure from the Manitoba Ministry of Education to anglicize the schools as part of a general mood of nativism which developed in World War I. Redekop's study confirms Harder's theory of structural disequilibrium whereby a vital relationship to society was sacrificed for a rigorous separatism. In rejecting the Manitoba establishment the Old Colony Mennonites created an established church and society which negated their Anabaptist voluntaryism. Now the young people are born into an Old Colony society from which they cannot, for all practical purposes, escape. In many ways this has been the central dilemma of many Mennonite, Amish and Hutterite attempts at developing a counter-culture. The counter-culture becomes a new culture in which deviance and dissent are rendered inoperative.

Redekop has also contributed to the debate on Troeltsch in arguing that powerful sectarian traits can operate even when voluntaryism is eroded by the counter-culture establishment of birthright membership. Meanwhile, Leo Driedger and associates at the Univeristy of Manitoba are breaking fresh ground in Winnipeg urbanization studies among the largest urban concentration of Mennonites in Canada—17,850 to be exact. These studies are also unique because in

---

[3] *Steinbach and its Churches* (Elkhart: Mennonite Biblical Seminary, 1970).

[4] Calvin Redekop, *The Old Colony Mennonites* (Baltimore: The Johns Hopkins Press, 1969).

1974 the Canadian Mennonite population became more urban than rural. Driedger notes that "the number of Mennonites living in Cana-dian cities is of little significance unless we can ascertain whether they are maintaining their identity in the city or whether they are assimilating. Furthermore, the urban quality of the identity maintenance by those living in the city must be assessed as either a transferral of rural community into the city forming islands of ethnic villagers who cling to rural values, or a metropolitan remnant which loves the city but does not succumb to urban seductions."[5]

Mennonite sociologists describe the Mennonite rural community as a social structural community in equilibrium: "a stable, predictable, little changing small community where gemeinschaft living is the ideal."[6] Driedger's studies indicate that this ethnic village model can be transplanted into the city. The ethnic village traits of territorial control, institutional completeness, cultural identity and social distance are flourishing in the city on the basis of cross-cultural research with the French, Jewish, German, Ukrainian, Polish, Scandinavian and British populations of Winnipeg. The territorial control is working in North Kildonan, suburban satellite village of Winnipeg with scores of Mennonite businesses in the center and the outskirts of the area. Letkemann and Siemens describe similar concentrations in Vancouver and Martensville, the urban Mennonite halfway house near Saskatoon. Driedger's studies suggest that the Mennonite identity is above the Scandinavians and Poles but below the Jews and French.

After establishing that territorial control, institutional completeness, cultural identity and social distance were successfully transferred to the city, Driedger declares that it is not acceptable as a model for Mennonites. The ethnic villager cum urban villager is incompatible with the dynamisms of Christian community which require the villagers to recruit new members from untypical backgrounds and, in general, to increase interaction and sophistication.

Driedger is also a sociologist with historical imagination. His essay, "Native Rebellion and Mennonite Invasion: An Examination of Canadian River Valleys,"[7] tests the thesis that "Mennonites, although historically suspicious of governments, have on numerous occasions reaped settlement benefits from government eviction of minority groups. Specifically, we hypothesize that Mennonites were able to settle in large concentrations on Canadian prairies only because the Canadian gov-

---

[5] Leo Driedger, "Canadian Mennonite Urbanism: Ethnic Villages or Metropolitan Remnant?" *MQR*, XLIX, 3 (July, 1975), p. 226.

[6] *Ibid.*, p. 228. By 1975 Driedger finally refined his methodology for studying urban Mennonites, principally in Winnipeg, in relation to other minorities and the host society. He is a vigorous opponent of assimilation as the deterministic fate of minorities.

[7] *Mennonite Quarterly Review*, XLVI (1972).

ernment had cleared away Indians and Metis in the West. Ironically, such settlement opportunities were associated with violence, while Mennonites were greatly concerned with establishing nonviolent communities."[8]

Driedger warns that sociologists have been preoccupied with the establishment and equilibrium of Mennonite communities leaving the impression that "radical theology, migrations and conscientious objection to war were but minor events in Mennonite preoccupation with building stable communities. Very little has been written about Mennonite relations with the peoples they contacted and often replaced. Such contact creates a dynamic which reveals conflict and stress as an integral part of Mennonite life and history, and which could perhaps be examined better with a change or dialectical method."[9]

In contrast to the Manitoba cross-cultural studies in urbanization and the minor motif of out-group relations in the nineteenth century settlements, Anderson of Saskatchewan University used cross-cultural methods in a rural setting of Saskatchewan to test the reality of the Canadian cultural mosaic which grants considerable autonomy to ethnic groups rather than melting them down to a bland consensus. The nine groups studied lived in bloc settlements in the north central part of the province. Included were Hutterites and Russian Mennonites.

Considering rankings on preservation of identity, speaking the mother tongue, traditional religious affiliation, folkways of food and dress, Anderson added them together and concluded that the Hutterites have "by far" the best defined identity followed by Ukrainian Catholics, Polish Catholics, French, Ukrainian Orthodox, Mennonites, and Doukhobors in fairly close sequence. Only the Scandinavian and German Catholics were rapidly moving toward assimilation.

Driedger's research in urban culture placed Mennonites at the very top of identity in cross-cultural studies. In rural Saskatchewan the Mennonites are near the top and clearly separated from the two groups moving toward the mainstream. Anderson believes that a more sophisticated approach is needed to understand a long continuum form a segregated non-assimilated type to an integrated assimilated type. On this continuum Anderson appears to doubt that the vertical mosaic can survive the assimilatory trends in Canadian society. But, his doubts are surrounded by many qualifications which deny a simple answer. "The study described in detail," Anderson concluded, "how the assimilation of each ethno-religious group may have been related to complex sets of conditional, causal and concomitant factors."[10]

---

[8] *Ibid.*, p. 290.

[9] *Ibid.*

[10] Alan Betts Anderson, "Assimilation in the Bloc Settlements of North Central Saskatchewan" (unpublished Ph.D. dissertation, University of Saskatchewan, 1972), p. 375.

If the best sociological research in recent years has focused on Canadian Mennonites who migrated from Russia, it is appropriate to note
that the dean of Mennonite sociologists, J. Winfield Fretz of Conrad
Grebel College, University of Waterloo, has been studying the Waterloo County (Ontario) Mennonites for the past ten years with plans for a
comprehensive book utilizing these researches due for early completion.

Nearly 13,000 Mennonites live in the county with a variety of backgrounds and patterns unequalled in North America. Fretz has paid
particularly close attention to technological change among the Old
Order Mennonites and the inter-Mennonite "ladder" whereby shifts
toward conservative or liberal can take place *within* the spectrum of
Mennonites by changing conference and congregational affiliation.
Fretz conducts research like an anthropologist with a minimum of conceptualization and a maximum of descriptive data on family,
economic practice, customs, technology and religion. The completion
of his work will add much to our knowledge of the "Plain People" and
the continuum on which the different Mennonite groups are found.

These samples of current direction in sociological research concerning Canadian Mennonites are meant to reveal the richness and sophistication of current scholarship. They cannot reveal the enormous
output of scholars in at least six major universities of Canada and
interaction with scholars in the States with similar and often identical
interests. The increasingly sophisticated tools of research clearly suggest deepened understanding of the Mennonites in Canada.

If sociologists were looking for an ideal source for research it would
be difficult to improve on the Hutterites of North America who have
400 years of social and genetic continuity within isolated communities.
For Canadians there is an additional asset: most of the colonies are in
their country within the prairie provinces.

Starting with Lee Emerson Deets' *The Hutterites: A Study of Social
Cohesion* (Gettysburg, 1939) scholars have been impressed with the
clarity of their ideology, the effectiveness of their nurture and discipline, the homogeneity and the high birth rate. Concurrent with the
scholarship of the sociologists, psychologists and geneticists, two historians of distinction clarified the rich background in European history: A. J. F. Ziegelschmid recovered and published the remarkable
diary which the Hutterites have kept for four centuries; and Robert
Friedmann delineated their originality as Christian communists and
wrote on their unique pottery (Haban Fayence), barber-surgeons,
marriage patterns and social structure.[11]

---

[11] Ziegelschmidt was affiliated with Northwestern University and Friedmann with
Western Michigan University. See Robert Friedmann, *Hutterite Studies* (Goshen, Ind.:
Mennonite Historical Society, 1961).

Thus the work started by Deets was operating in the widening context of historical and sociological understanding. His work was followed by the mental health studies of Eaton and Weil, later supplemented by Kaplan and Plaut. The outside world was surprised by the minimal amount of mental illness among an isolated group which would appear to be under-stimulated and repressed.

The Canadian Mental Health Association study of 1953 extended research into social psychology among the Hutterites of Saskatchewan, noting the misconceptions which lead to scapegoating because local farmers see the colonies as threats to the cohesion, prosperity and educational growth of their communities.

Karl Peter studied the Weberian thesis on Protestantism and the development of a capitalistic outlook. While the Hutterites have many of the traits of the Protestant ethic such as frugality, innovation, and hard work, the social relations of the Hutterite colonies block the development of a capitalistic spirit. Liberated by a progressive view of technology (unlike the Amish and Old Colony Mennonites) the economic success of the Hutterites has continued to impress students of their social patterns.

In the vast output of research on the Hutterites the most impressive finding is innovation without acculturation: "Innovation is selective, managed and tends to be consistent from the viewpoint of the dominant goal of communal living. Innovation does not alter the internal heirarchy and social structure." This is a finding of Hostetler's definitive work, in *Hutterite Society* (Baltimore: Johns Hopkins, 1974). This represents skilled social management and planning of the highest order. In any case, the Hutterites have cooperated with many scholars making field studies since Deets published 38 years ago. On the whole, the results of this research have been positive for the oldest example of Christian communism in the world. Against the background of the precarious existence of communes in the contemporary youth culture the Hutterites are not social curios but communities which have survived persecution, migration, hostile legislation and empirical sociologists.

Future agendas for research should include a cross-colony comparison of the more progressive Hutterite colonies in New York, Pennsylvania, and Ontario with those in the Prairies in order to assess the effects of the progressive colonies in permitting educational and cultural sophistication while maintaining rigorous discipline and group cohesion. An additional problem for research is the impact of corporate wealth of the colony as a vicarious substitute for private property. Finally, research should probe into the continued intranisgence of the Hutterites toward all forms of government welfare and agricultural subsidy; and, the possibility of providing all of these services in health care outside of government plans.

In sharp contrast to the number of Hutterite studies in Canada is the paucity of work on the Amish with the plausible explanation of smallness in numbers here (nine congregations with 906 members in Ontario compared to eighty districts and 6,808 members in Ohio). Moreover, this is an area of research dominated by one man, John Hostetler of Temple University. Born and raised in the Amish fellowship, Hostetler has continued in rapport with his people despite rejection of their ban on higher education and movement to other religious affiliation. Hostetler's *Amish Society* supplemented by twenty scholarly articles and monographs are the definitive publications on Amish culture.

Using Redfield's concept of little communities (small, self-sufficient, distinctiveness) and Malinowski's conception of charter as the normative features of a social system, Hostetler describes how the charter is applied and, most important, the changes such as the continued use of propane gas in the kitchen stove in place of the electric stove which is banned.

The Amish restraint of technology is one of the most interesting struggles in a technological society. Unfortunately, this intransigent stand has become a tourist attraction in Lancaster, Pennsylvania and Nappanee, Indiana, where thousands of people come to observe these strange people who are holding out against some of the clearest symbols of the twentieth century, such as cars and TV. It is now possible that Ontario may duplicate this tourist culture in connection with the Old Order Mennonites of Elmira. Sociological research itself may strain the right to privacy, but tourism changes these people into the inhabitants of a sociological zoo.

Hundreds of books, graduate theses and articles provide data of increasing reliability to understand the diverse minorities known as Mennonites, Amish and Hutterites. As the Canadian identity is more clearly delineated, these studies will likely stay in the context of the cross-cultural as the nation seeks that highest goal of a democratic society, unity in diversity.

I. Bibliography and Social Theory

Abbreviations used throughout the bibliography include: *ME* for *Mennonite Encyclopaedia*; *ML* for *Mennonite Life*; *MQR* for *Mennonite Quarterly Review*.

A. Bibliography and Social Theory

BENDER, HAROLD S.; KRAHN, CORNELIUS; and GINGERICH, MELVIN (ED.)
The Mennonite Encyclopedia. 4 vols. Hillsboro, Kansas: Mennonite Brethren Publishing House; Newton, Kansas: Mennonite Publication Office; and Scottdale, Pennsylvania: Mennonite Publishing House, 1955-1959.

> This four-volume work is a major bibliographic resource for research on Mennonites throughout the world. Although its focus is more historical than sociological, it is still important to consult this encyclopedia on most topics. A second edition appeared 1969-1973. A full revision is scheduled for 1980.

CANADIAN DEPARTMENT OF CITIZENSHIP AND IMMIGRATION: ECONOMIC AND SOCIAL RESEARCH BRANCH
Citizenship, Immigration and Ethnic Groups in Canada: A Bibliography of Research, Published and Unpublished Sources, 1920-1958; 1959-1961; 1962-1964; and 1964-1968. Ottawa: Queen's Printer, 1961, 1962, 1964, and 1970.

> This bibliography provides an up-to-date account of material written on Canadian ethnic groups. Included in the section on

specific ethnic groups are the Mennonites and Hutterites. The
bibliography is far from being an exhaustive one.

CLASEN, CLAUS-PETER
*Anabaptism, A Social History 1525-1618, Switzerland, Austria, Moravia,
South and Central Germany.* Ithaca: Cornell University Press, 1972.

A carefully crafted book of major importance by a scholar claim-
ing to be free of all value commitments.

The social history of the Anabaptists and Hutterites is crucial to
grasp the early radical views of revolution, government, war, law,
oaths, property, commerce, usury, marriage, divorce and the
position of women.

In assessing the social and political impact of the Anabaptists
and Hutterites Clasen finally reveals his own conservative value
commitments (p. 425) in viewing the Anabaptists as a potential
threat to civilization. The descriptive material can be read without
affirming the author's conclusions.

CRYSDALE, STEWART and MONTMINY, JEAN-PAUL
*Religion in Canada. Annotated Inventory of Scientific Studies in
Religion—1945-1972.* Downsview: York University Press; Quebec:
Les Presses de L'Universite Laval, 1974, 189 pp.

The first bilingual survey of religious life in Canada stressing
formal research design conceived in empirical terms. Ten social
science disciplines are considered. In Mennonite research the
studies of Leo Driedger in Winnipeg are featured. A useful
addition to bibliographic tools but not comprehensive enough in
all aspects of current research dealing with Mennonites, Hutterites and Amish.

CRYSDALE, STEWART and WHEATCROFT, LES (EDS.)
Religion in Canadian Society. Toronto: Macmillan of Canada, 1976.
498 pp.

A compilation of thirty-three articles by sociologists, historians and
anthropologists on nine topics including Bennett on the Hutterites
and Driedger and Peters on Germanic connections of Winnipeg
Mennonites. It is the first symposium of this type providing the
wider Canadian context for Mennonites, Hutterites and Amish
studies. The fifty-six page introduction is mainly devoted to the
theories and methods in sociology of religion with only twelve pages
given to the interpretation of religion in Canadian society. The
introduction also contains a debatable definition of religion.

DRIEDGER, LEO
"In Search of Cultural Identity Factors." *The Canadian Review of
Sociology and Anthropology,* 12:2 (May, 1975), pp. 150-162.

Concentrating on the largest group of urban Mennonites in the world, Leo Driedger of the University of Manitoba has found Winnipeg to be the best laboratory to develop a multi-dimensional approach to cultural identity based on the six factors of religion, endogamy, language use, ethnic organizations, parochial education and choice of in-group friends. In this study which climaxes similar research for the past twenty years, Driedger locates Mennonites as Germans in the mosaic with British, Ukrainians, French, Dutch, Poles, Scandinavians and Jews.

Mennonite-Germans emerge in their identity below the Jews and French but above the Scandinavians and Poles, stressing *gemeinschaft*, high church participation, parochial education, endogamy; but they are weakest of all groups in voluntary associations.

Driedger's Ethnic Cultural Inventory is a major contribution to the study of cultural identity in Canada and now awaits his application of it to another large group of urban Mennonites in Windsor, London, Kitchener-Waterloo, Toronto and Ottawa, Ontario. And, of course, the relation of these Mennonites to their cultural neighbors in the vertical mosaic.

The appended bibliography includes important background literature which has made minority studies one of the exciting parts of social science in recent years. Over-simplified assimilationist views have been countered by empirical studies and conceptual revision by many scholars.

EPP, FRANK H.
Mennonites in Canada, 1786-1920. The History of a Separate People. Toronto: Macmillan of Canada, 1974, 480 pp.

Although Epp writes primarily as a historian, this book is indispensable to the social scientist because of its painstaking research of original sources, comprehensive bibliography, massive footnotes, twenty maps and charts, forty-five tables and critical analysis of issues. Chapter Nine, for example, "The East and West Reserves," can be read with profit by any sociologist seeking to understand the failure to recreate the Russian Commonwealth in Manitoba. If the reader wants to pursue the topic of Reserves further the twenty-seven footnotes provide a quick guide to the sources.

In any case, it is a major tool for the study of Canadian minorities.

FRANCIS, E. K.
"A Bibliography on the Mennonites in Manitoba." *Mennonite Quarterly Review*, XXVII (July 1953), pp. 238-248.

This bibliography was compiled in connection with a research project on the Mennonites in Manitoba. Special works on the

Manitoba Mennonites and their authors are presented in the introduction. The bibliography is divided into subject headings such as, From the First Immigration to World War I, The School Question, From the End of World War I to the End of World War II, and the Mennonite Churches and Brotherhoods in Manitoba.

FRETZ, J. WINFIELD
Mennonite Colonization; Lessons from the Past for the Future. Akron, Penn.: The Mennonite Central Committee, 1944.

This is a general introduction to the field of Mennonite migration and colonization with practical suggestions for future action. The booklet begins with a valuable summary of the religious, economic, social, and psychological causes of Mennonite migration. This is followed by a description of the types of colonization and the reasons why Mennonites colonize rather than settle in scattered areas as independent farm units. Author states that the nature of the Mennonite Church, with its emphasis on Christian brotherhood and on separation from the rest of society, is the basic reason for Mennonite colonization. Also discussed are the factors contributing to success in Mennonite colonization which include religion, the practice of Christian mutual aid, willingness to work hard and live simply, geographic and economic conditions, and adequate financial credit. Colonization failure is shown to be a result of inadequate preparation, lack of leadership, absence of group consciousness, and internal conflicts.

FRETZ, J. WINFIELD
"Mennonite Mutual Aid: A Contribution Toward the Establishment of a Christian Community." Unpublished Ph.D. dissertation, Chicago, 1941.

In this thesis, the author shows that mutual aid as demonstrated by the Mennonites is a contributing factor toward the development of Christian community. The study is divided into three main areas: the general nature and background of mutual aid; historical data concerning Mennonite mutual aid; and the interpretation of the significance of Mennonite mutual aid for the development of a Christian community. This final division is of primary importance in understanding Mennonite mutual aid. For example, the author describes how mutual aid is closely identified with the characteristic behavior of a religious sect. It developed from a folkway to a religious principle and a basic code of ethics. He also shows how mutual aid has served to perpetuate large sections of Mennonites, to reduce social stratification to a minimum, and to distribute economic gains fairly equitable. This dissertation was a pioneer work in the sociological study of Mennonite communities.

FRIESEN, ABRAHAM
Reformation and Utopia, The Marxist Interpretation of the Reformation and Its Antecedents. Wiesbaden: Franz Steiner Verlag GMBH, 1974. 271 pp.

Friesen is a Canadian Mennonite scholar teaching at the University of California who spent two years in Europe researching this book. He has written a critique of Marxist historiography ranging from the pioneering work of Engels and his mentor W. Zimmerman in the nineteenth century to Ernst Bloch and the East German Marxist scholars of today. Pondering the place of the Peasants' War and the violent apocalyptic vision of Thomas Müntzer, the Marxists have wanted to locate crypto-Communism in the left-wing of the Reformation. This book is an achievement of the highest order for an understanding of the explosive moment in European history out of which the Mennonites and Hutterites emerged. Although Friesen is a non-Marxist he is not a polemical ideologist. An important book for intellectual history and social theory.

FRIESEN, J. W.
"Mennonites and Hutterites in Twentieth Century Alberta Literature With Special Reference to Educational Implications." *The Alberta Journal of Educational Research*, XXII, No. 2 (June, 1976), pp. 102-128.

This paper reports on an analysis of a variety of sources of literature dealing with the attitudes of Albertans toward two minority groups, Mennonites and Hutterites, from the turn of the century to the present. The format of the research was to identify, categorize and analyze literature such as personal correspondence, newspaper articles, government documents and research studies, noting specific attitude orientations for each decade. In addition to the primary sources the author includes a valuable forty-three item bibliography of secondary materials. The study questions the depth of acceptance for a pluralist culture and makes recommendations for inter-cultural education.

GIESBRECHT, HERBERT
The Mennonite Brethren: A Bibliographic Guide to Information. Winnipeg: The Christian Press, 1971.

This bibliography, although not complete, includes many significant works on the Mennonite Brethren. It is largely a bibliography of published books and pamphlets, although several of the more revealing articles and theses pertaining to the Mennonite Brethren have been included. The immediate purpose of the bibliography is that of providing a study and research guide for pastors, teachers, and students.

HARDER, LELAND
  Fact Book of Congregational Membership. Newton, Ks.: The General
  Conference Mennonite Church, 1971.

  A statistical book on the census of the General Conference Mennonite Church in Canada and the United States. Census-takers
  from each congregation were used to collect data. Author also
  includes charts, pyramids, and tables to indicate the statistical
  information, and a chapter on instructions for congregational
  self-study. An index of churches is given at the end of the study.
  This is now the most definitive study on the census of the largest
  group of Mennonites in Canada.

HORVATH, MARIA
  A Doukhobor Bibliography. Vancouver: University of British Columbia
  Library, 1972.

  This bibliography includes forty-two entries on Mennonites and
  Hutterites primarily in German. Although a Doukhobor bibliog-
  raphy, it is useful to review the entries when researching the
  Russian Mennonites of Europe and Canada.

HOSTETLER, JOHN A.
  Annotated Bibliography on the Amish. Scottdale, Pa.: Mennonite Publishing House, 1951.

  The focus of this bibliography is intended to be primarily on the
  Old Order Amish and on any directly related Amish group. It
  includes items that are historical, sociological, religious and
  genealogical in nature and its scope includes both Europe and
  America and extends from the origin of the Amish in 1693 to
  1950. The items are classified into ten divisions: general; settlement history; church doctrines and practices; Amish admonitory
  and miscellaneous writings; literature, language and art; hym-
  nology; bibliographies; genealogy; feature articles; and modern
  scientific studies. This was Hostetler's first publication in a distinguished career as bibliographer and scholar. Superceded by subsequent publications by him; but, still valuable.

HOSTETLER, JOHN A.
  "A Bibliography of English Language Materials on the Hutterian
  Brethren." *MQR*, XLIV (January, 1970), pp. 106-113.

  "The objective of this bibliography is to make available a comprehensive bibliography of literature in the English language that
  will be of use both to the specialist and to the general reader." It
  includes many of the most important articles, scattered in a wide
  variety of journals, and dissertations, along with pamphlets, short
  newspaper reports, and purely general descriptions.

KAUFFMAN, J. HOWARD
"Report on Mennonite Sociological Research." *MQR*, XXXVII (April, 1963), pp. 126-131.

The study of Mennonites as a social group has emerged because of a growing concern for strengthening Mennonite rural community life, a concern which arose out of the possibility that the increasing urbanization of Mennonites may be leading to the disintegration of Mennonite beliefs and practices. Also this sociological research has arisen out of a desire to understand the nature and extent of the process of assimilation and a desire to discover how Christian social relationships may be expressed in the Mennonite brotherhood. The report includes a list of writers and a bibliography of doctoral dissertations on contemporary Mennonitism. This bibliography confirms the trend toward sociological study of North American Mennonites since 1945. (See the updating of this survey by Prof. Kauffman in *MQR*.)

KAUFFMAN, J. HOWARD
"Toward a Sociology of the Mennonites." *MQR*, XXX (July, 1956), pp. 3-52.

The main feature of this article is a comprehensive bibliography on the sociology of Mennonites, which includes items that provide some original, empirical data, that are concerned with one or more substantial aspects on the social aspects of Mennonite life and thought, and that are primarily published journal articles and books. This article also discusses reasons for the rising interest by scholars in the sociology of Mennonites as well as providing a classification of topics for research in Contemporary Mennonite life, a survey of the literature on the sociology of Mennonites, and some methodological considerations for the application of the scientific approach to the study of Mennonites.

KAUFFMAN, J. HOWARD and HARDER, LELAND
Anabaptists Four Centuries Later. A Profile of Five Mennonite and Brethren in Christ Denominations. Kitchener, Ontario: Herald Press, 1975, 400 pp.

This is the first comprehensive sociological study of Canadian and United States congregations financed with a $50,000 budget and a staff of forty-four led by two professionally trained sociologists. Developing a sophisticated methodology similar to Lenski and Glock, the chief researchers also drew upon the national survey of Lutherans conducted in 1970 and the National Opinion Research Center in Chicago. Researchers can profit from the Appendix, "How the Study Was Conducted." With this book Mennonite sociologists join the mainstream of research in the sociology of religion.

The data is massive. There are eighty-seven Tables presenting the data. There are 391 footnotes which serve as a definitive bibliography of all literature relevant to the sociology of the Mennonites and useful studies of other religious groups.

The author's conclusions are optimistic that (a) assent to the Anabaptist vision (the normative Mennonite view rooted in the left wing of the sixteenth century Reformation) is a potent influence which exceeds age, education and socioeconomic status in predicting the behavior of Mennonites; and, (b) the functional value of the Anabaptist vision in relation to the variables has a rival in fundamentalist orthodoxy which undermines pacifist commitment, social concern and inter-Mennonite activities and clusters with reactionary thinking at many levels.

KAUFFMANN, DUANE R.
"Mennonite Bibliography." Unpublished. Goshen, Indiana: Goshen College, 1973.

This bibliography of sources on the sociology and the psychology of Mennonites covering the years from 1955-1972 is an update of a bibliography published by J. Howard Kauffman in July, 1956 in the *Mennonite Quarterly Review*. It is an exhaustive bibliography with items arranged under twelve headings, such as demographic data, Mennonite family patterns, education, Mennonite community organizations, urbanization, recreational patterns, and technology and economic activities among Mennonites.

KRAHN, CORNELIUS (ED.)
"Radical Reformation and Mennonite Research, 1973-74." *ML*, 30 (March, 1975), pp. 19-33.

Excluding articles from Mennonite publications, the editors of this bibliography and report of research in progress have published every five years since 1956. Included are titles of Ph.D. dissertations, M.A. theses, journal articles and books from Canada, the U.S. and Europe. Titles include sociological, historical and theological. Five of these bibliographies can be obtained from the publisher, Bethel College, North Newton, Kansas, 67117.

KRAHN, CORNELIUS and GINGERICH, MELVIN
The Mennonites: A Brief Guide to Information. Newton, Kansas: Faith and Life Press, 1967.

This is a brief guide to selected information pertaining to the Mennonites. It is particularly designed to aid students in high schools and colleges who are interested in the study of some phase of the Mennonites. The first part of this guide consists of a brief account of the origin and spread of the Mennonites. The second part is a selected bibliography helpful in research in dealing with the Mennonites.

MALLEA, J. R. and PHILIP, L.
"Canadian Cultural Pluralism and Education: a Select Bibliography." *Canadian Ethnic Studies*, VIII, No. 1, 1976, pp. 81-88.

A valuable new bibliography in the rapidly growing area of Canadian ethnicity including the best books, articles and theses on pluralism, immigrants and language. Helpful for national and regional contexts and cross-cultural studies. It also reveals the paucity of bibliographic knowledge concerning Mennonites, Hutterites and Amish despite scattered items in the list.

MALYCKY, ALEXANDER (ED.)
"Bibliographic Issue." *Canadian Ethnic Studies*, V, No. 1/2, 1973, 426 pp.

Twenty-eight Canadian ethnic groups included. Mennonites cited under German and Russian rubrics. Hutterites considered separately. Theses, periodical literature, creative writing and books are listed. Comprehensive, excellent addition to the scholar's tools.

MANN, W. E.
Sect, Cult and Church in Alberta. Toronto: University of Toronto Press, 1955.

This pioneering book describes the burgeoning of new forms of religious organization in Alberta after World War I by distinguishing between "sects" which seek to recover first-century Christian doctrine and "cults" as a syncretistic mix of Christianity and alien religious or psychological notions. Both are seen in the social context of an insecure frontier, primarily rural culture. The Mennonites and Hutterites are sects in Mann's definition.

Mennonites arrived in Alberta from Manitoba in 1892 well ahead of the flood-tide of religious zealots described by the author. Surviving the strident voices (via radio and tabernacle) of competing sects and cults would appear to be one of the major achievements of the Mennonites and Hutterites of Alberta.

A unique achievement of Alberta fundamentalists was the capture of the provincial government by William Aberhart and colleagues for many years. Elsewhere in North America the Protestant "right" were outsiders who were powerless critics of establishment apostasy, political and religious.

MARTENS, HELEN
"The Music of Some Religious Minorities in Canada." *Ethnomusicology*, XVI (Sept., 1972), pp. 360-371.

In an issue of *Ethnomusicology* entirely devoted to Canada, the article by Martens analyzes the music of Mennonites (Old Order, Old Colony and progressive Russian), Amish, Hutterites and Doukhobors. The goal is to illustrate the crucial significance of music as symbolic of the culture, history and religion of each group.

The basic formula among the ultra-conservative groups is a freezing or canonization of the tradition preceded and followed by borrowing. The Amish hymnbook, the *Ausbund*, was first published in 1583, the Old Colony uses a collection dated 1796 and the Old Order churches have a book which has been used in Ontario since 1836.

One of the tunes in the Hutterite hymnbook comes from the Gregorian chants of the Middle Ages. Forty Hutterite hymns come from the *Ausbund*. At an Old Order songfest held Sunday night in an Ontario farm home, the author heard Gospel songs set to country and western music. Symbolic of their rejection of fixed order, the Doukhobors have a totally aural musical tradition without any hymnbooks; and, they have choirs without directors.

Only the progressive Mennonites utilize hymns from the full range of sources again, a symbol of their openness to new influences. But, the progressives selected hymns which suited their understanding of Christianity.

MOIR, JOHN S.

"Sectarian Tradition in Canada." *The Churches and the Canadian Experience*. Edited by John Webster Grant, Toronto: Ryerson Press, 1963.

Defining "sect" as a form of religious organization involving division, protest, separation and smallness of numbers usually fundamentalist and anti-traditionalist, Moir accepts E. T. Clark's classification of sects as pessimistic (second coming), perfectionist (holiness), legalistic, communistic (Hutterite), hedonistic and esoteric (Baha'i).

He notes that the Prairies have been the hotbed of sectarianism with the synthesis of frontier fundamentalism and political activism and success. He asserts that the perfectionist sects —Methodist and Baptist—provide the center of Canadian sectarianism; not British, not American but a peculiar amalgam of both.

Moir deals only marginally with Mennonites and Hutterites because their language barriers have prevented them from contributing much to the main sectarian traditions, a questionable view because of the acculturation of the Mennonites and the public struggles of the Hutterites; and, the considerable number of studies available in 1963.

PEACHEY, PAUL
Die soziale Herkunft der Schweizer Täufer in der Reformations-zeit: Eine religionssoziologische Untersuchung. Schriftenreihe des Mennonitischen Geschichtsvereins, IV. Vol. IV. Karlsruhe, 1954.

The key to this pioneering work is the argument that the radical social views of the Anabaptists must be interpreted in the light of their religious outlook and not vice versa. Also, the social composition of the sixteenth century Anabaptists was too diverse to justify a Marxist class conflict interpretation.

Peachey does insist on the legitimate place in the sixteenth and seventeenth centuries of urbanism, mercantilist nation states and the impact of modern theories of society on the peasantry.

The author is also well known for his emphasis on the *corpus Christianum* as the tragic error of European Christianity against which the Anabaptists made the first, painful protest which was finally realized in the rejection of state churches in nineteenth century North America.

For shorter versions of this book see *MQR*, XXVIII (1954) and "Social Background of Anabaptists," *ME*, Vol. IV, pp. 558-60.

PETER, KARL
"Ethnological and Sociological Study of Hutterites in Alberta." Unpublished paper, Glenbow-Alberta Institute, Calgary, 1967.

In this study Peter illustrates the typology of Max Weber of "gesellschaft" and "gemeinschaft," interpreting the Hutterites as an excellent illustration of the "gemeinschaft" life. To do this, he analyzes the individual, marriage, economic systems, leather and textiles, gestures and signs, doctrine and faith, and totality of culture.

REDEKOP, CALVIN
"A New Look at Sect Development." *Journal for the Scientific Study of Religion*, 13:3 (Sept., 1974).

The premier Mennonite analyst of sect development goes beyond his mentors—Troeltsch, Niebuhr, Becker, Yinger, O'Dea and Wilson—to suggest that hitherto studies have concentrated on nonradical sects confronting relatively tolerant societies. Previous studies have not dealt with radical sects operating in hostile environments. In this paper it is argued that sect development involves a dialectical process between sect and host society: illustrations are drawn from Old Colony Mennonites and Mormons.

"To use a word, therefore, to refer to a religious group requires a specification as to where it is in history. One should know the history of a particular sect before it can be meaningfully placed within a classification scheme."

REDEKOP, CALVIN
   "Religion and Society: A State Within a Church." *MQR,* 37:4 (Oct.,
   1973), pp. 339-357.

   One of the leading Mennonite sociologists trained in the Chicago
   school skillfully states the central dilemma of a separatist sect as
   follows: ". . . if it achieves the environmental freedom to follow its
   own inner dynamics, it will by necessity create its own secular
   society and state and will thus compromise its committed objectives. The relatively new information this thesis provides us with
   is that the believers' church, or sect, . . . can become secularized
   not by adopting or accepting the values of the world to become
   respectable, but by becoming the world from within by remaining
   separate."
   For social theory and for the sociology of Mennonites this is an
   essay of central importance. Yet, the essay has the specificity to
   satisfy the researchers—especially in the context of Russian Mennonites of three continents.

REDEKOP, CALVIN
   "The Relation of Research to the Sectarian Self-Image." *Conference
   on Mennonite Educational and Cultural Problems,* XIII (June, 1961),
   pp. 43-53.

   The conflict between sectarianism and scientific research for the
   Mennonite Church is discussed. Since the Mennonite Church
   adheres to the sectarian ideal and also engages in scientific research, it is caught in a dilemma. Author says that when a sectarian feels doubt and needs to experiment, he is no longer a
   sectarian. An example of this dilemma is education since a school
   that is only sectarian cannot be really academic. Also the mental
   health movement indicates that the Mennonite Church is de-
   pending more on scientific truth and is, therefore, not totally
   sectarian. Author concludes by saying that a religious group will
   need to retain a substantial amount of sectarian thinking.

REDEKOP, CALVIN
   "The Sect Cycle in Perspective." *MQR,* XXXVI (April, 1962), pp.
   155-161.

   It is the purpose of this article to evaluate the concept of the sect
   cycle and to evaluate the concept "sect" since the cycle depends
   upon the nature of the different groups in question. Author
   hopes that this will provide a better basis for analysis of the social
   dimension of religious phenomena. He argues that the old typology, that consisted of a ledger of traits for the church type and the
   sect type, is not too useful and concludes that it is no longer
   relevant "to ask whether a certain group is a 'sect' or a 'church', or
   whether it is going through the 'sect cycle'."

REDFIELD, ROBERT
"The Folk Society." *The American Journal of Sociology,* LII (January, 1947), pp. 293-308.

A general theoretical study of the folk society that can be applied to a study of the Hutterites, Amish, and some Mennonite groups. A folk society, according to the author, is "small, isolated, nonliterate, and homogeneous with a strong sense of group solidarity." Other characteristics of the "folk mentality" are: lack of experiment and reflection for intellectual ends; behavior is traditional, spontaneous, uncritical, and personal; the sacred prevails over the secular; the economy is one of status rather than of the market; and kinship, its relationships and institutions, are the type categories of experience. The principal conclusion of the study is that the less isolated and more heterogeneous the folk society becomes, the more it will be secular and individualistic and increasingly characterized by disorganization of culture.

RILEY, MARVIN P.
The Hutterian Brethren: An Annotated Bibliography with Special Reference to Hutterite Colonies in South Dakota. South Dakota State College Experimental Station, Summer 1965. Classification of sources by topic with alphabetical listing of author's name.

Although emphasis is placed upon the South Dakota Hutterites, consideration is given to the Hutterian brotherhood elsewhere in the United States, Canada and in other parts of the world.
  A large number of the items are works that contain findings of "field studies and surveys on the culture, intergroup relations, social organization, agriculture, and the mental and physical health of the Hutterites."
  Although twelve years old it is still valuable.

SPRUNGER, KEITH L.; JUHNKE, J. A.; and WALTNER, J. D.
Voices Against War: A Guide to the Schowalter Oral History Collection on World War I Conscientious Objection. North Newton, Kansas: Bethel College, 1973.

This study records the movement of World War I draft dodgers from the United States to Canada indicating that draft dodging covered two wars. It also reveals that a new methodology in research has developed in the study of Mennonites in the form of oral history.

WILLIAMS, GEORGE HUNSTON
The Radical Reformation. Philadelphia: Westminster Press, 1962.

For sociologists who want to probe the origins of the Mennonites and Hutterites in the radical reformation of the sixteenth century this *magnum opus* by the dean of Harvard church historians is highly recommended. For a brief, sound but popular history from a fresh perspective see Walter Klaassen's *Anabaptism: Neither Catholic nor Protestant*. Waterloo: Conrad Press, 1973.

WILSON, BRYAN R.
"An Analysis of Sect Development." *American Sociological Review*, XXIV (February, 1959), pp. 3-15.

"This paper seeks to distinguish and characterize distinctive types of sects, and to use such characterizations to determine the specific elements, and combinations of elements, which promote or retard such development." Sects are faced with the problem of maintaining their original value orientations in the face of changing external or internal social circumstances. "Some sects are markedly successful in the preservation of undiluted values of protest; others, notably those which gradually become denominationalized, are much less so." The Mennonites are discussed as an example of a group that has, through several ways, been able to preserve its sectarian nature. For example, schisms are a common occurence among Mennonites and, as the author states, "the schismatic groups tend to become the keepers of each other's consciences in relation to the maintenance of traditional values." Also the isolation of Mennonites, through language, social separateness, and distinctive dress, has been important in maintaining their original values.

YODER, DON
"Plain Dutch and Gay Dutch." *Pennsylvania Folklife*, VIII (Summer, 1956), pp. 34-35.

This article contrasts the life-styles of two different types of Pennsylvania Dutch people. The two classifications are based on religious beliefs. The "Gay Dutch" (Lutherans, Reformed, etc.) are those who live "in the world." The "Plain Dutch" (Mennonites, Amish, Brethren, etc.) are those who prefer to live apart, "in the world yet not of it." Author examines the origins of both groups, the evolution of the plain costume, the plain way of life, patterns in architecture, and survival of "plainness."

Since 1956, "Gay" has become a term of sexual identity lessening the viability of the word in relation to Pennsylvania Dutch. But the fact of the dichotomy among the Pennsylvania Dutch is still present, and, it applies to the "Plain Dutch" Mennonites who migrated to Ontario in 1783 and after; and the dichotomy is also present in Ontario today where a German Lutheran has a different social strategy than a German Mennonite. "Dutch", of course is a transliteration of the German word for German.

II. Mennonites

A. Books and Pamphlets

ANDERSON, J. T. M.
The Education of the New Canadian. Toronto: J. M. Dent and Sons, Ltd., 1918.

Deals with the general educational problems posed by the Canadians of non-British extraction. Particular reference is made to the Mennonites, pages 65-79, in which author presents a hostile point of view. He says that the parochial schools are marring the whole Western Canadian school system and that if firm treatment is handed out to these Mennonites, they will be grateful in the end. A period piece, revealing attitudes of World War I.

BAUSENHART, W.
"The Waterloo Pennsylvania German Dialect Community." *The Waterloo County Area Selected Geographical Essays*. Edited by A. G. McLelland. Waterloo: University of Waterloo, 1971, pp. 31-40.

The purpose of this linguistic survey was to discover the extent to which the dialect is still alive today, to collect sociolinguistic data about the speakers of the Pennsylvania German Dialect, to determine its geographic limits, to determine the dialect's future and to furnish data for a linguistic atlas of the area. Other influences on the dialect such as religion, schools and urbanization are presented.

BENDER, URIE A.
Soldiers of Compassion. Scottdale, Pennsylvania: Herald Press, 1969.

The purpose of this book is to tell the story of Pax, an organization sponsored by the Mennonite Central Committee, and to
paint a picture of Paxmen in their natural habitat. Pax is a program of service overseas in church-related projects instead of
military service. Author describes Pax involvement in eight different countries and also attempts to describe the motivations of
these men to join this program. References are made to Canadian
participation.

BURKHOLDER, J. R. and REDEKOP, C.
*Kingdom, Cross and Community. Essays on Mennonite Themes in Honor of
Guy F. Hershberger*. Kitchener, Ontario: Herald Press, 1976.

A *Festschrift* tribute by sixteen Mennonite scholars and one
Church of the Brethren writer to a sociologist and historian who
published over 300 books, reviews, and essays between
1922-1976 while teaching at Goshen College.

The agony of the new era of outreach is reflected in the essays
by theologians, political scientists, sociologists and historians. Any
assessment of North American Mennonites will have to take into
account the sophisticated methods by which Mennonites now
analyze themselves. Nowhere is this as well set forth as in this
symposium.

BURKHOLDER, LEWIS J.
A Brief History of the Mennonites in Ontario. Toronto: Livingstone
Press, 1935.

This history of the Mennonites in Ontario gives descriptions of
conditions in early Ontario, the coming of the Mennonites into
Canada, their settlements, congregations, conferences, and
nearly 400 ordinations. Author describes the several sections of
the Mennonite Church in Ontario and plainly outlines the
reasons, for and the results of certain schisms. Such topics as
evangelism, missions and Sunday School are discussed as factors
in division. A chapter on military service describes the efforts of
these Mennonites to remain true to their non-resistant principles.

DAWSON, C. A.
Group Settlement: Ethnic Communities in Western Canada. Vol. VII of
Canadian Frontiers of Settlement. Edited by W. A. Mackintosh and W.
L. G. Joerg. 9 vols. Toronto: The Macmillan Company of Canada
Ltd., 1936.

The Canadian Mennonites are one of several ethnic group
studies in this book which, the author says, "reveal how land
settlement is affected by homogeneous groups, their inevitable

transformation into heterogeneous groups, under Canadian conditions of mobility, and the burden placed on Canadian institutions and Canadian patience during the long period of their economic and social readjustment." The section on Mennonites begins with a discussion of the meaning of "sect" and proceeds to outline the changes that have occurred among Mennonites which are indicative of a move toward a secular community. Author appears to view assimilation of the Mennonites, and of any ethnic groups, as a natural and a necessary process.

DETWEILER, RICHARD C.
Mennonite Statements on Peace, 1915-1966. Scottdale, Pennsylvania: Herald Press, 1968.

This booklet contributes toward clarification of Mennonite Church peace witness developments from 1915-1966. It attempts to do four things: review the main aspects of the early Anabaptist-Mennonite position on church and state; evaluate the peace witness documents representing the Mennonite Church during 1915-1966; develop some theological implications of Mennonite Church peace witness trends; and bring the findings to a focus in order to help bring about a consensus on peace witness in the Mennonite Church.

DRIEDGER, LEO (ED.)
Mennonites in Urban Canada. Winnipeg: Proceedings of the 1968 Conference on Urbanization of Mennonites in Canada, University of Manitoba, 1968.

A series of articles on urban Mennonites that were taken from *Mennonite Life*. These articles represent a beginning in urban Mennonite research in Canada. They look at such problems as the struggle for identity in the urban community and the adjustment within the religious life of Mennonites. For those who do not have direct access to *Mennonite Life*, this collection of essays is a valuable one.

DRIEDGER, LEO
"Urbanization of Mennonites in Canada." *Call to Faithfulness: Essays in Canadian Mennonite Studies*. Edited by Henry Poettcker and Rudy A. Regehr. Winnipeg: Canadian Mennonite Bible College, 1972, pp. 143-155.

While five times as rural as the average Canadian, Canadian Mennonites are rapidly urbanizing with variation by provinces (B.C. Mennonites most urbanized; Alberta the least) and cities with two-thirds living in Winnipeg, Vancouver, Saskatoon and Kitchener. All four of these cities have large Mennonite rural hinterlands which feed into the cities and all four cities have heterogeneous ethnic populations inviting comparisons. Having established the facts of urbanization, Driedger then indicates how urban social organization affects Mennonites via specialization, social interaction, cultural patterns—mainly language—and religious life. The essay concludes on an optimistic note and even invokes the tradition of early Christianity and early Anabaptist history to suggest that Christianity flourishes better in cities than rural areas.

DYCK, CORNELIUS J. (ED.)
An Introduction to Mennonite History. Scottdale, Pa.: Herald Press, 1957.

A history of Anabaptist-Mennonite life and thought from the sixteenth century to the present. It describes in simple terms who the Mennonites are in relation to their forefathers and in relation to each other. The author has intended this book to serve as an introductory study of the basic historical and doctrinal developments during the four centuries that Anabaptism and Mennonitism have existed. Walter Klaassen of Conrad Grebel College, University of Waterloo, is a major contributor.

ENGLAND, ROBERT
The Central European Immigrant in Canada. Toronto: MacMillan Company of Canada Ltd., 1929.

A study of the assimilation in Canada of the Continental immigrants. Particular reference is made to the Mennonites on pp. 50-54 where author criticizes the privileges granted to the Mennonites by the government and talks of the great problems created by the more conservative Mennonites because of their refusal to participate in civic duties, to bear arms, and to take oaths.

EPP, FRANK H.
Education With a Plus: The Story of Rosthern Junior College. Waterloo, Ontario: Conrad Press, 1975, 460 pp.

This study is of great value for understanding the attitudes of Russian Mennonites of Canada toward education, how these attitudes changed over the years, and the conflicting views over the goals of education. It describes in detail the development of a Mennonite parochial school first known as the German-English Academy and it shows how Mennonites in Saskatchewan realized the need for church-related education for their own survival. The study goes on to reveal the conflicts that arose over the goals of this education.

EPP, FRANK H. (ED.)
I Would Like to Dodge the Draft-Dodgers But . . . . Winnipeg and Waterloo: Conrad Press, 1970.

Over 60,000 young Americans fleeing the draft and militarism
came to Canada in the 1960's. This book, composed of articles by
nine different authors, is an attempt to interpret the situation, to
increase understanding among Canadians, and to widen the base
of moral and material support for the new immigrants.

EPP, FRANK H.
*Mennonite Exodus: The Rescue and Resettlement of the Russian Mennonites
Since the Communist Revolution.* Altona, Manitoba: D. W. Friesen &
Sons, 1962, 571 pp.

As the title indicates, the central and unifying theme of this book
is the rescue and resettlement of Russian Mennonites. It is an
extensive coverage of the causes and settlements of the major
migrations from Russia to Canada and South America in
1923-30, of the migrations during 1947 and 1954, and of subsequent minor movements. The author presents not only the story
of the migrations and the establishment of settlements, but also
relates the difficulties the immigrants encountered in their new
environment and their adjustment to the economic, cultural,
social, and political life of the adopted countries. Much of the
story is biographical, telling of the courage and dedication of
outstanding Mennonite leaders. But the weaknesses of the Mennonites are also revealed, especially in their encounter with
Communism. The book includes many maps, illustrations, tables,
detailed footnotes and bibliography. A definitive volume.

EPP, FRANK H.
Mennonites in Canada 1786-1920. (See annotation under Bibliography and Social Theory.)

EPP, FRANK H.
The Glory and the Shame. Winnipeg: Canadian Mennonite Publishing
Association, 1968, 79 pp.

This small book consists of a series of editorials by Frank H. Epp,
published in *The Canadian Mennonite,* in which Epp makes an
assessment of the Mennonite Church, pointing to both positive
and negative. Through such topics as ecumenicity, communism,
church and state, and evangelism, the author shows a "deep
appreciation for the best of the Anabaptist heritage," but he also
points out the failure of Mennonites in upholding this heritage.

EPP, FRANK H.
"The Struggle for Recognition." *Call to Faithfulness: Essays in Cana-
dian Mennonite Studies.* Edited by Henry Poettcker and Rudy A.
Regehr. Winnipeg: Canadian Mennonite Bible College, 1972.

The Canadian Mennonites entered a new phase in their aspirations for material and spiritual survival after World War II which

the writer calls the "struggle for recognition." This desire for social recognition by their fellow Canadians and for spiritual recognition by other Christians was a result of the humiliation and embarrassment suffered in World War II when they were accused of being "enemy aliens" and "war profiteers." Evidence of this struggle can be seen in the many changes that have taken place in the last twenty-five years such as the movement from rural to urban areas, the change from German to English in worship, the movement to the top of professions, business, art, and politics, and the creation of prestigious homes and churches. Author also discusses what these changes accomplished and why they have not been completely satisfying.

FRANCIS, EMERICH K.

In Search of Utopia: The Mennonites in Manitoba. Altona, Man.: D. W. Friesen & Sons Ltd., 1955.

This book attempts to reveal the search of the Manitoba Mennonites for a form of social life based on Christian principle and to outline the problems this may create for the social stability of the major society. A large part of the book is historical with accounts of the migration of these Mennonites from Russia to Canada, of the settlements on the Reserves, and later of the exodus to Latin American countries. But the sociological scope of this study is evident as the social system of the Manitoba Mennonites is analyzed in detail. Of particular interest is a discussion on the relation of the Mennonite colonies to the larger society, the breakdown of the communal organization, and the state of flux in which the Manitoba Mennonites found themselves after the war. Author is particularly concerned with the problem of creating an equilibrium acceptable to the large society and to the minority group.

FRETZ, J. WINFIELD

(See annotations in Introduction and Graduate Theses)

FRETZ, J. WINFIELD

Christian Mutual Aid: A Handbook of Brotherhood Economics. Akron, Pennsylvania: The Mennonite Central Committee, 1947.

This booklet was written to encourage Mennonite churches to develop a program of mutual aid. It advocates that "the members of the Christian community, locally and as a whole, bear one another's economic burdens." Author has combined Scripture teaching and historical illustrations with a summary of mutual aid principles and some practical operating suggestions to produce a helpful handbook for Mennonites.

FRETZ, J. WINFIELD
The Mennonites in Ontario. 2nd ed. Waterloo, Ontario: The Mennonite Historical Society, 1974.

This brief pamphlet answers questions frequently asked about Mennonites in Ontario such as, who are the Mennonites, why are there so many varieties, the church as a community, asking if they are a religious or a cultural group, the purpose of education, and government as friend or foe. It also discusses Mennonite economics, their struggle against change, and whether they will survive or become extinct in the future. The author treats Ontario Mennonites as a total group and classes them into three divisions, the conservatives, the moderates, and the progressives. Within this small group is an extremely wide range of social practices and fragmented organizations. The sociological differences which range among them are the primary concerns of this book.

GERBRANDT, HENRY J.
Adventure in Faith. Altona, Manitoba: D. W. Friesen and Sons Ltd., 1970.

The background in Europe and the development in Canada of the Bergthaler Mennonite Church of Manitoba is the subject of this book. It is useful for gaining an understanding of the origins, the present situation and destination of this church and how it fits into the larger Manitoba, Canadian, and North American Mennonite communities. Although the story often becomes lost in the many details and facts, the author does reveal some major themes such as the socio-economic evolution of these Mennonites, the school question, and the resulting schisms. The book has many illustrations as well as a chart at the end of the book called the Manitoba Mennonite Family Tree which is very helpful for sorting out all the schisms and different Mennonite groups in Manitoba which originated from the Chortitza and Molotschna Colonies in Russia.

GIBBON, JOHN MURRAY
Canadian Mosaic: The Making of a Southern Nation. Toronto: McClelland and Stewart Ltd., 1938.

A valuable story of the various immigrant nationalities which make up the Canadian people. The contributions of each group are dealt with in a scholarly fashion. Chapter VII, "Germany and Canada," provides a summary of the various Mennonite settlements in Canada, commenting briefly on the war experiences and assimilation of these Mennonites.

GINGERICH, MELVIN
Mennonite Attire Through Four Centuries. Breiningsville, Pa.: The
Pennsylvania German Society, 1970.

This comprehensive, well-illustrated study of the history of Mennonite costume seeks to learn what practices in dress were followed by the Anabaptists in the 150 years before coming to North
America and also what the Mennonite immigrants were wearing
when they first settled here. The book then looks at changes that
occurred as a result of the impact of the American culture upon
them. Although primarily historical, this study also surveys the
psychological and social factors which helped establish their
mores in America. The author also presents reasons for the
Mennonites' nonconformity in dress and for their simplicity of
life.

GINGERICH, MELVIN
Service for Peace. Akron, Pennsylvania: The Mennonite Central
Committee, 1949.

The story of Civilian Public Service for all branches of Mennonites in North America. The chapter on Canadian C.O.'s discusses
the Conference of Historic Peace Churches, the work camps,
and service on farms and in industry and provides a list of the
number of C.O.'s in each province. Author says many of the
Canadian C.O.'s felt that the position they had taken was not
being adequately supported by the church, since an educational
and a religious program were not provided for them and since
the church had not organized any systematic visitation of the
camps.

GOOD, E. REGINALD
*Anna's Art, the Fraktur Art of Anna Weber, a Waterloo County Mennonite
Artist 1814-1888.* Kitchener: Pochauna Publications, 1976, 48 pp.

Forty reproductions with commentary and bibliography introduce the reader to the peculiar art form brought to Canada in the
nineteenth century by the Pennsylvania German Mennonites
who utilized a technique found within the folk cultures of the
German Rhenish Palatinate. The book is valuable as social history
which reveals the impact of the cultural backgrounds of the
Mennonites and the creativity of self-taught people making the
common life of birds, animals and flowers fascinating and beautiful. The story of Anna Weber herself provides an inside view of
the early culture of the Ontario Mennonite settlements.

HARDER, LELAND
*Comparative Demographic Analysis: Mennonite Church and General Con-
ference Mennonite Church.* Elkhart, Indiana, 1967.

This comparative analysis of the (Old) Mennonite Church and the General Conference Mennonite Church required several lines of research. One was a further development of a theory of "structural disequilibrium" in the free church, and another was a demographic survey based upon data previously gathered independently for the two conferences. Data primarily came from the 1960 "Mennonite Mobility Study," the "Mennonite Family Census" of 1963, and the doctoral research of J. A. Hostetler entitled "The Sociology of Mennonite Evangelism." The present study examines trends in overall church membership, and compares the two conferences according to rural-urban place of residence, age and sex composition, age of baptism, educational attainment, and occupational classification. Many conclusions are set forth. For example it was found that upward social mobility is more evident in the General Conference than in the Mennonite Church, and that the age of baptism is much lower in the Mennonite Church than in the General Conference Mennonite Church. Both conferences have a continental structure.

HARDER, LELAND
Steinbach and Its Churches. Elkhart, Indiana: Mennonite Biblical Seminary, 1970.

This detailed account involves two types of field study. The first surveys the cooperating churches, historically, geographically, and demographically, and the second pertains to the community itself—its population growth, schools, economic institutions, level of prosperity, and its relation to the agricultural hinterland. The author also uses such techniques as a congregational membership graph, age-sex pyramids, and a spot map.

HARDER, LELAND
See annotation for *Anabaptists Four Centuries Later* with J. Howard Kauffman.

HERSHBERGER, GUY FRANKLIN
The Mennonite Church in the Second World War. Scottdale, Pennsylvania: Mennonite Publishing House, 1951.

Hershberger gives a complete report and evaluation of the experiences of one Mennonite group, the Mennonite Church, during World War II. This book covers all phases of "war relations" of the Mennonite Church in Canada and the United States. There are also chapters on missions, education, relief, voluntary service, and inter-group relations both within and without the Mennonite family. Generally this study contributes to an understanding of the war's effect upon the life and work of the Mennonite Church.

HERSHBERGER, GUY FRANKLIN
War, Peace and Nonresistance. Scottdale, Pennsylvania: The Herald Press, 1964.

Nonresistance, as a total way of life for Mennonites, is described in detail with reference to the Biblical foundations, the historical development, and the present state of the nonresistant faith. A major section of the book describes the experiences of the Mennonites during World War I and II. The author explains that in Canada the hysteria of wartime led to opposition to Mennonites in western Canada, and to legislation preventing further Mennonite immigration to Canada for a time and demanding the use of the English language in schools. This book also attempts to analyze and classify the various types of pacifism that exist today, to explain the Anabaptist attitude toward the state, and to reveal the contribution of nonresistance to society.

HOSTETLER, JOHN A.
Mennonite Life. Scottdale, Pa: The Herald Press, 1959.

This brief, general summary of the Mennonites is useful for those who are unfamiliar with this religious group. It attempts to define the Mennonites with a discussion on religious beliefs, discipleship, and their type of worship, as well as to make the reader aware of the many different Mennonite groups and their many varying lifestyles and attitudes.

HOSTETLER, JOHN A.
The Sociology of Mennonite Evangelism. Scottdale, Pennsylvania: The Herald Press, 1954.

This study deals with selective mobility, the movement of persons in and out of the Mennonite Church. The discussion centering around evangelism is concerned with how much mobility there is, what the personal characteristics of the religious migrants are, and the social and religious sources that they come from. The objectives are not only to form an adequate picture of the growth through evangelism and the social-psychological factors associated with numerical growth, but also to discover what kind of contacts have been most fruitful for gaining out-group persons into the Mennonite Church. The study is also valuable for providing an understanding on the disorganizing factors associated with persons who leave the Mennonite Church. Some of these are the desire for greater freedom, conflicting views with the Mennonite Church, and feelings of nonacceptance in the church.

JUHNKE, JAMES C.
A People of Two Kingdoms. The Political Acculturation of Kansas Mennonites. Newton, Kansas: Faith and Life Press, 1975, 215 pp.

If Frank Epp's doctoral dissertation in Minnesota in 1965 was the first important study of Canadian Mennonite political behavior, Juhnke's book is the first comprehensive study providing a wider context in the American environment but with many implications for the Russian Mennonites in Canada. In any case, it is in direct conflict with Harder's use of disequilibrium theory since Juhnke sees the Mennonite political pattern as adjusting but not succumbing to nationalism thrust upon them from the outside. Reminiscent of Luther, Juhnke restates the theory of two kingdoms. Most surprising he interprets the Mennonite Central Committee's good works as an acculturating response to American nationalism. Original data combined with excellent bibliography.

His methodology has located the use of voting records in one predominantly Mennonite county in Kansas. He has delineated a method for political analysis for future studies in Canada.

JUHNKE, JAMES C.
"Conflicts and Compromises of Mennonites and the Draft." *Conscience and Conscription*. Papers from the 1969 Assembly. Sponsored by the Mennonite Central Committee Peace Section, Chicago, November 20-22, 1969. Akron, Pennsylvania: Peace Section, MCC, 1970.

This paper emphasizes the problems facing the Mennonite Church in light of the Vietnam War and the United States government's claim to conscript Mennonite young men into national service. There is a need for the Mennonite Church to once again work out a satisfactory relationship to the government and to the problems posed by American military conscription. This is crucial to the self-understanding of the Mennonite Church. Author briefly reviews the history of the Mennonites and the draft and suggests that Mennonites compromised at each turn in the story. Acceptance of the principle of the draft, the rise of the Mennonite Central Committee and the focus of Mennonite energies upon relief programs are viewed as elements in a compromise with government and society. Article goes on to show the benefits of these compromises and states that compromise with the world at some level is inevitable.

KAUFFMAN, J. HOWARD and HARDER, LELAND
Anabaptists Four Centuries Later. See annotation in the Introduction.

KAUFMAN, EDMUND GEORGE
The Development of the Missionary and Philanthropic Interest Among the Mennonites of North America. Berne, Indiana: The Mennonite Book Concern, 1931.

A doctoral dissertation at Chicago, Kaufman's study was the first attempt in North America to utilize the typology of Troeltsch for the analysis of Mennonites as a sectarian group. The interest of the Mennonite Church in missions is a rather recent development as compared with that of other Christian bodies. This study is concerned with this late development and attempts to discover how this interest began, to what extent it has permeated the whole group, and how this interest is being expressed among Mennonites. Author provides an explanation for the loss of early Anabaptist missionary outreach and the development of a distinctly nonmissionary mind, by defining the religious sect and the sect cycle. He says every sect goes through a cycle from fusion with the community, to complete isolation, to assimilation. It was in the period of isolation, which was paritally caused by persecution and the lack of educated leaders, that the nonmissionary mind began among Mennonites. The author then describes the gradual awakening of the missionary activity among the General Conference Mennonites and the "Old" Mennonites. The Russian Mennonites of Canada and the United States are viewed as catalysts of outreach and missions.

KRAHN, CORNELIUS (ED.)
From the Steppes to the Prairies, 1874-1949. Newton, Kan.: Mennonite Publication Office, 1949, 115 pp.

A series of essays that discuss the coming of the Russian Mennonites to the prairie states and provinces. Among the articles, are descriptions of the hardships of the pioneers, and of how the Mennonite pioneer fared in Canadian and American literature. Of particular value is an essay by Melvin Gingerich on Jacob Y. Shantz and the Mennonite immigration to Manitoba.

KRAHN, CORNELIUS and SCHMIDT, JOHN F. (ED.)
A Century of Witness: The General Conference Mennonite Church. Newton, Kansas: Mennonite Publication Office, 1959.

An account of how the General Conference Mennonite Church came into being, how various streams of Mennonitism became a part of it, how the conference organization functions, and an evaluation of its strengths and weaknesses. Two charts are valuable for clarifying the complex background of North American Mennonites.

LEDERACH, PAUL M.
Mennonite Youth. Scottdale, Pennsylvania: Herald Press, 1971.

A report by Mennonite Youth Research which attempts to outline what Mennonite young people have reported as true about themselves, their beliefs, understandings, and concerns. This report provides only one perspective on Mennonite youth since it is limited to what Mennonite youth have said about themselves. Several of the conclusions are: Mennonite youth provide a distinct sub-culture; youth from the east to the west are very much alike; in general they are happy with the church; Mennonite youth want more participation in the decision-making process of the church; they are interested in living a life of service; they are committed to nonresistance; there are few differences between Mennonites from public high schools and those from church-related schools; and one-half of Mennonite youth are interested in getting a college education.

LITTELL, F. H.
The Origins of Sectarian Protestantism. New York: Macmillan Co., 1964.

Littell has given impressive support to the master-motif of the Anabaptist-Mennonites as seeking the restitution of the early church after the Fall of the church in the fourth century under Constantine. This Fall was a lapse into a coercive, militaristic monolithic state-church culture. Prior to the Fall was the apostolic golden age in which pacifism was the cardinal principle.

Littell sees crypto-modern percursors of twentieth century pluralism in the sixteenth century voluntaryism of the radical sectarians or Anabaptists. Catholics, Lutherans and Calvinists were perpetuating archaic views of church, state and culture, according to Littell's basic argument.

LYON, LOUISE C. and FRIESEN, JOHN W.
Culture Change and Education: A Study of Indian and non-Indian Views in Southern Alberta. University of Calgary: Department of Educational Foundations, 1969.

This interview study was undertaken to obtain some realization of the opinions of native peoples about present day events which portend change. The areas probed are those of Indian social system management, changing cultural conditions, socialization of Indian children, the meaning of Indians' world view, and Indian need. This research is broad in conceptual scope and in data and Lyon and Friesen believe it provides a useful framework with which to study other minority groups such as the Mennonites.

LYON, LOUISE C.; FRIESEN, JOHN W.; UNRUH, W. R.; and HERTZOG, RAYMOND L.
Intercultural Education: A Study of Interperson-Perceptions upon Indian and Non-Indian Pupils in Southern Alberta. University of Calgary: Faculty of Education, 1970.

This study considers delineations of culture similarities and differences as a beginning approach in intercultural education. Its purpose is to seek effects of similarities and differences in interpersonal-perceptions of the pupils and teachers involved. "The research attempts to provide some understandings whereby teachers and administrators may gain more insights into their task of trans-cultural linkages." Because of the scope of this study, it becomes a very useful approach for understanding how the self-identifications and solidarities of Mennonite pupils may contrast with non-Mennonite children and thus may lead to better educational procedures in dealing with Mennonite and non-Mennonite pupils.

MacEWAN, GRANT

Between the Red River and the Rockies. Toronto: University of Toronto Press, 1952.

This review of western agriculture briefly mentions the contributions made by the Mennonites on pages 53-54. Author states that the early settlers generally avoided the prairies, but the Mennonites who came in 1871, 1874, and 1875 set a new pattern in settlement. They chose the open country between the Red River and the Pembina Mountains. It is also stated that the Mennonites are "peace-loving, hard-working, and devoted people," and have stayed on the land more than any other group of settlers.

MACKINTOSH, W. A.

Prairie Settlement: The Geographical Setting. Vol. I of *Canadian Frontiers of Settlement.* Edited by W. A. Mackintosh and W. L. G. Joerg. 9 vols. Toronto: The Macmillan Company of Canada Ltd., 1936.

This book briefly outlines the Mennonite settlements up to 1929 in Alberta, Saskatchewan, and Manitoba on a map and states that the Mennonites of the Manitoba colony led the way in opening up the "high plains."

MARTENS, HILDEGARD M.

Mennonites from Mexico: Their Immigration and Settlement in Canada. Ottawa: Canada Manpower and Immigration, 1975, 134 pp.

It is almost unknown for Mennonites of any type to display social disorganization. Sociologists can examine this classic case of social disorganization among the Old Colony Mennonites upon their return to Canada in recent years after leaving in 1922 to protest what they perceived as cultural and educational imperialism. The conditions in Mexico with respect to civil disorder, land and citizenship caused departures to British Honduras in 1957, Bolivia in 1967 and Canada more recently. In Canada the Mennonite Central Committee and one of the Russian Mennonite conferences are now providing assistance at many levels of need. Working under Frank Epp, Martens has made an important, comprehensive study supplemented with many government documents and letters.

MARTIN, ISAAC G.
The Story of Waterloo-Markham Mennonite Conference. Unpublished paper, Conrad Grebel College Archives, 1953.

This is a valuable historical account of the Mennonite Church in Ontario. It contains some original information on controversies and divisions that occurred among the Mennonites throughout the years. Also included is a detailed description of the ministers, deacons, and meeting houses of the Old Order Mennonites of the Waterloo district.

MEYERS, ROBERT
Spirit of the Post Road: A Story of Self-Help Communities. Altona, Manitoba: Federation of Southern Manitoba Cooperatives, 1955.

An account of the economic and social rebirth of a rural region in Southern Manitoba which is largely populated by Mennonites. The success of their communities is a result of the development of cooperatives. Author carefully describes the growth of each major cooperative at Rhineland, Altona, Gretna, Plum Coulee, and Winkler, and the background out of which each emerged. Author of the foreword, J.W. Fretz, states that the central value of this book is that it demonstrates some of the essential ingredients necessary to bring economic vitality and social growth to rural communities in any part of the world.

MOIR, JOHN S. (ED.)
Church and State in Canada, 1627-1867. Toronto: McClelland and Stewart Ltd., 1967.

A section of the book, pages 152-155, entitled "Disabilities of Dissenters," presents the statutes drawn up by the Canadian government specifically for the Quakers, Mennonites, and Tunkers "because of their uncompromising obedience to the Biblical injuction against killing and swearing."

MURDIE, R. A.
"The Mennonite Communities of Waterloo County." *The Waterloo County Area Selected Geographical Essays*. Edited by A. G. McLelland, Waterloo: University of Waterloo, 1971, pp. 21-30.

This essay deals with the population and economic and cultural aspects of the Mennonites. The population charts are from the Census of Canada 1861-1961. Special attention is given to a comparison between the Old Order Mennonites and the Mennonite Conference of Ontario.

NORRIS, JOHN
Strangers Entertained: A History of the Ethnic Groups of British Columbia. Vancouver, British Columbia: Evergreen Press Limited, 1971.

This book is an account of the ethnic groups in British Columbia who came to this province in the last century, and of their contributions to its developing society and culture. Pages 185-190 describe the adaptation of the Mennonite community to British Columbia. It is a short but valuable description of the interactions between Mennonites and non-Mennonites. Author reveals that the Mennonites became unpopular with the main society because of their refusal to assume some of the normal duties of citizenship and because of their "economic success arising from a co-operative devotion to material achievement." He also explains how the desire to justify themselves in the eyes of their neighbors by superior industry, morality, and material success has destroyed the Mennonite community as a distinct, separate entity. But it is concluded that a strong sense of solidarity still exists among the Mennonites of British Columbia.

OFFICER, E. R.
"Waterloo County—Some Aspects of Settlement and Economy before 1900." *The Waterloo County Area Selected Geographical Essays*. Edited by A. G. McLelland. Waterloo: University of Waterloo, 1971, pp. 11-20.

In 1799 Joseph Schorg and Samuel Betzner from Franklin County brought the first Mennonite families to settle on land purchased by Richard Beasly (Block 2). This essay also gives an outline of the immigrant groups, patterns of settlement and statistics on population growth.

PALMER, HOWARD
Land of the Second Chance: A History of Ethnic Groups in Southern Alberta. Lethbridge: The Lethbridge Herald, 1972.

This book includes a chapter on Mennonites, pp. 91-107, which tells of Mennonite settlement in Western Canada after World War II. Immigration was often blocked by government restrictive policies toward a German-speaking, non-violent minority. Today the greatest unifying factors for Mennonites are their religious and historical tradition and the common hardships they have had to overcome. Contemporary social trends such as in acculturation, politics, education, and music are also briefly discussed.

PATTERSON, NANCY-LOU
Mennonite Traditional Arts. Toronto: Canadian Antiques Collector, 1971.

A survey of Waterloo County Mennonite traditional arts such as 'Fraktur'-writing, paper-cutting, tree-carving, furniture-making, needlework including embroidery and quilt-making, and "fancy" cooking. The author describes these "arts of humility" in detail and gives special attention to 'Fraktur'-writing and quilt-making.

PATTERSON, NANCY-LOU
Mennonite Folk Art of Waterloo County. Toronto: Ontario Historical Society, 1969.

Author begins this study of objects within the Mennonite folk art tradition with a definition of art. She says folk art is the combination of useful and/or beautiful handmade objects produced by cultures operating at a relatively primitive level of technical life. The study then looks at four areas of this folk art: the basic decorative style; how this style is used to produce the objects; those objects which are useful but not decorated; and the Russian Mennonite folk art.

POETTCKER, HENRY and REGEHR, RUDY A. (EDS.)
Call to Faithfulness: Essays in Canadian Mennonite Studies. Winnipeg: Canadian Mennonite Bible College, 1972.

A book of essays dealing with almost every aspect of the Canadian Mennonites. The subject matter ranges from their origins, to their struggles in Canada, to the present state of Canadian Mennonites. In general the purpose of this book is to delineate the essence of the Mennonite faith and to appraise Mennonite performance. The articles, which are listed and annotated separately, are both historical, covering such topics as the development of the Conference of Mennonites in Canada and the rise of Mennonite private schools, and sociological studies, concerned with such issues as urbanization, the family, the ministry, fine arts, and Mennonite identity.

QUIRING, WALTER and BARTEL, HELEN
In the Fullness of Time, 150 Years of Mennonite Sojourn in Russia. Kitchener, Ontario: Aaron Klassen, 1974.

The Russian Mennonites were avid photographers, permitting a vivid grasp of their lifestyle, costume, architecture, economic enterprises, schools, churches, welfare institutions and tragic experiences during and since the Communist revolution. This book contains hundreds of pictures which are important in understanding the triumph and tragedy of the Russian sojourn. Another photographic collection which includes the Danzig, Germany settlements and recent visits to Soviet Mennonites is: *Heritage Remembered* by Gerhard Lorenz, Winnipeg: CMBC Publications, 1974, 221 pp.

REAMAN, GEORGE ELMORE
The Trail of the Black Walnut. Toronto: McClelland and Stewart, 1957.

A study of the Pennsylvania Germans and related ethnic groups who migrated to Ontario during the American Revolution. It is

the author's aim to discover how and where these groups originated, what they have in common, and what contributions they
have made as pioneers in Upper Canada. Among the groups
studied are the Mennonites and the Amish. In his conclusion, the
author states that assimilation has taken place to a large extent
among these ethnic groups, except in Waterloo County where the
Mennonite groups are increasing in numbers. But he also states
that Mennonite membership went down during the struggles
over the use of German or English in church services, over the
issue of higher education, and becuase of enlistment by Mennonite youth in World War I.

REDEKOP, CALVIN
The Free Church and Seductive Culture. Scottdale: Herald Press, 1970,
189 pp. A preface by Gibson Winter.

Using historical data and several original sociological case studies,
the author shows that the central problem of the Christian church
is self-deception, a temptation which seduces all men and institutions. The uniqueness and incongruity of the self-deception of
the Christian church is that it lays claim to a divine perception of
reality, yet contradicts this divine orientation at every turn.

With this sharp statement of the problem, the author draws on
his background in free church life to call for a church of account-
ability where the several members and the institution, *per se*,
subject themselves to continuous criticism and judgment.

Redekop combines sociological training with theological and
historical insight in a mentality which is rugged and unsentimen-
tal.

REIMER, DAVID P. (ED.)
Erfahrungen der Mennoniten in Canada während des zweiten Weltkrieges.
Steinbach, Man.: Derksen Printers Ltd., n.d., 177 pp.

The minutes of forty meetings in Manitoba during the Second
World War with a summary of developments with regard to
conscientious objectors.

REIMER, GUSTAV EDUARD and GAEDDERT, G. R.
*Exiled by the Czar: Cornelius Jansen and the Great Mennonite Migration,
1874*. Newton, Kansas: Mennonite Publication Office, 1956.

The question particularly treated in this book is how did the
Mennonite migration, from Russia, Poland, and Prussia to the
prairie states and provinces in the 1870's, come into being, and
what were the factors that gave it such magnitude? The book is
also very much the story of one man, Cornelius Jansen, since it
attempts to show how he was, to a very large extent, responsible
for the initiation and scope of the migration.

ROBINSON, HEATHER
Grass Roots. Toronto: James Lewis and Samuel, 1973.

Vivid impressionistic sketches of five prairie towns based on a month's interviews in each place. Winkler, Manitoba is described as "a Mennonite Bible belt boom town devoted to free enterprise."

Robinson believes there is a uniform rural culture in western Canada based on a code which is Anglo-Saxon, Protestant middle class and materialist. It enforces a single standard of behaviour which represses deviance.

Winkler is depicted as a consumer society haunted by spiritual desolation. Robinson's journalistic sketches provide an alternative to empirical studies but they are also open to bias and distortion until the empirical method delivers a reliable sample of the whole. The only certainty is that Robinson is totally negative towards small towns in the prairies.

The book also contains a four-page analysis of the Hutterite colony at Miami, Manitoba which emphasizes the hostility and resentment of the local people.

SAWATZKY, HARRY LEONARD
They Sought a Country. Mennonite Colonization in Mexico. London: University of California Press, 1971.

The main account of this book deals with the exodus of Canadian Mennonites to Mexico, their relocation in Mexico, and their adaptation to the new physical environment and to cultural change. But a section of the book is also devoted to the experiences of these Russian Mennonites in Canada. A summary of the background and areas of settlement of the four groups, Bergthal, Kleine Gemeinde, Chortitza, and Fürstenland, is provided. Of particular value is a discussion on the causes of the Mennonite migrations to Mexico. Some of the reasons discussed are the scarcity of land, the loss of certain exemptions, in particular as to schools, and the conscription question.

SMITH, C. HENRY
The Story of the Mennonites. Fourth Edition. Newton, Kansas: Mennonite Publication Office, 1957.

This book continues to be the best single volume dealing with Canadian and American Mennonite history. The author describes the Mennonites, not only in terms of their religious experiences, but also as a distinct economic or social group. Two chapters are significant from a sociological point of view and out of Canadian interest. One is the chapter on culture and progress in which the Mennonites are arranged into three broad groups—Conservatives, Progressives, and Moderates—and in which such topics as the "sense of otherworldliness," the German language, education and missions are discussed. Also a chapter entitled "Witnessing in War and Peace" is significant in that it discusses the problems that arose out of the World Wars.

SMITH, C. HENRY
The Coming of the Russian Mennonites. Berne, Indiana: Mennonite Book Concern, 1927.

An historical account of the migrations of the Mennonites of Southern Russia to North America. One chapter centers on their settlements in Manitoba on the East and West Reserves and on the four different Russian Mennonite groups: Kirchliche Mennoniten, Brueder-Gemeinde, Krimmer Brueder, and the Kleine Gemeinde. A pioneering work.

SOMMERVILLE, E.
"Waterloo County: A Population Profile, 1951-1971." *Waterloo County Area Selected Geographical Essays.* Edited by A. G. McLelland. Waterloo: University of Waterloo, 1971, pp. 41-62.

This essay provides a straightforward descriptive account of the demographic composition of Waterloo County and its constituent communities, based upon elementary analysis of the most recently available census data. It provides the demographic context for understanding Waterloo County Mennonites.

SWALM, E. J.
Nonresistance Under Test. Nappanee, Indiana: E. V. Publishing House, 1949.

The Historic Peace Churches of United States and Canada have subscribed to a "philosophy of non-resistance and peace." This book shows how the nonresistant witness found expression during both World War I and World War II. Author describes the Biblical and historical backgrounds of the nonresistant philosophy and doctrine, the filing of claims with the American and Canadian governments for liberty during World War II, the Civilian Public Service and Alternate Service as work of national importance, and the public relations to the peace witness of the nonresistant groups.

TOEWS, JOHN A.
Alternative Service in Canada During World War II. Winnipeg: Publication Committee of the Canadian Conference of the Mennonite Brethren Church, 1957, 127 pp.

Alternative service was a religious venture during a crisis that involved national emergency and that affected the people of Canada as a whole. The purpose of this book is to evaluate this service from the point of view of its national importance. The author is in sympathy with the cause of the conscientious objector and his service during World War II. The first part of the book gives an historical account of the immigration of four pacifist groups for whom the Canadian government made provision for exemption from military service. They are the Mennonites, Quakers, Hutterites, and Doukhobors. Of the 6,158 objectors registered in the four mobilization districts 4,425 were Mennonites, 482 Hutterites, 406 Doukhobors and eight Quakers. There were forty-five United Church, four Anglican and one Roman Catholic.

TOEWS, JOHN B.
Lost Fatherland. Scottdale, Pennsylvania: Herald Press, 1967.

A detailed examination of the Mennonite emigration from Russia between 1921 and 1926. It attempts to reconstruct the events which led to the breakup of the Russian Mennonite settlements and the forces which alienated the colonists and finally led to the exodus to Canada. The book is particularly concerned with the general bankruptcy confronting the Russian Mennonites during this period and the internal processes related to the emigration.

VOGT, R. H.
"Economic Questions and the Mennonite Conscience." *Call to Faithfulness: Essays in Canadian Mennonite Studies*. Edited by Henry Poettcker and Rudy A. Regehr. Winnipeg: Canadian Mennonite Bible College, 1972.

"There is no question that in the past few decades Mennonites have entered the mainstream of economic life in Canada." This economic success has led to social differentiation and to breakdown of the brotherhood concept which appear to be at odds with Mennonite ideals. This paper deals with the ways in which the Mennonites of Canada seem to be coming to terms with their conscience during the present period of prosperity. Response to this problem has ranged from total rejection by some groups, resulting in migration, to wholehearted acceptance by others. Author presents two "Anabaptist" approaches to economic life that fall between these two extremes. They are the "nonresistant" approach and the "new community" approach. After a description of these ideas, the writer outlines his own approach to economic questions which is partly based on the Mennonite heritage but also points in new directions.

WARKENTIN, A. and GINGERICH, MELVIN (EDS.)
Who's Who Among the Mennonites. North Newton, Kansas: Bethel College Press, 1943.

This book contains biographical sketches of Mennonites who have either had some influence on the growth of a community, or have been church leaders, pastors with seminary training, administrators, editors, missionaries, physicians, master farmers, etc. Covers all of North America.

WARKENTIN, ABE

Reflections on our Heritage: A History of Steinbach and the R. M. of Hanover from 1874. Steinbach, Manitoba: Derksen Printers, 1971.

This history of Steinbach and the East Reserve reveals the pioneering hardships, the unique Mennonite communities, and the consequent growth of an entire area up to modern times. The book follows the immigration of the Mennonites from the Ukraine to the East Reserve in Manitoba which is now roughly contained by the Rural Municipality of Hanover. Although a local history, this book provides some insight into Mennonites as a whole, particularly concerning aspects of Mennonite patterns of settlement.

WIEBE, BERNIE

"Canadian Mennonite Families: Foundations and Launching Pads." *Call to Faithfulness: Essays in Canadian Mennonite Studies.* Edited by Henry Poettcker and Rudy A. Regehr. Winnipeg: Canadian Mennonite Bible College, 1972.

"Mennonites have to this date accepted the primacy of family living." Wiebe is interested in discovering what makes Mennonites emphasize family life. He also considers the significance of a rapidly changing culture upon Mennonite family life. The large size, the traditional male-female roles, and the functions of the Mennonite family are all undergoing changes. Urbanization and industrialization have introduced Mennonite families much more directly to the materialistic aspects of everyday living, have removed the togetherness of families, and have increased mobility and leisure time. It is suggested that the Mennonite family is in a position to demonstrate a Christian alternative. This means moving from an authoritarian relationship in the family to increased personal involvement and self-giving.

WIEBE, GEORGE

"Faithfulness to the Arts." *Call to Faithfulness: Essays in Canadian Mennonite Studies.* Edited by Henry Poettcker and Rudy A. Regehr. Winnipeg: Canadian Mennonite Bible College, 1972.

The rapid development of the arts in the last thirty years is the theme of this essay. The article begins by revealing how Mennonite views on art have changed from the suspicion that too much preoccupation with the arts could be a deterrent to a vital personal faith, to the view that fine arts are desirable because of the "ennobling" effect they have on the development of character and personality. The essay is predominantly concerned with the musical development among Mennonites and emphasis is placed on its roots, choral culture, music festivals and competitions, orchestras, and professionalism. Other topics of discussion include musical sophistication, "the frustrated artist," the gap between professional musicians and laymen, "the artist as synthesizer of past and present," and the artist of the future.

WIEBE, MENNO

"Mennonite Adaptation and Identity." *Call to Faithfulness: Essays in Canadian Mennonite Studies*. Edited by Henry Poettcker and Rudy A. Regehr. Winnipeg: Canadian Mennonite Bible College, 1972.

The focus of this paper is on consideration of three questions from the point of view of Mennonite identity and adaptation. They are: 1) the nature of human alignments; 2) the relationship of man to his environment; and 3) religious ideologies as they relate to the predicament of human survival. Throughout the article it is emphasized that, before Mennonites can talk about themselves as a religio-ethnic group, they must rid themselves of their self-consciousness about the Mennonite identity. Also the post-rural pastor and post-rural congregation is described since the strains that have arisen out of this new environment have weakened Mennonite cohesiveness which depends upon the solidarity of church conference structures. An attempt is also made to understand what the Mennonites are sociologically. Author strongly believes in Mennonite solidarity, in rediscovering the genius of Mennonitism, and in "hammering out a theology that will provide for contemporary Mennonites a valid reason to be."

WIENS, HENRY J.

The Mennonite Brethren Churches of North America: An Illustrated Survey. Hillsboro, Kansas: Mennonite Brethren Publishing House, 1954.

A survey of the churches of the Mennonite Brethren Conference, their locations and surroundings, as well as a brief historical outline of each. Included are the churches of Alberta, British Columbia, Manitoba, Ontario, and Saskatchewan.

WILLMS, H.

At the Gates of Moscow; or God's Gracious Aid Through a Most Difficult and Trying Period. Yarrow, B.C.: Columbia Press, 1964.

This is a descriptive and personal report of the experiences suffered by the Mennonites in Russia beginning with the First Five Year Plan in 1928 which finally led to the mass flight of Mennonites from Moscow to Canada.

YODER, SANFORD C.
  *For Conscience Sake: A Study of Mennonite Migration Resulting from the
  World War*. Goshen, Ind.: Mennonite Historical Society, 1940.

  At least 50,000 Mennonites have had to "flee home and country
  for conscience' sake." Half of them settled in Canada and the
  other half found their way into Mexico, Brazil, and Paraguay.
  This study states the grounds upon which the Mennonites base
  their beliefs, considers the attitude of the state toward them,
  attempts to discover the circumstances that made it necessary for
  them to leave their homes, and follows the migrations that resulted during and after the War. As H. S. Bender states in the
  foreword, this book is "an interpretation of the whole of Mennonite history and faith."

B. Graduate Theses

ANDERSON, ALAN B.
  "Assimilation in the Bloc Settlements of North-Central Saskatchewan: A Comparative Study of Identity Change Among Seven
  Ethno-Religious Groups in a Canadian Prairie Region." Unpublished Ph.D. dissertation, University of Saskatchewan, 1972.

  This study is primarily concerned with a cross-ethnic analysis of
  assimilatory trends in the bloc settlement context and with the
  factors affecting those trends. Author defines group identity in
  terms of four components: ethnic origin, mother tongue, religious affiliation, and unique group customs. In the study, identity
  change is related to such conditions as age and generation differences, community size and homogeneity, and rural depopula-
  tion. The major conclusion that arises out of the ranking of the
  seven ethno-religious groups in north-central Saskatchewan is
  that "1) the Hutterites have by far the best-defined identity,
  succeeded by 2) Ukraininan Catholics, 3) Polish Catholics, 4)
  French, 5) Ukrainian Orthodox, 6) Mennonites, and 7)
  Doukhobors, in fairly close sequence, and finally by the rather
  assimilated 8) Scandinavians and 9) German Catholics."

AUGSBURGER, AARON DON
  "The Influence of Formal Control Patterns Upon Behavior and
  Personal and Social Development among Freshmen from Several
  Mennonite Colleges." Unpublished Ed.D. dissertation, Temple
  University, 1963.

  Author defines control as the system of disciplinary influence
  exerted by an individual or group such as the church and the

home, which has a great influence on behavioral development. Purpose of the study was to gather and present empirical data which would throw light upon a segment of Mennonite youth who have been influenced by the divergent control patterns.

BERGEN, JOHN J.
"The Manitoba Mennonites and Their Schools from 1875-1924." Unpublished M.A. thesis, University of Manitoba, 1950.

An excellent study to understand the two different strategies at work among the Mennonites: the intransigent policies of the Old Colony conservatives and the more flexible bilingual pattern of the progressive groups. Since this struggle is a prototype of the central division among Mennonites, the study of Bergen sheds much light on the problem of social change, particularly when government regulations stand at the center of the struggle. His study also reveals the larger context of patterns in Russia which influenced the struggle in Manitoba from the first Russian Mennonite settlements in 1874.

BERGEN, JOHN J.
"School District Reorganization in Rural Manitoba." Unpublished Ph.D. dissertation, University of Alberta, 1967.

The Mennonite content of this dissertation is minimal. The author's main purpose for doing this study is to examine the factors related to the progress of school reorganization in rural Manitoba. He feels that education programs provided for rural pupils are less than adequate and that centralization of schools is requried. But the rural communities which are mostly French and Mennonite neither seek nor demand change.

BERGEN, PETER FRANK
"The Mennonites of Alberta." Unpublished M.A. thesis, University of British Columbia, 1953.

This introductory account of the Mennonites in Alberta focuses mainly on the two largest denominations: the Mennonite General Conference and the Mennonite Brethren. The more liberal outlook of these two groups has given them an economic and cultural dominance. The land settlement policies, the economic development and the general problems of the Mennonites in relation to the community are discussed in detail.

BOON, HAROLD W.
"The Development of the Bible College or Institute in the United States and Canada since 1880 and Its Relationship to the Field of Theological Education in America." Unpublished Ph.D. dissertation, New York University, 1950.

Not specifically on Mennonites but this thesis is important for a background on the Bible college movement. Author discusses the reasons for the rapid growth of Bible institutes which tend to be conservative in theology and ethics; and evangelical in function. A chart of the denominational affiliation of forty-nine Bible institutes includes those that are Mennonite. Deficient in overlooking the role of politics associated with Bible institutions. Especially the mixture of populism and fundamentalism in Alberta.

BURKHOLDER, J. LAWRENCE
"An Examination of the Mennonite Doctrine of Nonconformity to the World." Unpublished M.A. thesis, Princeton Theological Seminary, 1951.

"The doctrine and practice of nonconformity to the World is the distinctive emphasis of the Mennonite Church. Except for the emphasis of this doctrine there would be no essential basis for cleavage between the Mennonite Church and the larger denominations. It is this doctrine alone which accounts for the sectarian character of the Mennonites." It is the aim of this thesis to discover the meaning of the Mennonite doctrine of nonconformity, the methods used by selected Mennonite groups in the application of the doctrine, the problems encountered by the Mennonites, and the extent to which their efforts may be regarded as successful. The study is divided into discussions on the Swiss Brethren of the Reformation period, the conservative application of the doctrine of the Hutterites and Amish, the moderately conservative program of the "Old Mennonites," and the doctrine of nonresistance "which is possibly the most essential aspect of the Mennonite nonconformist attitude."

DEAN, WILLIAM WARD
"John Funk and the Mennonite Great Awakening." Unpublished Ph.D. dissertation, University of Iowa, 1965.

This study describes and evaluates the spiritual awakening which occurred among North American Swiss Mennonites in the late nineteenth and early twentieth centuries. Its primary purpose is to deal with the relationship of John Funk to the Mennonite awakening in the years 1860-1900. Author gives the historical background of the Mennonite Church, and considers the brief period after 1900, when the awakening was consummated. The study goes on to report on definite changes that occurred after this spiritual awakening, such as the formation of the Mennonite Publication Board, the rise of programs for missions and higher education, and the beginnings of a merger between the Mennonites and the Amish Mennonites. Above all, the author says, the Great Awakening led to an upward trend in membership of the Mennonite Church.

DOERKSEN, JOHN G.
"History of Education of the Mennonite Brethren of Canada." Unpublished M.Ed. thesis, University of Manitoba, 1963.

The Mennonite Brethren of Canada are an education-minded
brotherhood. They stress the spiritual as well as the intellectual
and physical development of the child. To some extent they
subscribe to a philosophy of separatism in education since they
are reluctant to share in cooperative educational ventures with
other denominations. The aim of this study is to trace the beginning, development and present status of each institution as it
exists in Canada, to point out underlying principles which have
guided Mennonite Brethren thought and action in the past, and
to focus attention on present-day trends. These institutions have
an effect on the religious and moral life of the country's national
culture.

DRIEDGER, LEO
"A Sect in a Modern Society: A Case Study: The Old Colony Men-
nonites of Saskatchewan." Unpublished M.A. thesis, University of
Chicago, 1955.

A very brief chapter is devoted to the heritage of Mennonites
while the major proportion is centered on the history, community
organization value system and way of life of the settlements. The
author includes a chapter for a conclusion and his predictions of
the Old Colony Mennonites.

DYCK, HENRY DIETRICH
"Language Differentiation in Two Low German Groups in
Canada." Unpublished Ph.D. dissertation, University of Pennsyl-
vania, 1964.

The aim of this study is to record the present state of Low German
and the linguistic changes that have taken place between 1870
and 1920 by comparing the Chortitza and the Molotschna
dialects. The dissertation is divided into four areas: a brief history
and linguistic background of the Low German Mennonites; the
sub-dialects of the Chortitza dialects among the Low German
Mennonites; a description of the Chortitza dialect; and a description of the original and derived Russian Mennonite dialect. Author concludes that linguistic change is most evident among the
Manitoba Mennonites from the Chortitza colony in Russia who
tended to adopt the Molotschna dialect and to strive for the
refinement of High German. Also discussed are the effects of the
English language and the dangers of losing Low German among
the various Russian Mennonite groups in Manitoba.

ELLIS, WALTER E. W.
"Some Aspects of Religion in British Columbia Politics." Unpublished M.A. thesis, University of British Columbia, 1959.

This study on the relationship between religion and politics in British Columbia is divided into three areas of discussion: the attitudes of clergymen to their role in political affairs; the history of a religiously based pressure group, the temperance movement; and the religious affiliation of members of the British Columbia legislature and the relationship between religion and cabinet appointments. Mennonites are not treated in any detail and, thus, this paper is not a clear indication of Mennonite participation in politics.

ENS, ADOLF
"The Relation of the Western Canadian Mennonites to the Government." Unpublished Ph.D. dissertation, University of Ottawa, 1975.

Against the background of the Russian privilegium (special rights negotiated by a specific group of people) the Western Canadian Mennonites came to Canada with a modified equivalent of this pattern in the more complicated milieu of a democratic government where rights are applied with much broader sweep.

Today Mennonites have M.P.'s and M.P.P.'s and civil servants posing new problems and new opportunities which did not exist under privilegium.

EPP, FRANK H.
"An Analysis of Germanism and National Socialism in the Immigrant Newspapers of a Canadian Minority Group, the Mennonites in the 1930's." Unpublished Ph.D. dissertation, University of Minnesota, 1965.

This dissertation is an analysis of pro-Germanism, in the political context of National Socialism, in the Canadian Mennonite immigrant press of the 1930's. It begins with a description of the background and beliefs of Mennonites with emphasis on their identification with German cultural and national life. Author also defines the concept of National Socialism and shows how it was a German movement with support from most German minorities abroad. The study goes on to reveal that the Canadian Mennonite press also insisted on asserting its Germanism. Author does this by determining the amount and the nature of Germanism content by subject, by direction, and by source in the newspaper, *Der Bote*. He then comments on the extent to which this Germanism mirrored Mennonite thinking in general. Author concludes that the newspaper was fairly representative of the Mennonite immigrant mind which was strong in its identification with racial Germanism and "sympathetic to the political Germanism of the *Third Reich*."

FRETZ, J. WINFIELD
"Mennonite Mutual Aid: A Contribution Toward the Establishment
of a Christian Community." (See annotation in Introduction.)

FREY, KENNETH D.
"Comparative Occupational Aspirations of Old Order Mennonite
and Non-Old Order Mennonite Farm Youth." Unpublished M.Sc.
thesis, Guelph University, 1971.

Old Order Mennonite youth have one occupational choice
—farming—while only two-thirds of the Mennonite young people outside of the Old Orders share this aspiration. The one-third
with other occupational goals perceived lack of capital and insufficient government control as reasons for rejecting farming; and,
positively, parental challenge, white collar goals and intellectual
outlook led to commercial and professional vocations. Not sur-
prisingly, Old Order youth planned to farm with only limited
modernization of production methods.

Frey also makes six recommendations the key of which is to
protect the right of Old Order Mennonites to survive in an era of
large-scale farming. In the study he used a stratified occupational
sample.

FRIESEN, I. I.
"The Mennonites of Western Canada with Special Reference to
Education." Unpublished M.A. thesis, University of Saskatchewan,
1934, 200 pp.

The educational attitudes of the Mennonites today can be traced
from the Reformation. This essay centres on the educational
process of the Russian Mennonites on the prairies. The first few
chapters deal with their history, customs, and beliefs, with special
emphasis on Johann Cornies who started the educational reform
in South Russia.

The causes of the Manitoba school controversy are discussed in
detail and the resulting emigration of the opposing groups to
Mexico and Paraguay. The last chapter briefly states the progressive view to education and gives an account of the various Bible
schools.

GAEDE, JIM
"Mennonites and Social Work: A Study of the Influence of Mennon-
ite Culture on the Choice and Practice of Social Work as a Profession."
Unpublished M.S.W. thesis, University of Southern California, 1960.

"The Mennonite social welfare program is continuing to grow.
There is a greater need for professionally trained Mennonite
social workers to serve in these agencies. This study will attempt
to understand some of the attitudes of social workers of Mennonite background toward Mennonite church related social service

agencies. Also an attempt will be made to find out how social segregation, which has an important relation to the maintenance of a cultural pattern of beliefs, affects the individual as it relates to social work; and how the profession affects the individual as it relates to his cultural background." The study is generally limited to social workers with the Association of Mennonite Social Workers. In general these postulations were supported: the expression of "separation from the world" deters a Mennonite from selecting social work as a profession; and the expression of "Christian love through service" motivates a Mennonite to choose social work. Also the Mennonite Church expresses cultural values which cause stress and frustration for social workers as they practice their profession.

GIBSON, JAMES R.

"A Comparison of Anglo-Saxon, Mennonite, and Dutch Farms in the Lower Fraser River Valley: A Methodological Study in Area Differentiation and the Relative Influences of the Physical and Cultural Environments." Unpublished M.A. thesis, University of Oregon, 1959.

This thesis compares Anglo-Saxon, Mennonite, and Dutch farms in order to determine their differences and similarities and the relative parts played in the causes thereof by the physical and cultural environments. This last point is studied in view of the controversy between the environmental determinists who hold that the physical environment determines man's activities, and the cultural determinists who believe that the human environment determines man's behavior. The comparison technique of the farm types took into consideration many factors such as farm size, ethno-religious background, land use and soil type. The findings revealed several interesting conclusions concerning the Mennonites: "there seems to be a breaking point in both the settlement ratio of Mennonites to Anglo-Saxon and in the density of Mennonite settlement itself beyond which the culture of the Mennonites begins to crumble"; similar use of land by Mennonites from two different areas where the physical environment was radically different revealed that the physical environment is of little importance as a differentiating factor in the thesis area; and Mennonites seem to be characterized by high standards of cleanliness and neatness, a large measure of self-sufficiency, and a high degree of intensity in their land use.

GLICK, OREN W.

"The Effects of Behavioral Norms on the Selection of Associates." Unpublished M.A. thesis, University of Kansas, 1962.

Students primarily from the General Conference Mennonite constituency were chosen as subjects "to document further the nature of the relationship between attitudinal variables and interpersonal choice behavior in a real life setting." The study assumes that Mennonites have emphasized certain standards of behavior which are implied by Scripture. Nine of these behaviors are selected for study to determine: the informal groupings among subjects; the extent of normative agreement within such groupings; the extent of the normative agreement within the total population; and the extent of intra-group normative agreement as compared to the extent of total population normative agreement. It was found that individuals possessing similar norms for behavior will tend to associate with one another.

GOERZEN, JACOB W.
"Low German in Canada: A Study of 'Ploutdits' as spoken by Mennonite Immigrants from Russia." Unpublished Ph.D. dissertation, University of Toronto, 1952.

A study of the language and history of the Mennonite immigrants from Russia. It is also a study of the influences which have been at work in shaping the language as it is spoken in Canada today. "Ploutdits" which is described in the thesis is the continuation of the Molotschna Low German. Glimpses of European history and a history of settlement in Canada open the account. The most important part of the study is the chapter on compatibility which describes eight phonemic tables. Other chapters include the phonology, the morphology, the historical developments, and present-day trends in Ploutdits. The last chapter discusses the beginnings of a literature in the old country and shows how it is developing in Canada today.

HARDER, LELAND D.
"The Quest for Equilibrium in an Established Sect: A Study of Social Change in the General Conference Church." Unpublished Ph.D. dissertation, Northwestern University, 1962.

Harder's study seeks to understand and explain the way sects develop and change. As he states, his purpose is to develop a structural disequilibrium theory of social change in a sect and to examine the relevance of this theory in a case study of a Mennonite sect. Harder retains the church-sect typology, as developed by Troeltsch, as a tool in understanding the many facets of socio-religious behavior. To observe and specify those aspects of disequilibrium, the dissertation is concerned with a detailed study of social change in the General Conference Mennonite Church. The changes in behavior in this sect group were interpreted within reference to two factors: culture contact and structural disequilibrium. Author believes that certain socio-religious factors are not adequately explained by culture contact alone. Rather "inner tensions" or structural disequilibrium are more and more forces of change in a sect group.

HEINTZ, GLADYS
"German Immigration Into Upper Canada and Ontario from 1783 to the Present Day." Unpublished M.A. thesis, Queen's University, Kingston, 1938.

This study includes a section on the Pennsylvania Mennonites who came to Ontario. The purchase of block number two by these Mennonites, the coming of Christian Naffzigger and the Amish, the activities of these pioneers, and the development of the Mennonite Church are some of the topics discussed. The author makes generalized statements without much evidence. For example, she says, "Today there is no distinct group in Ontario more keenly interested in the political welfare of the country than the Pennsylvania Dutch and the Germans of Waterloo."

IUTCOVICH, MARK I.
"A Comparative Study of the Process of Acculturation Among Certain Groups of Immigrants in the Province of Manitoba." Unpublished M.A. thesis, University of Manitoba, 1962.

The process of acculturation by the Hutterite and Romanian peasants who immigrated to Manitoba prior to 1930 is the subject of this study. As a comparative study, the author attempts classification of the groups under study in relation to three variables: the mode of migration, the mode of existence in the original milieu, and the cultural and social characteristics of the group. These variables provide a broad classification of immigrants into three types: the specialized category, the compact, and the isolated. The groups for this study were chosen because the Hutterites are a clear-cut example of the "specialized category" type and the Romanians represent the "isolated" immigrant type. The study then proceeds to analyse the processes of acculturation undergone by each group and to explain why these two groups differed dramatically in their adjustment to Canadian society. The chapter on the Hutterites considers historical background, factors contributing to group unity, religion, economic and political organization, and value orientations.

KAUFFMAN, J. HOWARD
"A Comparative Study of Traditional and Emergent Family Types Among Midwest Mennonites." Unpublished Ph.D. dissertation, University of Chicago, 1960.

This study, based on families affiliated with the Mennonite Church in Canada and the United States, has four purposes: 1) to present empirical data which bear on the question of the relative "success" of "traditional" families as compared with families which evidence the newer, emerging forms of family life; 2) to discover factors related to successful child development; 3) to make an ethnological contribution on aspects of family life among Mennonites; and 4) to provide more reliable information for use in family life education and family counselling programs among Mennonites. The principle hypotheses are: Mennonite families differ as to type and may be placed on a continuum ranging from traditional norms to emergent norms; traditional families are related positively with rural residence, farming, lower education, and lower income; there is no significant relationship between traditional—emergent family types and the marital success variable; and acceptance of Mennonite values is greater among parents and children from traditional families.

KLASSEN, PETER GEORGE
"A History of Mennonite Education in Manitoba." Unpublished M.Ed. thesis, University of Manitoba, 1958.

"This thesis is an attempt to develop the story of Mennonite education in Manitoba and to show how, in spite of problems, a religious philosophy has been maintained in the new land." It begins by providing an outline of Mennonite history which is necessary for understanding the development of Mennonite education in Manitoba. The general subject of the thesis is treated chronologically with the discussion divided into four stages: Mennonite education during the time of complete school autonomy; the period of religious and language conflicts; the struggle for better education among the Mennonites; and Mennonite education in modern times. Trends in Mennonite education are also presented. They include an increasing interest in secular education and the trend to abandon the cause of bilingualism. But, author concludes, Mennonites retain the belief that education is a special function of the church and that it is a means to preserve their way of life.

KLASSEN, PETER G.
"A History of Mennonite Education in Canada, 1786-1960." Unpublished Ph.D. dissertation, University of Toronto, 1970.

By tracing the history of Mennonite education, author hopes to answer questions concerning the values that Mennonites wish to retain and propagate, their attempts to perpetuate these values by education, the differences in Mennonite denominations in attitudes toward education, and their educational contributions to Canadian society. Several periods in this history stand out as having particular impact on Mennonite unity. For example, the Manitoba School Question, the establishment of three institutions of higher learning by the more progressive Mennonites, and the coming of twenty thousand Mennonite immigrants in the 1920's were events that caused conflict not only between the Mennonites and the authorities, but also between the conservative Mennonites and the more progressive-minded Mennonites who felt their own schools were inadequate. Author concludes that there are still too many barriers among Mennonites and that some Mennonite denominations will be forced to close some of their schools. He also feels that secular aspects of education have been advanced at the expense of the religious element.

KRAHN, JOHN JACOB
"A History of Mennonites in British Columbia." Unpublished Ph.D. dissertation, University of British Columbia, 1955.

The purpose of this dissertation is to analyse the Mennonites in British Columbia historically and sociologically with final consideration of the integration of Mennonites into the Canadian social structure. The author puts the story of the Mennonites in the context of the development of British Columbia. After a resume is given of the Mennonite origins in Europe, the author describes three Mennonite communities, Yarrow, Black Creek, and South Abbotsford, as well as the major Mennonite groups—the General Conference, Mennonite Brethren, Evangelical Mennonite Brethren, Sommerfelder Mennonites, Old Colony Mennonites, and the Church of God in Christ. Sociologically, the author provides information on the family, marriage, schools, and beliefs, ministry, and organization of the church. The degree of assimilation in certain areas of Mennonite life is also discussed. On the whole, this is a generalized study lacking in depth and conclusions.

LAURENCE, HUGH
"Symbolic Change and Root Metaphor—A Study of Boundary Interaction and Change in Religion and Economics Among Amish Mennonites in Southwestern Ontario." Unpublished Ph.D. dissertation, McGill University, 1977.

Changing structures in religion and economics are described in the transition from the old, closed community and ideology based on shared labour to a religion of individual salvation and individually operated farms and businesses. This is a breakdown of community in both religion and economics. Conceptually Laurence affirms a dialectical relationship between the economic forces which change religion and the religious forces which change economics. The dissertation is based on two years of field residence in the Amish Mennonite communities of Ontario.

LEATHERMAN, DANIEL R.
"Political Socialization of Students in the Mennonite Secondary Schools." Unpublished M.A. thesis, University of Chicago, 1960.

This study is a beginning in providing an understanding of Mennonite political behavior. Its motives are to raise a major problem faced by pluralistic, democratic political systems—the satisfactory intergration of deviant minority groups—and to provide information which the sect in question "may find useful in evaluating its own position vis-a-vis the 'outgroup' society." The study begins with a consideration of the relevant theological and historical factors on which the Mennonite norm of nonparticipation in politics is based. In his final analysis, author states that Mennonite youth's degree of political deviancy is related to "1) the specificity in political content of the aspect of socialization and 2) the degree of general cultural sectarianism in the youth's environment." Also two hypotheses are tested and supported. One is that males tend to be more politicized than females, and the other is that basic political socialization occurs at the pre-adolescent level.

MILLER, IRA E.

"The Development and the Present Status of Mennonite Secondary and Higher Education in the United States and Canada." Unpublished Ed.D. dissertation, Temple University, Philadelphia, 1953.

This study is concerned with the general development of Mennonite secondary and higher education with particular reference to the philosophy on which it is based. It also seeks to determine the present status of these schools in the United States and Canada. The study is based on forty accredited educational institutions which are located in eleven states and in five provinces. Data is provided which may be useful to Mennonites for readjusting their educational programmes to fit changing conditions.

MOTT, MORRIS

"The Foreign Peril: Nativism in Winnipeg, 1916-1923." Unpublished M.A. thesis, University of Manitoba, 1970.

This thesis is indirectly of value for a study on Mennonites. It is primarily concerned with an Anglo-Saxon Protestant culture group, which had established its predominance in the city of Winnipeg and which became acutely suspect of the loyalties of those who were not of British ethnic origin during World War I. The overt nativism of this strongly pro-British group was evident during the war years as they maintained a defensive vigilance against "the subversive elements in their midst." Suspicions of the Germans were particularly intense which led to the stereotyping of all Germans as gruff and barbaric. The Mennonites, although not specifically mentioned, were frequently objects of suspicion, hence this study is useful for revealing the atmosphere and the harassments they suffered during the war.

MURDIE, ROBERT

"A Geographical Study of the Mennonite Settlement in Waterloo County." Unpublished B.A. thesis, Waterloo Lutheran University, 1961.

This thesis is primarily concerned with providing an awareness of the exact location of Waterloo County Mennonites and of the marked differences between Mennonite orders or groups. The number of Mennonites living within county subdivisions for ten year periods beginning with 1861 was available from census data. The farmsteads of six major Mennonite and Amish Mennonite orders were located with the assistance of Mennonite clergy and laymen. These were then plotted on topographic maps. To arrive at an objective view of Mennonite life, questionnaires were sent to members of the Old Order Mennonites and Mennonite Conference of Ontario. From the questionnaire results, tables were drawn up comparing the two groups in relation to occupations, agricultural practices, household conveniences, transportation and shopping habits. It is concluded that today only about one quarter of Waterloo County's Mennonite population, the Old Order group, have retained their cultural identity, and it is apparent that they cannot retain this identity in a highly urbanized area. They must either become assimilated or move to a remote area.

MURRAY, STANLEY N.
"A History of Agriculture in the Valley of the Red River of the North, 1812-1920." Unpublished Ph.D. dissertation, University of Wisconsin, 1963.

The central theme of this study is the changing patterns of settlement and nature of farming as they occurred in the Red River Valley of Manitoba from 1812-1920. This area was settled by many different groups who adapted to the land in various ways. The Mennonites are regarded as one of the important migrant groups in the settlement of the Red River Valley and reference is made to them throughout the paper. In particular, a detailed description of the Mennonites who came from the Ukraine in the 1870's is provided on pages 133-141. This section carefully describes the movement of the Russian Mennonites to Canada, and outlines the arrangements made with the Canadian Government for religious freedom, exemption from military service, and the right to live in closed communities with their own form of local government. It is emphasized that the Mennonites were a "determined and resourceful group" but they did not achieve the prosperity that they had known in the Ukraine. Also described are the Mennonite settlements of Rosenort and Rosenhof.

NIGH, HAROLD D.
"Factors that Effect the Growth of the Rural Brethren in Christ in Ontario." Unpublished B.D. thesis, McMaster University, 1958.

The rural Brethren in Christ in Ontario are described in detail with special emphasis on the church's organization and leadership, its methods of church extension and its distinctive doctrines and practices. These aspects of the church are examined as factors that affect the growth of the rural Brethren in Christ with the hope of providing information that will be useful in promoting growth in the rural churches. Author suggests that the Brethren in Christ Church will have to place less importance on some of its traditions and will have to allow for new ideas or it will lose the present fervor within the church. He also concludes that the Brethren in Christ will remain within Anabaptist tradition, especially as it is preserved among the Mennonites, with emphasis on nonresistance and some form of the "agape" or love feast, a form of communion.

NYMAN, JOHN S.

"The Mennonite Vote." Unpublished B.A. thesis, University of British Columbia, 1956.

A study on some aspect of Mennonite political behavior is valuable since this is an area in Mennonite life that remains generally unresearched. The aim of this thesis is to attempt to assess the relative importance of various factors determining the voting behavior of a specific and limited group, the Mennonites. The first part of the study determines the political allegiance of the Mennonites of the Fraser Valley in the provincial election of 1952 and asks the following questions: Do the Mennonites vote as a bloc? For whom do they vote? and What is the extent of their political participation? With this established, the major part of the study examines the characteristics of the Mennonites and attempts to ascertain if the party which captured their vote employed any special techniques designed to appeal to their particular needs. Nyman concludes that "the perception of the Social Credit image as being congenial to their values—values derived from Christian principles—was the decisive factor in the provincial general election of 1952."

OSWALD, C. EVAN

"A History of Sports in the Mennonite Church of North America Since 1900." Unpublished M.S. thesis, University of Illinois, 1957.

The modern recreation movement has influenced many churches but the extent of this influence on the Mennonite Church is questionable. "It is the purpose of this study to determine the place of sports in the life of the Mennonite Church of North America and to analyse the activities and attitudes of the church towards sports. The specific purposes of this study are: to present an objective description of the developmental history of sports in the Mennonite Church since 1900; to analyse the trends and to present and contrast the development of sports in society through the Mennonite Church since 1900. To understand the basic patterns of living which have influenced the twentieth century philosophies and practices of the church, it was necessary to study the church from its beginnings."

PALMER, HOWARD
   "Responses to Foreign Immigration: Nativism and Ethnic Toler-
   ance in Alberta, 1880-1920." Unpublished M.A. thesis, University of
   Alberta, 1971.

   This thesis attempts to find manifestations of nativism in Alberta,
   to discover its origins and causes, and to examine stereotypes
   which English-Canadians had of various ethnic groups. An up-
   surge of nativism occurred between 1898-1922 in response to the
   rapid increase in the number of eastern Europeans coming to
   Alberta. Fears were expressed that they would undermine
   Anglo-Saxon political institutions, that they would destroy the
   religious social homogeneity of the west, and that they would
   threaten middle class patterns of life. Native Canadians saw three
   solutions to "threats" which these immigrants posed: either assimilation, or immigration restriction, or both. The predicament
   of the Mennonites in light of these sentiments is best seen during
   World War I, a period of intense and pervasive anti-German and
   anti-enemy sentiment. The thesis briefly outlines the resentment
   which arose over the pacifism of all Mennonite groups, and the
   use of German by the Holdemanites of Linden and General
   Conference Mennonites near Didsbury. It states that hostility
   toward the Mennonites was further aroused with the arrival of
   the Hutterites in Alberta and reveals how this hostility finally led
   to the passing of a law in 1917 which barred Hutterites,
   Doukhobors, and Mennonites from entering Alberta.

PETER, KARL
   "Social Class and the Conception of the Calling: Toward a Construc-
   tive Revision of Max Weber's Hypothesis." Unpublished M.A.
   thesis, University of Alberta, 1965.

   "The German sociologist, Max Weber, traced the spirit of
   capitalism to the workings of religious psychological sanctions
   which operated in a number of Protestant sects. In the present
   study the author looks at one of the sects, the Anabaptist-
   Hutterite group, and finds that this group has similar religious
   psychological sanctions but never developed a spirit of capitalism.
   To explain this the author hypothesizes that social relations
   characteristic of the Anabaptist-Hutterite membership have an
   influence on the institutional and religious development of this
   sect. The particular social relation characteristic of the
   Anabaptist-Hutterite membership is determined through an
   analysis of two Medieval social structures. By analyzing the
   emergence of the Anabaptist-Hutterite group as a social movement, the author finds the hypothesis to be confirmed. From
   these findings it can be suggested that the social relations characteristic of a social class did have an influence on the nature of the
   emergent institutional behavior of the Protestant sect."

PETERS, FRANK C.
"A Comparison of Attitudes and Values Expressed by Mennonite and Non-Mennonite College Students." Unpublished Ph.D. dissertation, University of Kansas, 1959.

Author states that "if the Mennonite doctrine of separation from the world is actually implemented in the daily lives of Mennonites, a difference between the value-systems of Mennonites and non-Mennonites should exist." He sets out to test this as well as the supposition that Mennonite private schools are justified because they submit certain values to the students, values which students would not receive in the public schools. The study deals with three Mennonite groups: the Old Mennonites, General Conference Mennonites, and Mennonite Brethren. These groups stress education, support educational systems of their own, and communicate with the non-Mennonite world about them. Author discovered that the Mennonites and non-Mennonites differed significantly in their attitudes but that Mennonites who attended church high schools did not differ greatly from Mennonites who went to public schools.

PETERS, JACOB
"The Association of Religious Affiliation, Socio-Economic Status, Generation, and Segregation with German Ethnocentrism." Unpublished M.A. thesis, University of Manitoba, 1971.

This study attempts to investigate the association of religious affiliation, socio-economic status, generation, and segregation with ethnocentric behavior and attitudes exhibited by German speaking university students. German ethnocentrism was measured by ingroup choice and German language proficiency. The findings partially supported the hypotheses, although the levels of association were negligible or low. German university student behavior, excluding Mennonite students, indicated low loyalty toward the German ethnic group. Mennonite students expressed high German language proficiency supported by positive attitudes, and they depended heavily on intra-ethnic group friends. "This study suggests that religious affiliation is a crucial variable in the analysis of German ethnocentrism. The traditional image of Mennonites as a distinct group among the Germans was strongly supported by the data."

REDEKOP, CALVIN
"The Sectarian Black and White World." Unpublished Ph.D. dissertation, University of Chicago, 1959.

A research into sectarian behavior is the object of this work. One part of the study attempts to advance our understanding of the social phenomenon which is called the sect since it is felt that the typology of the sect and of the sect cycle are in need of re-evaluation. A second part is a close analysis of a typical sect, the Old Colony Mennonites, with the purpose of keeping the theoretical analysis close to empirical data. The data from this case study is used in the reconceptualization of the sect type. For example, analysis of the Old Colony Mennonites in Canada and Mexico permits the author to test the following hypotheses: the sect emerges through economic protest; the sect is an unstable social phenomenon, continually moving toward the church type; and the sect type is a "protest" against social and cultural organization. A number of postulates were also supported or contradicted by this case study. The stratification in the Old Colony system contradicted the belief that the sect is a true brotherhood, but the postulate that the sect is basically concerned with rejection of the "world" was supported.

REID, ERNEST H.
"A Comparative Study of Secondary and Higher Educational Interests Among The Different Racial Groups of Manitoba." Unpublished M.Ed. thesis, University of Manitoba, 1937.

It is the purpose of this study to determine the extent to which the various ethnic-religious groups (mistakenly called "races") in Manitoba participate in the facilities for higher education apart from such factors as economic and social status and the geographical situation of the race. It is based upon the assumption that those groups most active educationally will be the ones which will influence the culture of the province to the greatest extent. The Germans, largely made up of Mennonites in Manitoba (who are originally Dutch), constitute one of the six groups chosen for this comparative study. Topics of discussion include the European background and educational tradition of each group, the education problems created in Manitoba by extensive immigration, the ethnic composition of secondary school enrolment, and analysis of the enrolment of teacher training classes and of the enrolment of the University of Manitoba. It is revealed that the hostility of Mennonites toward education was replaced by a strong desire for education and "the result is an enthusiasm for various types of higher education on the part of their young people."

SAWATSKY, RODNEY
"History as Ideology: The Identity Struggle of An American Minority—the Mennonites." Unpublished Ph.D. dissertation, Princeton University, 1977.

Developing a new approach in Mennonite identity analysis, the Dean of Conrad Grebel College notes the transition from ethnicity to denominationalism which suggests that scholars must go beyond sociological and theological categories to understand the vast historical scholarship of Mennonites during the past fifty years as an *ideological* tool. Until 1950 almost all Mennonite intellectuals delineated their identity through historical study. In this quest Sawatsky finds and labels normative history with a right and left wing. A fresh approach which is a complex follow-up to his 1967 M.A. thesis at Minnesota, "The Influence of Fundamentalism on Mennonite Nonresistance, 1908-1945."

SAWATZKY, ARON
"The Mennonites of Alberta and Their Assimilation." Unpublished M.A. thesis, University of Alberta, 1964.

This study focuses on the impact of the Alberta environment on the Mennonites, how they have responded to external influences, and how effective have been their endeavors to preserve their faith under new circumstances. Attitudes of various groups of Mennonites are also considered to see what effect they have had on the primary objective of Mennonites to maintain the faith. Author found that some Mennonite groups, like Old Colony Mennonites and the Holdemanites, sought to preserve their faith and traditions by migrating whenever these were threatened. As a result, he states, these groups have experienced stagnation and frustration. Other groups like the Old Mennonites, Mennonite Brethren, and General Conference Mennonites chose to accept innovations and assumed leadership in religious, social and political matters. Since these Mennonites "have made use of new methods and technology to advance their faith, 'they have achieved' stability and expansion."

SCHELBERT, LEO
"Swiss Migration to America: the Swiss Mennonites." Unpublished Ph.D. dissertation, Columbia University, New York, 1966.

Although not specifically Canadian, this study is of great value for anyone studying the Swiss Mennonites. The author tries to understand the cultural background, the dislocating forces, the migratory experience, and the final settling and acculturation of this particular immigrant group. The study suggests that the central role of religious persuasion emerges as a main characteristic of Swiss Mennonites coming to America and that these Mennonites represent a social group with a different outlook and motivation than other Swiss immigrants.

SCHELLENBERG, ARNOLD
"A Study of Acculturation Proneness of an Ethnic Subculture Within an Urban Community: Mennonite Musicians in Winnipeg." Unpublished M.A. thesis, University of Manitoba, 1968.

As Canadian Mennonites urbanize, new patterns emerge for acculturation as this study of Winnipeg Mennonite musicians reveals. By sound research Schellenberg shows the crucial significance of advanced training in its effect of receptivity to change in the Winnipeg milieu. The less trained and less talented have little receptivity to social change, view music as a means to the end of churchmanship, and have different musical tastes.

Because Winnipeg has the largest concentration of Mennonites in any urban center of North America, the many studies stimulated by the University of Manitoba will eventually constitute the first reliable body of evidence dealing with the effects of urbanization on the progressive Mennonites who migrated from Russia since 1924.

SCHRAG, M. H.
"The Brethren in Christ Attitude Toward the World: A Historical Study of the Movement from Separation to an Increasing Acceptance of American Society." Unpublished Ph.D. dissertation, Temple University, 1967.

Using the refinement of Troeltsch's sect typology developed by Yinger, Schrag shows that the Brethren in Christ (known in Canada as the River Brethren or Tunkers) are an established sect on the way to status as a denomination. The key shift in the direction of denominational status is the individualistic understanding of sin without reference to social structure. Brethren in Christ in both the Unived States and Canada cooperate with the Mennonite Central Committee.

SIEMENS, ALFRED H.
"Mennonite Settlement in the Lower Fraser Valley." Unpublished M.A. thesis, University of British Columbia, 1960.

"This study attempts to trace the historical geography of Mennonite settlements in Fraser Valley, to single out for analysis significant changes in their structure and function and to summarize their distinctive characteristics by means of statistics, maps, photos, and description. All this is to lift a segment of one ethnic group out of the mosaic of the Canadian population and show what has been its part in the shaping of the landscape of British Columbia's densely settled southwestern corner. The individual holdings, the small nucleation, the sizeable Mennonite centers of Yarrow and Clearbrook, as well as the urban communities in Vancouver were described and analysed in turn with a view toward capturing peculiarities and finding some definite marks of the degree of acculturation experienced by the people themselves." It is concluded that the Mennonites have retained a number of peculiarities in the nature of their settlements but cultural and economic change is moving them toward farm rationalization and urbanization so that in many cases the only peculiarities that persist are theological and ethical.

SMELTZER, MORRISON F.

"Saskatchewan Opinion on Immigration, 1920-1939." Unpublished M.A. thesis, University of Saskatchewan, 1950.

The general nature of this study can be applied specifically to a study of the Mennonites since it examines the changing opinions of the Saskatchewan people concerning immigration at a time when Mennonites were attempting to enter this province. Outlined in this paper are immigration policies, such as the consistent opposition of farmers' organizations to immigration projects, the greater support for immigration during prosperous times, the preference for British immigrants, and the attempts to assimilate and absorb the foreign groups into one pattern of life, which had a great impact upon the Mennonites. Problems discussed specifically concerning Mennonites are: the difficult situation the Saskatchewan government encountered when Bishop Toews, head of the Mennonite Church in Canada, appealed on humanitarian grounds to allow 1000 Russian Mennonites to enter Canada at a time when Saskatchewan desired only British immigrants; and the demand for special consideration by Mennonites which was inconsistent with the emphasis on "Canadianization" of all immigrants.

THIELMAN, GEORGE GERHARD

"The Canadian Mennonites: A Study of an Ethnic Group in Relation to the State and Community with Emphasis on Factors Contributing to Success or Failure of Its Adjustment to Canadian Ways of Living." Unpublished Ph.D. dissertation, Western Reserve University, 1955.

Mennonites interpreted as a distinct ethnic group with common language, religious faith and behaviour patterns. Individualism has split the Mennonites into liberal, moderate and conservative.

As colonizers Mennonites are high achievers because of mutual aid, first class agriculture and economic zeal. Among the liberals technology and urbanization have caused Canadianization to triumph over old world Mennonitism. Data is provided to show that acculturation and assimilation have taken place in politics, military service and education.

"Kultur Mennonitism" now exists in tension and conflict with Biblical Christianity. Empirically based, the writer has made a powerful attack on the assumption that Canadian Mennonites have not succumbed to the erosion of their radical ethical traditions. An important work.

TOEWS, JACOB JOHN

"The Cultural Background of the Mennonite Brethren Church." Unpublished M.A. thesis, University of Toronto, 1951.

"Whatever religious causes may have contributed to the beginning of the Mennonite Brethren Church, it can hardly be denied

that strong social and economic factors played their potent role to
a much greater degree than it may appear on the surface." The
role of these factors is the theme of this thesis and the author is,
therefore, primarily concerned with discovering the social and
economic factors which contributed to the controversy leading to
the origins and growth of a new group. The findings indicate that
one of the major factors in the conflict was the change in the
Mennonites of Russia from a homogeneous society to a highly
stratified one. The rebellion of the lower classes "constituted a
powerful social reorganizing agency." Other factors which contributed to the birth of the Mennonite Brethren Church include
the following: the decline of church authority; a well-to-do ministry which weakened their spiritual zeal; introduction of Mennonites into civil offices; and interaction with the outside community.

URRY, JAMES
"The Closed and the Open: Continuity and Change Amongst the
Mennonites in Russia, 1789-1889." Unpublished D. Phil. disserta-
tion, Oxford University, 1975.

Specializing in anthropology at Oxford, Urry did most of the
research for this doctoral dissertation through interviews of
Canadian Russian Mennonites and perusal of the Mennonite
archives in Canada. It is an important contribution to the understanding of closed communities which move to new patterns
of socialization by new forms of discourse and new ranges of
knowledge. Johann Cornies, a marginal Mennonite, was the key
agent of change as he mediated between a government which
blessed the hard-working, creative Mennonites as model colonists
and the colonists themselves who had no idea that their virtues of
the Protestant work ethic and scientific agriculture could lead to
the vices of assimilation. The terminal date of 1889 does not cover
subsequent events leading to the Revolution and its brutal discon-
tinuity. The Mennonite vision of a culture within a culture is
seriously challenged by this original, comprehensive study.

WARKENTIN, JOHN H.
"The Mennonite Settlement of Southern Manitoba." Unpublished
Ph.D. dissertation, University of Toronto, 1960.

Warkentin's thesis is an endeavour to explain the changing geography of the Mennonite Reserves of Southern Manitoba. Settlement geography is concerned with the facilities men build in the
process of occupying an area. The author, therefore, outlines the
agricultural developments that have led to significant changes in
both Reserves. Since the two Reserves are dissimilar in resources
and location, the dimension of comparative geography is added.
Also discussed, are the distinctive features of these Mennonite
settlements. For example, their mode of settlement was nucleated
rather than dispersed, and they wished to avoid being absorbed

into the rural society about them. From this study, the author makes three conclusions: the Mennonites' unique settlement pattern did not survive in Canada; from 1930-1950, important changes in agricultural geography occurred; and significant changes in the role of central places in the Reserves were made.

WIESEL, BARBARA BOWIE
"From Separatism to Evangelism: A Case Study of Social and Cultural Change among Franconia Conference Mennonites." Unpublished Ph.D. dissertation, University of Pennsylvania, 1973.

This study complements the McGill dissertation of Laurence in Ontario. Rapid social change has come to previously conservative Mennonites and Amish. Wiesel charts the movement from communal to individualistic patterns. The *MQR* reviewer believes that Wiesel's study represents an important new model which combines anthropological field research with oral history and traditional history (XLVIII, 3, pp. 391-392).

WILLOWS, ANDREW
"A History of the Mennonites, Particularly in Manitoba." Unpublished M.A. thesis, University of Manitoba, 1924.

A survey of Mennonite history with special consideration of Ontario, Manitoba and Saskatchewan focusing primarily on the clash in Manitoba between provincial educational policy requiring English language instruction contrasting the attitudes of the progressive Mennonites who came from Russia in 1874 and the Old Colony Mennonites who would not yield on the language question. Written on the eve of the second great wave of migration from Russia in 1924.

ZOOK, MERVIN D.
"Measurement of Attitudes toward Religious Conscientious Objectors in Selected Magazines of World War II Years by Evaluative Assertion Analysis." Unpublished M.A. thesis, Indiana University, 1969.

Measurement of attitudes expressed in the content of messages written about religious conscientious objectors in some selected magazines during the World War II years, 1939-1947 inclusive, is the focus of this study. It emphasizes that the Mennonites, Quakers, and Brethren constituted 65 per cent of all conscientious objectors in World War II and were the subject of a great deal of publicity during the wartime years. Also discussed are the Mennonite conscientious objectors who served in the Civilian Public Service and gave more than $4 million worth of labor to their country without a cent of pay. The hypothesis that conscientious objectors would be treated unfavorably in magazines was not supported.

C. Articles

AUGSBURGER, A. DON

"Control Patterns and the Behavior of Mennonite Youth." *MQR*, XXXIX (July, 1965), pp. 192-203.

The purpose of this study was to gather statistical data which would throw some light upon the influence of control factors in both home and church upon behavior and personal and social development of Mennonite youth. The differences in opinions of control patterns to be used in child rearing are presented, as well as methods of group control. Some findings revealed that too little restriction may be a definite handicap to the child as a prospective adult and that the church offers valuable assistance as a supplement to home influence.

BAEHR, KARL

"The Secularization Process Among Mennonites." *Conference on Mennonite Cultural Problems*, I (August, 1942), pp. 35-40.

A sociological description of the secularization process in the form of five diagrams. First the Mennonite sect is in conflict with the larger society. Next Mennonites are granted religious freedom and they are tolerated by the rest of society. Lastly there are three stages of interaction. Usually the sect moves up the Mennonite ladder rather than moving directly out into the larger society.

BAKER, O. E.

"The Effects of Urbanization on American Life and on the Church." *MQR*, XIX (April, 1945), pp. 117-142.

Author implies in this study that modern urban culture is ephemeral and that the Christian rural culture, for example the Mennonites, is much more lasting. The family is described as a basic institution of human society and its functions are primarily the reproduction of the race and the transmission of wealth and of culture from generation to generation. But, author states, when the family fails to function in these three ways, the society, based on this declining institution of the family, will die out. Article states that Mennonites must endeavor to "row against the drifting tide of urbanism and build a new civilization that emphasizes peace rather than war, economic cooperation, family integrity, loyalty and continuity."

BARGEN, PETER F.

"The Coming of the Mennonites to Alberta." *ML*, XI (April, 1956), pp. 83-87.

There were four definite periods of migrations to Canada: the movement into Upper Canada from the United States in 1786; the movement in the 1870's from Russia into Canada; the coming of the Russian Mennonites, 1923-1930; and the movement after World War II. Article discusses these movements and their contributions to the Mennonite population of the province of Alberta.

BARGEN, PETER F.
"Mennonite Land Settlement Policies." *ML*, XV (October, 1960), pp. 187-190.

An explanation of the tendency of the Mennonites to settle in groups and to obtain land in "blocks." Author also tells of the type of farming land the Mennonites chose, where the group settlements were established, and the functions of the Mennonite Provincial Committee. Author says that traditionally the Mennonites belong to the land and that the large number of landless families in the 30's caused great concern. Lack of unity among Mennonites is also discussed as a detrimental factor in the Mennonite land settlement policy.

BENDER, H. S.
"Kleine Gemeinde." *ME*, III, pp. 196-199.

Account of a dissatisfied group who originated in 1814 in the Molotschna Mennonite settlement in Russia. Their basic characteristics, leaders, and immigration to Manitoba are discussed. Author also tells what happened to this congregation as change began to take place after World War I. He says the Kleine Gemeinde has remained until recently one of the more conservative and traditional of Russian Mennonite groups in North America.

BENDER, HAROLD S.
"New Data for Ontario Mennonite History." *MQR*, III (January, 1929), pp. 42-46.

Article briefly describes the claims by Mennonite residents of Waterloo County, outlines the journeys from Eastern Pennsylvania to Waterloo Township, and gives statistics regarding Mennonite ministers and Mennonite population in Ontario.

BENDER, HAROLD S.
"Church and State in Mennonite History." *MQR*, XIII (April, 1939), pp. 83-103.

The functions of the state involve the collection of taxes, economic benefits, and law and order. There is seldom a conflict with these functions. But when the state enters a field which relates to the real values of life, such as morals, religion, and family life, there is often conflict. This situation has created problems for Mennonites especially when the oath and military service have been involved. This study gives an account of Mennonite participation in the organized political forms of the state and of their obedience to the state.

BENDER, H. S.
"Ohio and Canada West Mennonite Conference." *ME*, IV, p. 30.

The Canada-Ohio Conference was organized in 1855 under the formal name, "Conference of the United Mennonite Community of Canada West and Ohio." The Canadians were a small dissident group from Waterloo and Lincoln Counties. It continued until 1869 when members began to join other conferences.

BENDER, HAROLD S.
"Mennonite Inter-group Relations." *MQR*, XXXII (January, 1958), pp. 48-57.

Inter-Mennonite relationships are growing today on an intercontinental as well as on an inter-denominational and international basis. This growth reflects the developing mutual understanding and enlarging good will among Mennonites of the distinct denominational bodies. Such programs as the Mennonite Central Committee, the Conference on Mennonite Cultural Problems, and the Mennonite World Conference enable Mennonites to work alongside each other.

BENDER, PAUL
"Mennonite Secondary and Higher Education: A Report of the Study Conducted for the Study Commission on Mennonite Secondary and Higher Education." Mennonite Board of Education, Goshen, Indiana, 1964.

"The study arises out of efforts of Mennonite school administrators to set up ten-year budgeting plans for the schools they administer, and the need to do this planning so as to accomplish most effectively the purposes of Mennonite secondary schools and colleges." Although this study recognized the need for a clarification of the philosophy of education for the Mennonite Church and its schools, it is confined to the compilation and interpretation of the more objective data related to Mennonite schools. The report is divided into several areas, with each portion showing all pertinent statistical data and supplemented by concise tables and graphs. They are: Mennonite Family Census, 1963; enrolments at Mennonite colleges; Mennonite students beyond high school; Mennonite students and student fellowships at universities; the impact of Christian education at the various age levels; facts and opinions from church workers regarding Mennonite schools; and nursing education.

BERGEN, JOHN and FRIESEN, DAVID
"Changing Attitudes of Mennonite University Students." *ML*, XXIII (October, 1968), pp. 169-172.

This survey was compiled with the help of Edmonton students. It gives the beliefs and views of contemporary university students to such issues as Mennonitism, religious convictions, vocational involvement, etc.

√ BREUGELMANS, R.
"Dutch and Flemings in Canada." *Canadian Ethnic Studies*, II (December, 1970), pp. 83-115.

A section of this article considers the Mennonite claims to "Dutch" parentage. It explains the change in origins among Mennonites from "German" to "Dutch" as revealed by the 1921 and 1931 census returns. Author says this gave rise to a controversy among Mennonites since some pointed with pride to their "Dutch" origins while others saw it as an "historical error." The names of Canadian Mennonites from Russia—Dyck, Claassen, Cornies, etc.—reflect the earliest origins in Holland, followed by residence in Prussia before migrating to Russia and Canada.

BURKHOLDER, J. LAWRENCE
"The New Mennonite Community." *ML*, XXVII (December, 1972), pp. 104-105.

Urban Mennonites are faced with the problems of retaining their religious identity and of transmitting the Mennonite faith to their children without the support of a Mennonite community. Author states that Mennonites today are looking for a viable form of Christian community but the Mennonite Church seems to offer only two possibilities: the "classical rural Mennonite community" or the "commune." What is needed, he says, is a model that tries to preserve some of the values of the traditional rural Mennonite community while taking into account the facts of urban life. Suggestions given for this "new Mennonite community" are provision for depth relations through the house church, appreciation of a high degree of freedom, and also perpetuation of what is best in the Mennonite tradition without apology.

BURKHOLDER, J. LAWRENCE
"Peace Churches as Communities of Discernment." *The Christian Century*, LXXX (September 4, 1963), pp. 1072-1075.

This article considers one problem facing the peace churches: "How can today's congregation be designed in order to express the underlying intentions of faith as interpreted by the peace churches?" It is specifically concerned with structuring the congregation to make ethical decisions and to become a "discerning community." It emphasizes that a discerning community must be seen in relation to a fundamental change in the cultural situation of peace churches. This, the writer states, is especially true for the Mennonites who must realize that the city is now the fundamental sociological context of the church and that they are facing a whole new set of ethical problems. In terms of structure, the article mentions that house churches, prayer cells, study groups, and lay preaching are indigenous to the peace churches of today, and it outlines methods for setting up an effective decision-making instrument. Above all, it stresses that the church should not move toward pietism or secularism but should "bring cultural relativity and the spirit of Christ into creative interaction."

BURKHOLDER, J. R.
"Christ, Conscience, Church, and Conscription." *Conscience and Conscription*, papers from the 1969 Assembly Sponsored by the Mennonite Central Committee Peace Section, Chicago, November 20-22, 1969. Akron, Pennsylvania: Peace Section, MCC, 1970.

Burkholder examines the theological and ethical validity of the draft resistance position, in the light of the historic Anabaptist-Mennonite understanding of discipleship and nonresistance. He employs a paradigm for ethical analysis in order to sort out the patterns of thought. In his conclusion, the author states that he believes draft resistance is a possible, but not a necessary implication of the Mennonite ethic of nonresistance. Also he believes that the central ethical issue can be stated in this way: "On what grounds, if any, can the act of civil disobedience represented by draft resistance be justified?"

BURKHOLDER, PAUL H.
"Highlights of Mennonite History in the Markham Community." Waterloo: Mennonite Historical Society, 1970.

This article outlines the arrival of Mennonite settlers to York County, Ontario, their farms, and business enterprises. Also included is a discussion on the influence of other faiths such as the Methodist Church which gained members at the expense of the Mennonites, and on the schism of 1840 led by Daniel Hoch.

BURKHOLDER, PAUL H.
"Ontario." *ME*, IV, pp. 61-65.

Author provides a detailed description of the Mennonite settlements in Ontario and provides an excellent map indicating the churches from all Mennonite conferences in Ontario.

CHANDLER, RUSSELL
"The Mennonites: Pioneer Nonconformists." *Christianity Today*,
XIV (September 11, 1970), pp. 44-46.

This brief article discusses a question that is very often of concern
for Mennonites: "How do you express nonconformity to the
world but be involved in world need?" Mennonite involvement in
world need can be seen in their evangelism efforts, in their
alternative programs to military service, and in other programs
such as PAX and Voluntary Service. This discussion also reveals
how the Mennonite emphasis on dress as a means of nonconformity has been detrimental to church membership and has been a
source of embarrassment to Mennonite youth. Author feels that
nonconformitism does not grow out of a sentimental adherence
to tradition but out of a renewed sensitivity to the needs of the
world.

CORRELL, E. (ED.)
"Canadian Agricultural Records on Mennonite Settlements,
1875-1877." *MQR*, XXI (January, 1947), pp. 34-46.

A series of reports by various Government immigration agents on
Mennonite settlements in Manitoba and Ontario. They concern
the immigration of Russian Mennonites between 1875-1877.

CORRELL, ERNST
"Mennonite Immigration into Manitoba." *MQR*, XI (July, 1937),
pp. 196-227; XI (October, 1937), pp. 267-283.

Author presents a collection of various records on the movement
in the early 1870's of the Mennonites from Russia to Canada. It
reveals many broad problems significant not only in Mennonite
history but also in the general and economic history of Canada.
Academic recognition is given to the historical role played by, and
the socio-economic status assumed by, the Mennonites in Canada.

CORRELL, ERNST
"Sources on the Mennonite Immigration from Russia in the 1870's."
MQR, XXIV (October, 1950), pp. 329-352.

A series of primary sources on the migrations of the Mennonites
from Russia. The bibliography contains items on Canadian records, transportation, settlement contracts, and United States dip-
lomatic dispatches.

CORRELL, E. (ED.)
"The Mennonite Loan in the Canadian Parliament, 1875." *MQR*,
XX (October, 1946), pp. 255-275.

A series of documents relating to the latter half of an approxi-
mate 7,700 Mennonites who came from South Russia and settled

in Manitoba during the 1870's. The topics centre around the loan made to the Mennonites by the Canadian government, and the immigration from Russia in 1873-74. The support received from Canadian commercial agencies is also discussed.

CORRELL, ERNST
"The Sociological and Economic Significance of the Mennonites as Culture Group in History." *MQR*, XVI (July, 1942), pp. 161-166.

"As a culture group in history, the economic significance of the Mennonites is a distinct by-product of their religio-sociological existence." Correll notes that the life styles of Mennonites are based on the Biblical ideals of community living, conscientious objection to war, and a free church group. Persecutions drove them into isolated groups where they have historically practiced an agriculture or town handicraft economy. The uniqueness and relative economic strength of Mennonite agriculture is shown to be in its rural familistic philosophy.

CORRELL, ERNST H. and BENDER, HAROLD S.
"Marriage." *ME*, III, pp. 502-510.

A description of marriage among Mennonites including discussions on the marriage problem in the "separated" organized congregation, forms of courtship, the Anabaptist-Mennonite attitude on the indissolubility of marriage, divorce, and marital avoidance as a problem of church discipline. Early Anabaptist positions on these matters are given as well as marriage patterns among Mennonites in North America. Author notes an evolution in marriage attitudes among North American Mennonites. For example, prohibition of outside marriage, among most branches of Mennonites, has disappeared, and also courtship customs have changed to free selection of partners through a period of free and unchaperoned courtship. However, author says, high standards of marriage fidelity and lifelong monogamy are maintained, with divorce uncommon and separation rare.

DAVIES, BLODWEN
"From Militia Tax to Relief." *ML*, V (October, 1950), pp. 27-28.

During the first World War, Canadian Mennonites formed a Non-Resistant Relief Organization for relief of the suffering under war conditions. Between 1939 and 1949 the major area of concern centered on the Russian Mennonites.

DOERING, J. FREDERICK
"Pennsylvania German Folk Medicine in Waterloo County." *Journal of American Folklore*, XLIX (July-September, 1936), pp. 194-198.

This brief article outlines the primitive practices that Pennsylvania Germans of Waterloo County have used as remedies for certain illnesses such as appendicitis, ringworm, stomach troubles, and warts. Of these practices, charming is probably the most unusual. It is questionable if much of this primitive medicine is alive in the 1970's.

DOERKSEN, VICTOR
"Language and Communication among Urban Mennonites." *ML*, XXIII (October, 1968), pp. 182-185.

Author deals with several topics: the dynamic of change, the rural-urban shift, the present state of German, and the state of English. He feels that the movement to the city should increase religious vocabulary whether the language is German or English. At present he says, the Canadian Mennonite German and the adopted English are not truly communicative languages.

DRIEDGER, LEO
"Christian Witness in Race Relations." *ML*, XV. (January, 1960).

Analyzing the struggle of an all-white Mennonite General Conference, Driedger notes the multi-racial inputs from missions, overseas service of Mennonite Central Committee, the pioneering effort of Woodlawn Mennonite Church in Chicago (now closed after community conflict and a disastrous fire) and then suggests that the task of the church has just begun.

DRIEDGER, LEO
"Mennonite Graduate Fellowship: Its History, Purpose and Future." *ML*, XX (April, 1965), pp. 67-72.

The Mennonite Graduate Fellowship has grown to a complex group of university scholars, with various interests from scores of disciplines. Its aims of discussion, informality, fellowship, and freedom are discussed.

DRIEDGER, LEO
"Developments in Higher Education Among Mennonites in Manitoba." *Conference on Mennonite Educational and Cultural Problems*, XVI (June, 1967), pp. 60-72.

Focus of this work is on the assimilation and accommodation process of Manitoba Mennonites into the larger Manitoba educational stream. Author discusses social changes such as adjustment of a rural group to urban trends and a language transition from German to English, which caused great changes in Mennonite education. The study is well organized into three periods of educational development: a period of conflict, of accommodation, and of assimilation. The last part of the paper concerns itself with some models of higher education among Mennonites and with the struggle of this ethnic group to make its religious concerns relevant to this urban society.

DRIEDGER, LEO
"Developments in Higher Education Among Mennonites of Manitoba." *Manitoba Journal of Educational Research*, III (November,
1967), pp. 1-11.

The assimilation and accommodation process is studied among
Manitoba Mennonites through an analysis of higher education
from the early days of conflict over the English language
(1874-1922) to accommodation (1922-45) to assimilation (1945 to
the present).

The author rejects the possibility of Redfield's "little community" for Mennonites and this concludes by examining five educational models. It is clear to the author that the real question is
what kind of higher education the Mennonites will support.

DRIEDGER, LEO
"A Perspective on Canadian Mennonite Urbanization." *ML*, XXIII
(October, 1968), pp. 147-152.

This article outlines some Canadian urban trends, describes the
concentrations of Mennonites in Canadian cities and it explores
some possible types of urban Mennonite communities which may
be emerging in Canada.

DRIEDGER, LEO
"Louis Riel and the Mennonite Invasion." *The Canadian Mennonite*,
XVIII (August 28, 1970), p. 6.

The purpose of this article is to remind the Mennonites of Manitoba and Saskatchewan that their good fortunes grew out of the
displacement of the original people who lived there. Although
the Mennonites were not responsible for driving out the Indians
and Metis, they were still political pawns, used by governments to
occupy lands which were taken from unfortunate minorities by
force. Because of this, author concludes that Mennonites must
think before they condemn the Indians for their misfortunes
today, that Mennonite historians have not told the whole story,
and that Mennonites are obligated to become involved in politics.

DRIEDGER, LEO
"Native Rebellion and Mennonite Invasion: An Examination of
Two Canadian River Valleys." *MQR*, XLIV (July, 1972), pp.
290-300.

The thesis of this paper is that Mennonites, "although historically
suspicious of governments, have on numerous occasions reaped
settlement benefits from government eviction of minority
groups," specifically the Indians and Metis of the Canadian West.
Author tests this hypothesis by focusing on a study of the Mennonite settlements in the Red River Valley in Manitoba in 1869-74

and in the Saskatchewan River Valley in 1884-95. From this study the author asserts that it is highly probable that the Mennonites would not have settled in these areas if their direct negotiation with the government for their rights to land and freedom of life style could not have been secured. He concludes that this raises serious problems for the Mennonites since they compromised their principle of love of neighbor by agreeing to receive land and since they compromised their principle of nonresistance by accepting land from a government which used violence to get them these advantages.

DRIEDGER, LEO
"Impelled Group Migration: Minority Struggle To Maintain Institutional Completeness." *International Migration Review*, VII (Fall, 1973), pp. 257-269.

Driedger tests current migration theory in its present limited state by studying the Old Colony Mennonites who are the most persistent migrating group in Canada. It is a form of survival migration which is functional in the perpetuation of a traditional remnant.

The Old Colony people have a powerful ideology which leads to migration. After settlement they use four social patterns: European village, isolated community, suburban satellite and ethnic urbanism.

Since the most accommodating do not migrate and the most intransigent do migrate, Driedger points to analogues amongst the Jews, Puritans, Mormons and Hutterites confirming this tactic. His study, covering fifteen years, also requires a fresh statement of migration theory by scholars studying this phenomenon.

DRIEDGER, LEO
"Doctrinal Belief: A Major Factor in the Differential Perception of Social Issues." *The Sociological Quarterly*, XV (Winter, 1974), pp. 66-80.

Turning from his speciality of cultural identity among minorities, the author probes the relationship between doctrinal belief and positions on social issues by sending a questionnaire to the leading ministers of Winnipeg's 313 churches with a 42 per cent response.

Doctrinal orthodoxy was correlated with the affirmation of controls for public and private morality giving room for the power elite to use this support for opposition to social change. Doctrinal liberals were chiefly concerned with civil liberty, minority rights and social welfare and were restrained in relation to all uses of force. Education in both groups did not differentiate clergy significantly. On the whole the work of Stark and Glock was confirmed. Mennonites responded quite well to the questionnaire but this essay does not refer to them specifically.

DRIEDGER, LEO
    "Canadian Mennonite Urbanism: Ethnic Villagers or Metropolitan
Remnant." *MQR*, XLVIII (1975), pp. 226-241.

This article confirmed Driedger's more sophisticated methodology for studying Canadian urban Mennonites starting with a
study in 1968 (Mennonite Life, XXIII) which was limited to
updating the census figures.
    In 1974 the Canadian Mennonites became dominantly urban
with 17,850 or 22.2 per cent of all urban Canadian Mennonites
living in Winnipeg.
    The two models presented in the paper are ethnic villagers or
metropolitan remnant. The former are views as based on territorial control, institutional completeness, cultural identity and social distance. This is an Old Testament model. It works but it is
not fully acceptable.
    The New Testament model goes beyond in-group solidarity to
outgroup service and recruitment.
    This article is the best example of Driedger working both as an
in-group sociologist and an in-group theologian. More recently
his copious writings reveal refinements of empirical sociological
research exclusively.

DRIEDGER, LEO
    "In Search of Cultural Identity Factors: A Comparison of Ethnic
Students." *Canadian Review of Sociology and Anthropology*, XII, No. 2
(1975), 12 pp.

Primarily valuable for clarification of The Ethnic Cultural Identity Inventory (ECII) as a methodological instrument in identity
research.
    Compare this article with Driedger's "Ethnic Self Identity: A
Comparison of Ingroup Evaluations," *Sociometry*, XXXIX, No. 2,
pp. 131-141.
    Driedger has also utilized the Processionally Articulated Struc-
tural (PAS) model of Loomis, Bogurdus's social distance scale;
and the methodologies of Newman, Simmel, Gordon, Glazer,
Moynihan, Barth and Lewin in his relentless quest for his own
formulation of the most fruitful ways of studying minorities.

DRIEDGER, LEO
    "Towards a Perspective on Canadian Pluralism: Ethnic Identity in
Winnipeg." *Canadian Journal of Sociology*, II, No. 1 (1977).

Recommended for a full insight into the author's methodological
refinements of William Newman's approach to minority theory in
American Pluralism: A Study of Minority Groups and Social Theory
(New York, 1973). Newman, in turn, was refining Gordon's ear-
lier (1964) methodology in *Assimilation in American Life* (New
York).

Driedger affirms a multilinear, multidimensional pluralist option in addition to the unilinear assimilation outcome, the latter causing an overlook of those like the Mennonites and Jews who were not assimilated. This pluralist option is also in line with Glazer and Moynihan's *Beyond the Melting Pot* (New York, 1964).

Indispensable to anyone wanting to understand research into minorities in Canada and elsewhere. Excellent methodology for Mennonite research.

✓

DRIEDGER, LEO and PETERS, JACOB
"Identity and Social Distance: Toward Understanding Simmel's 'The Stranger.'" *Canadian Review of Sociology and Anthropology*, XIV , No. 2 (May, 1977), 25 pp.

Driedger's many studies in Winnipeg have raised serious questions concerning deterministic assimilation of the Canadian ethnics. Yet, if they do not assimilate can they cooperate in a minimal common life of the vertical mosaic? The answer is yes. Simmel's "stranger" is associated with social distance. This social distance is not incompatible with out-group individuals as friends, next door neighbors or as partners in work. Marriage with outsiders is the crucial point of intransigence. Prejudice and discrimination, therefore, do not necessarily follow. Germans (includes the Mennonites), Poles, Ukrainians and Jews illustrate his basic argument.

✓

DRIEDGER, LEO and CHURCH, GLENN
"Residential Segregation and Institutional Completeness: A Comparison of Ethnic Minorities." *Canadian Review of Sociology and Anthropology*, XI (January, 1974), pp. 30-52.

This study provides further testing of Joy and Lieberson's theory that residential segregation is crucial to the maintenance of ethnic solidarity. It was found that three patterns emerged in the study of Winnipeg ethnics: Community maintainers (French), Suburban invaders (Jewish, Ukrainian and Polish) and Ecological assimilators (Scandinavian and German). Of the Germans, the Mennonites originally settled in three tracts but are now scattering throughout metropolitan Winnipeg. The author's previous studies underscore factors other than residential segregation which maintain cultural identity. But, the high scores of the Jews and French in cultural identity *and* residence is a matter to ponder.

✓

DRIEDGER, LEO and PETERS, JACOB
"Ethnic Identity: A Comparison of Mennonite and Other German Students." *MQR*, XLVII (July, 1973), pp. 225-244. Also available in Crysdale, S. and Wheatcroft, L. *Religion in Canadian Society* (1976), pp. 449-461.

The central questions of this study by two Canadian scholars are whether assimilation undermines identity, and to what extent this is the case with Mennonites compared to other Germans. Various theories concerning factors relating to ethnic identity are discussed. This study focuses upon the relationship between identity factors and institutional completeness. Data was collected to test four hypotheses: 1) Mennonite identity will be significantly greater than that of other Germans in the six factors of religion, endogamy, language use, participation in ethnic organizations, parochial education, and choice of friends; 2) of the six cultural indicators of identity, participation in religion, endogamy, and choice of friends will be significantly greater; 3) type of community, socio-economic status and generation Canadian will not be significantly associated with ethnic identity; and 4) institutional completeness will be positively associated with maintenance of identity. In general, assimilation approaches were rejected and Mennonites possessed a higher identity supported by a greater institutional completeness than that of other Germans.

DRIEDGER, LEO and ZEHR, DAN

"Differential Perceptions of Social Issues: A Comparison of Canadian Mennonite Leaders and Students." Unpublished manuscript (forthcoming), 25 pp.

The sub-cultural experiences of youth and adults were considered to be sufficiently varied that they would think differently of social issues related to peace, the state, and social concerns. Religious leaders who had lived through the wars and the Russian revolution, it was proposed, would be more reluctant to become involved in issues related to the state. Youth, on the other hand, would be more broadly concerned with social issues.

DRIEDGER, OTTO H.

"Mennonite Family Stress in the City." *ML*, XXIII (October, 1968), pp. 176-178.

A description of the function, role, and place of the family in society. Special reference is given to the changing pattern of the Mennonite family in urban society, particularly concerning authority, the work ethic, and Mennonite discipleship. Religious beliefs and the rural background of the Mennonites are mentioned as having a great effect on their adaptability to city life.

DUNHAM, B. MABEL

"The Story of Conestoga." *Waterloo Historical Society*, XXXIII (1945), pp. 16-23.

The Conestoga wagon has become a part of Canadian folklore through its use by Mennonite immigrants during migrations from the United States beginning in 1795. It is a symbol of frontier courage and mobility. Author describes this wagon and the Mennonite migrations into Upper Canada.

DUNHAM, B. MABEL
"Beginnings in Ontario." *ML*, V (October, 1950), pp. 14-16.

This is a brief historical description of the Mennonites on the Niagara district, the Waterloo and Woolwich settlements, and the Markham and other districts in York County.

DYCK, HENRY D.
"Language Differentiation Among the Low German Mennonites of Manitoba." *ML*, XXII (July, 1967), pp. 117-120.

The linguistic differences between the Old Colony, Bergthal, Kleine Gemeinde and the Molotschna Mennonites are discussed in this paper.

DYCK, WILLIAM and SAWATSKY, JOHN
"Psycho-Social Changes within a Metropolitan Religious Minority." *ML*, XXIII (October, 1968), pp. 172-176.

This study is an analysis of the development and changes within a relatively small Mennonite congregation over a period of three decades in Toronto.

EBERSOLE, MYRON L.
"The Anabaptist View of the Church and the Therapeutic Community." *MQR*, XXXV (July, 1961), pp. 218-237.

This study attempts to provide an understanding of the Mennonite experience in the mental health program or more specifically, "to find some basis for integration of the work of the psychiatric hospital within the context of a strong religious tradition." The author compares the two communities to see whether the therapeutic community operates on the same presuppositions on which the church bases its life. Several conclusions are provided which indicate that the Anabaptist view of the church provides the theological basis for the therapeutic community.

ENNS, GERHARD
"Waterloo North and Conscription 1917." *Waterloo Historical Society*, LI (1963), pp. 60-69.

Waterloo North demonstrated anti-war and anti-conscription feelings during World War I. Author discusses the events leading up to the 1917 election of this riding and feels that the Mennonite population must have been a factor in the strong anti-conscription vote.

ENNS, J. H.
"Winnipeg, Manitoba." *ML*, XI (July, 1956), pp. 112-113.

There are more Mennonites in Winnipeg than in any other North American city. Article says this is primarily because they were seeking work and domestic employment could be found in well-to-do families. Author also describes the occupations and independent enterprises of Mennonites in Winnipeg.

ENS, ADOLF
"Mennonite Students—Statistical Background." *ML*, XX (April, 1965), pp. 54-57.

The increased trend among Mennonites towards more education is emphasized. Statistics are given from several surveys which give an overview of the combined student population of three Mennonite Church conferences.

EPP, FRANK H.
"National Socialism Among the Canadian Mennonites in the 1930's." *Conference on Mennonite Educational and Cultural Problems*, XV (June, 1965), pp. 123-131.

The pro-Germanism of some Russian Canadian Mennonites in the 1930's was rooted in past history. Mennonites had received help from Germany, especially while escaping from Russia, which created anti-communism sympathies. Author uses data received from a study of German-language Mennonite newspapers. A contrast is shown between the Mennonite attitudes of the 1930's and in the 1960's as new leaders emerged who were emancipated from the pro-German outlook. This article based on Ph.D. dissertation.

EPP, FRANK H.
"Mennonites and the Civil Service." *ML*, XXIII (October, 1968), pp. 179-182.

Involvement in civil service has always been considered outside of the Mennonite tradition until recently. The development of the Ottawa Canada Church in civil service is the major part of this article. The author believes that urbanized Mennonitism faces the challenge of finding both a new involvement and a new separateness.

EPP, FRANK H.
"Mennonites in Canada." *German-Canadian Yearbook I*, Toronto, 1973, pp. 141-143.

A skillful distillation of salient facts concerning Mennonites in Canada. A quick way to clarify the who, what, when and where of 182,000 Mennonites of all types.

EPP, FRANK H.
"The True North." *Mennonite Reporter*, IV (March 18, 1974), pp.
10-13.

Minorities develop a restless urge to migrate. Epp drove 10,000
miles in 1973 studying the nine migrations of Mennonites of
many types to fifty communities in Northern Alberta and Central
British Columbia between 1918 and 1970. The March 18, 1974
article was the first of fourteen reports in which the writer
analyzes what he calls "the destiny of a wandering people." Recommended as a study of the social effects of migration to isolated
areas of the Canadian frontiers. Other articles in this series were
published March 18, April 29, May 13 and 27, June 10 and 24,
July 22, August 5 and 19, September 30, October 28, December
29 during 1974. The final summary article was published February 3, 1975.

EPP, HENRY H. and ULRICH, WILFRED
"Mennonite Conferences in Ontario." *ML*, XVII (July, 1962), pp.
109-112.

This article describes very briefly nine Mennonite Conferences in
Waterloo county, an area with a great range of Mennonite styles
of life and patterns of belief. The term "Mennonite" needs qualification before it can be used with precision.

EWERT, H. H.
"The Mennonites." *The Historical and Scientific Society of Manitoba*,
1932.

This article attempts to demonstrate the strong points of the
Mennonites in Canada. For example, they are said to have the
following common characteristics: a spirit of independence, a
deep sense of the sanctity of human life, a democratic spirit,
strong conservatism, a commendable spirit of altruism, a desire
for perfection, and strong social ties. Ewert also provides a summary of Mennonite origins, persecutions, and migrations and
states that the determination of the Mennonites today is a result
of the historical experiences through which they have had to pass.
Descriptions of their church system, villages, cooperative institutions, and schools are included.

FRANCIS, E. K.
"The Origins of Mennonite Institutions in Early Manitoba."
Historical and Scientific Society of Manitoba, Season 1945-1946, pp.
56-71.

This paper proposes to deal with some of the distinctive culture
traits of the Manitoba Mennonites during the pioneer period. In
order to test whether their type of social organization was the
direct result of their "unhampered development" in Russia and

that their "economic institutions were distinct by-products of
their religious-sociological existence", the author attempts to
answer such questions as: To what extent are these culture traits a
logical consequence of the religious ideas of Mennonitism? Are
there any striking similarities between Mennonite culture traits
and those of other people with whom they came into contact in
the course of their migrations? The culture traits, which are
considered throughout the article as peculiar to this group of
Mennonites, are: a specific form of habitat and communal organization; certain institutions for mutual aid; a specific law of
inheritance; and close cooperation between church and civil government.

FRANCIS, E. K.
"Mennonite Institutions in Early Manitoba: A Study of Their Origins." *Agricultural History*, XXII (July, 1948), pp. 144-155.

This article begins with a detailed description of the most conspicuous institutions which characterized Mennonite culture in
Manitoba during the pioneer period. These traits are the habitat,
communal organization, inheritance, church and civil administration, and fire insurance. Author also examines the principal
tenets of the Mennonite creed that affect social life. From this, it is
concluded that it is highly probable that factors other than religious persuasion have contributed to the origin of these unique
institutions. By tracing the changing social conditions of these
Mennonites as they moved from West Prussia to Russia to
Canada, the author concludes that the following factors have
contributed to the development of Mennonite institutions: social
heritage, segregation, acculturation, and religion.

FRANCIS, E. K.
"The Russian Mennonites; From Religious to Ethnic Group."
American Journal of Sociology, LIV (September, 1948), pp. 101-107.

"This study of social change shows that generic characteristics of
different types of groups are conceived in sociological mutations.
In the case of the Russian Mennonites a religious group was
transformed within a comparatively short time into a distinct
ethnic and folk group when the ethnically heterogeneous par-
ticipants were allowed to segregate themselves by forming isolated territorial communities. While the specific religious system,
which afforded orientations in the formative stages changed and
even lost much of its appeals, the identity and cohesion of the
group did not suffer materially."

FRANCIS, E. K.
"Mennonite Contributions to Canada's Middle West." *ML*, IV
(April, 1949), pp. 21-23, 41.

This paper examines the contributions made by the Russian Mennonites to Canada's West such as their farm-credit system, the cooperative farm movement, and their general success as agriculturalists. Their importance in acting as spearheads in colonization and in contributing to the formation of major agricultural policies is also discussed.

FRANCIS, E. K.
"Tradition and Progress Among the Mennonites in Manitoba." *MQR*, XXIV (October, 1950), pp. 312-328.

Foresees that, as long as Mennonites retain their traditions based on religious principles, their existence as a group will not suffer substantially. Religion is the strongest single force preventing assimilation of the Mennonite ethnic group. The divisions between the Altkolonier, Bergthal, and Kleine Gemeinde and also the Manitoba School question are discussed as examples of the process of change among Mennonites.

FRANCIS, E. K.
"The Adjustment of a Peasant Group to a Capitalistic Economy: The Manitoba Mennonites." *Rural Sociology*, XVII (September, 1952), pp. 218-228. Reprinted in Gallagher, J. E. and Lambert, R. *Social Process and Institution*. Toronto: Holt, Rinehart and Winston, 1971, pp. 500-511.

"This paper examines the question whether the adjustment of ethnic groups is necessarily through acculturation and increasing conformity, and whether the process will always result in the destruction of the ethnic group as a functioning social subsystem within the larger society. Changes in the behavior of the Mennonite group in Manitoba over a period of seventy years are analysed as a test case. Ideal types for the parent and host societies are formulated. The early history and recent trends in the Mennonite colonies are described, and Dawson's 1932 conclusions about the acculturation of the Canadian Mennonites are reconsidered. The hypothesis that an ethnic group, particularly a rural group, will necessarily be absorbed by the larger society when forced to adjust itself to the capitalistic economy is rejected. It is concluded that adjustment is highly selective, and that by developing new behavior patterns, an ethnic group may be able to prevent assimilation."

FRANCIS, E. K.
"The Mennonite School Problem in Manitoba." *MQR*, XXVII (July, 1953), pp. 204-237.

This is a study of the Mennonite group as a dynamic system of social interaction subject to constant change. It precludes a full treatment of the social philosophy "myth" or "creed" which makes the Canadian nation what it is. Attention is given to this larger society in so far as it directly affected the Mennonite group. The school is shown to be the most powerful instrument to affect acculturation and to stimulate the assimilation of children. It was not until World War I that the Manitoba government adopted nationalistic ideas of general cultural uniformity and initiated a policy of systematic assimilation. The outcome of this issue was the withdrawal of the Fürstenland and Sommerfelder Mennonite groups from the struggle and their emigration to other lands.

FRANCIS, E. K.
"The Mennonite Farmhouse in Manitoba." *MQR*, XXVIII (January, 1954), pp. 56-59.

Early pioneer homes represent one of the most ancient monuments of folk culture in America. The Mennonite House in Manitoba has a characteristic austerity and a strong old world flavour. Article gives descriptions of various farmhouses.

FRANCIS, E. K. and BENDER, H. S.
"East Reserve, Manitoba." *ME*, II (1956), pp. 125-129.

Reserve was the name given to a tract of land set aside by the Canadian government for exclusive occupation by a homogenous group of settlers, to be divided according to their own plans. Two different reserves were provided for the immigrant Mennonites from Russia. A very detailed map indicates the original settlement of the East Reserve. Also a description is provided of the village organization which the author calls the solidaristic type of settlement since it fosters strong social coherence and a common value system.

FRETZ, J. C.
"The Early History of the Mennonites in Welland County, Ontario." *MQR*, XXVII (January, 1953), pp. 55-75.

A short history of the first Mennonite settlers in Welland County. It describes the location of land grants, family names, cemeteries, and provides a list of the early ordained Mennonites in Welland County. Brief descriptions are also given of the Mennonite Brethren, the Reformed Mennonites, General Conference Mennonites, and the Old Order Mennonites.

FRETZ, J. WINFIELD
"Mutual Aid Among Mennonites." *MQR*, XIII (January, 1939), pp. 28-58.

Mennonite mutual aid activities are an expression of the teachings of the Mennonite Church regarding the principles of love and brotherhood. Author states that this practice is one of the reasons that accounts for the existence of Mennonites as a separate group. By remaining loyal and helpful to each other, Mennonites have preserved their group solidarity and social institutions from generation to generation. Article discusses mutual aid among the Hutterites, the Russian Mennonites and the American Mennonites. Canadian aid programs involve an orphans' bank, a mutual aid burial society and homes for girls.

FRETZ, J. WINFIELD
"Recent Mennonite Community Building in Canada." *MQR*, XVIII (January, 1944), pp. 5-21.

Study focuses on Mennonite colonization efforts especially by immigrants who came to Canada from Russia between 1923 and 1930. Communities in Ontario, Alberta, and British Columbia are examples of Mennonite settlements.

FRETZ, J. WINFIELD
"Factors Contributing to Success and Failure in Mennonite Colonization." *MQR*, XXIV (April, 1950), pp. 130-135.

The colonization process involves a group of like-minded people who separate from a parent body and transplant themselves to a new locality with a separate organization. This pattern has occurred among Mennonites when they went from Russia to Canada, to Mexico, and to Paraguay. Author summarizes the success or failure of colonization efforts by the degree to which the colonists, as individuals and as a group, are committed to an unqualified following of Christ.

FRETZ, J. WINFIELD
"Sociological Aspects of Divorce Among Mennonites." *Conference on Mennonite Educational and Cultural Problems*, VIII (June, 1951), pp. 132-138.

Divorce as a problem of Mennonites must be considered. Article is based on findings from a study of twelve U.S. General Conference Mennonite congregations. Reasons are given for the lower divorce rate among Mennonites than for the rest of society. Author states that divorce is more common among those on the periphery of church life, and among those from mixed-marriages. Mennonite attitudes on divorce are also discussed.

FRETZ, J. WINFIELD
"Social Trends Affecting the Mennonite Family at Mid-Century." *Conference on Mennonite Educational and Cultural Problems*, XI (June, 1957), pp. 131-140.

Author discusses trends that are affecting Mennonite families such as change of family size, changing roles in marriage, and acquisition of new family functions. The disintegrating and integrating forces that play upon the family are listed. Author also discusses the need to develop a pattern of Christian family life with less secularization, to seek an answer to the problem of role confusion of Christian women, and to control the social behavior of the children.

FRETZ, J. WINFIELD
"The Role of the Laity in the Life of the Church." *The Lordship of Christ; Proceedings of the Seventh Mennonite World Conference*. Edited by Cornelius J. Dyck. Elkhart, Indiana: Mennonite Publishing House, 1962.

This study of the laity in the Mennonite Church is historical, sociological, and predictive. A discussion of the church of yesterday reveals that the Mennonite Church was a strong lay church. But today the tendency toward professionalization of the ministry is significantly affecting the laity in that the role of the laity has been a declining one while the role of the clergy has been a growing one. Reasons suggested for this shift in the ministry are the rising educational level of the laity which demands a better quality of preaching, and also the urbanization of Mennonites which has increased competition for the layman's time in occupational and community activities. Author reveals ways in which the layman can carry out his role and stresses that the role of the laity in the church today is to rediscover that the laity is the church.

FRETZ, J. WINFIELD
"Manitoba—A Mosiac of Mennonites." *ML*, XI (July, 1966), pp. 126-127.

The study of Mennonites in Manitoba is a fascinating one because it displays a mosaic of Mennonites. A description and a map of Mennonites on the "East" and "West" reserves is provided.

FRIESEN, JIM and VOGT, REINHARD
"The Mennonite Community in Winnipeg." *ML*, XIX (January, 1964), pp. 13-15.

This article describes the Mennonite attitudes and reactions toward its surrounding community. Some churches in Winnipeg are beginning to play an active part in the community. And, in the educational, artistic, commercial and political areas this largest urban Mennonite community of North America is demonstrating new powers of expression and outreach.

FRIESEN, JOHN W.
"Manitoba Mennonites in the Rural-Urban Shift." *ML*, XXIII (October, 1968), pp. 152-158.

Urbanization among the Manitoba Mennonites can be seen in the churches of Winnipeg. Here the Mennonites are moving away from their former ethnic identity towards an institutional group. The ethnic forces are taking second place to the religious influences in the community.

FRIESEN, JOHN W.
"Characteristics of Mennonite Identity: A survey of Mennonite and Non-Mennonite Views." *Canadian Ethnic Studies*, III (June, 1971), pp. 25-41.

The purpose of this study on Mennonites in southern Alberta is to determine to what extent unique characteristics of Mennonite culture still exist. The basic areas studied are the identification of elements of Mennonite identity, education, and the relation of Mennonite life to the process of assimilation. Data were collected through an interview-questionnaire technique and a statistical analysis was applied. For comparison purposes both Mennonites and non-Mennonites were asked the same questions. The statistics revealed that Mennonites have the same understanding of themselves as their non-Mennonite neighbors have of them. The major conclusion of this study is that a Mennonite culture exists; "the reality of a Mennonite identity in southern Alberta is confirmed." Evidence for this is the use of Low German and High German, avoidance of civil courts, and the attitudes of Mennonites toward everyday living with religion as the basis for this life. The possibility of assimilation is not overlooked.

FRIESEN, W.
"A Mennonite Community in the East Reserve: Its Origins and Growth." *Historical and Scientific Society of Manitoba* (Season 1960-1961), pp. 24-43.

The central topic of this article is the origin and growth of Steinbach. To serve as background, author provides an explanation of who the Manitoba Mennonites are, by describing their origins, migrations, and colonies in Russia. This is followed by a detailed and valuable description of their settlement in Canada on the West and East Reserves, of the various factions among these Russian Mennonites, and of the divisions that followed. But the major concern of this article is with the Mennonites who settled in Steinbach and thus the author presents an exact layout of the entire settlement and an account of each house, mill, and enterprise that was set up. Another concern of this article is the education of Mennonite children. It is revealed how Mennonites evolved in their attitudes toward education from the feeling that it was a threat to their way of life to the present attitude that education is desirable and necessary.

GEORGE, KATHERINE
"The Mennonites and the Protestant Ethic." *Historical and Scientific Society of Manitoba* (Season 1964-1965), pp. 83-99.

"There is no doubt that in recent and modern Mennonitism the Protestant ethic is present in full-bloom glory." The purpose of this paper is to test the Weberian thesis in regard to the nature of the origins and developments of capitalism by investigating the story of a Protestant sect, the Mennonites. To do this, the author begins by studying the meaning of Anabaptism for Menno Simons who, it is discovered, provides no ethic which is in agreement with the Protestant ethic of industry and frugality. This is followed by an evaluation of the movement of the Mennonites from Holland to Prussia to Russia and then to Canada. In each case there were Mennonites who were able to adjust to the changes that occurred and who prospered from it. In particular the Mennonites of Winnipeg "have penetrated all or almost all the bourgeois sanctums of industry, commerce and the professions in central Canada's major city." In general the author seriously questions the theory that maintains that this change has "sprung from the faith these people cherished and by which they sought to live."

GERBRANDT, H. J.
"The Conference of Mennonites in Canada." *Call to Faithfulness; Essays in Canadian Mennonite Studies*. Edited by Henry Poettcker and Rudy A. Regehr. Winnipeg: Canadian Mennonite Bible College, 1972.

A description of efforts to overcome the "curse of denominationalism" among the Russian Mennonites by the formation of church conferences. Controversies over political involvement, the issues of new birth and of eschatology, and the tension between faith and social action are discussed as decisive elements that came up at conference sessions. Laymen and youth participation in this conference are also topics of discussion.

GINGERICH, MELVIN
"Alternative Service Work Camps." *ME*, I, p. 76.

In June 1941 the Canadian government informed the Committee on Military Problems of the Conference of Historic Peace Churches (Ontario) that alternative service was to be provided for conscientious objectors to war. The C.O.'s were to serve in Alternative Service camps, operated by the Department of Mines and Resources, for the duration of the war. This article describes the camps in British Columbia and also their employment on individual farms and factories.

GINGERICH, MELVIN
"Jacob Y. Shantz, 1822-1909, Promotor of the Mennonite Settlements in Manitoba." *MQR*, XXIV (July, 1950), pp. 230-247.

Jacob Y. Shantz had a deep interest in the welfare of his fellow men and a strong faith in the economic possibilities of western

Canada. He had a spirit of adventure, a character marked by integrity, and a desire to serve. All this, the author states, combined to give Shantz an opportunity of leadership rarely surpassed as North American Mennonite history. Article relates the experiences of Shantz during his early years as a sawmill owner and as a member of the Board of Trustees in Berlin and describes his aid programs with the Russian Mennonite immigrants of Manitoba.

GINGERICH, MELVIN
"Mennonite Attitudes Toward Wealth—Past and Present." *Conference on Mennonite Educational and Cultural Problems*, IX (June, 1953), pp. 89-98.

Author first discusses the early Anabaptist position on materialism and Menno Simons' belief that sharing of goods should be practiced. Data on Mennonite occupations and income from four Mennonite Church areas, including Canada, is presented to show the distribution of high and low incomes. Author feels the churches are not aware of the problems produced by disparity of wealth and suggests that more discipline in standard of living and a better program of stewardship are needed.

GINGERICH, MELVIN
"The Mennonites of Alberta." *ML*, IX (April, 1954), pp. 56-59.

This article provides a brief description of the Mennonite settlements in Alberta, along with a map indicating these Mennonite communities.

GINGERICH, MELVIN
"Russian Mennonites React to Their New Environment." *ML*, XII (October, 1960), pp. 175-180.

The American and Canadian frontiers were the homes of migrating Russian Mennonites. Article describes the experiences of these immigrants with Indians, prairie fires, and other frontier problems when they first arrived.

GINGERICH, MELVIN
"Change and Uniformity in Mennonite Attire." *MQR*, XL (October, 1966), pp. 243-259.

The purpose of this study is to explore illustrative changes in costume, to discover causes for these changes, and to see how these changes came about in a culture that was conservative and that frowned upon innovation. In every period, Mennonite dress has represented an aspect of the culture of its environment. Today adaptation to the predominant culture is occurring so rapidly that an observer may wonder how effective the historic principle of simplicity will prove to be in guiding those who are departing from the garb.

GINGERICH, MELVIN
"The Virtue of Simple Dress." *ML*, XXVI (December, 1971), pp. 150-154.

This is an excerpt from the book *Mennonite Attire Through Four Centuries*. It is primarily concerned with the basis of thought behind simplicity of dress, the conflicts that arose over the meaning of simplicity, and the difficulties of enforcing a rigid garb. Author suggests that the struggles over bonnets, neckties, and 'plain coats' "often obscured the underlying principles of the issue which were Christian 'humility, stewardship, modesty, and simplicity.'"

GOERZEN, J. W.
"Plautdietsch and English." *ML*, VII (January, 1952), pp. 18-20.

Plautdietsch, a Low German dialect, is spoken in Canada, the United States, Mexico, Brazil, and Paraguay. The purpose of the article is to point out some similarities of Plautdietsch and English. Included is a short passage of the dialect in print.

GOOD, MILTON R.
"Canadian Public Welfare and the Mennonite Church in Ontario." *Mennonite Community*, V (May, 1951), pp. 20-21.

The major concern of this article is the effects of social legislation such as the Mothers' Allowance Act, Family Allowance Act, Old Age and Blind Pensions, and Unemployment Insurance upon the Mennonite Church. It is felt that the church dislikes to see her members turn to the state since this seems to involve some obligation to government. But, because of the higher standard of living and the increasing membership from urban areas, the Mennonite Church has no alternative but to allow her members to apply for government assistance.

GREEN, DAVID
"Waterloo County's Militia." *Waterloo Historical Society*, LIV (1966), pp. 62-68.

A description of military activity in Waterloo County since 1812. Author feels that this is a very vital part of Waterloo County's history and that it is paradoxical that this county is known more for its peaceful men, the Mennonites, than its warriors.

GROH, IVAN
"Disabilities of the Dissenters; Part II—Holding Church Property." *Canadian-German Folklore*, II (1967), pp. 28-41.

A section of this article describes the Ontario Mennonites in the early years before they got their own churches in 1834. Examples are given to show that Mennonites of the first generation in Waterloo were not like those of a later generation. There is evidence, the author says, that they were "men of affairs, business men, men of the world, and 'disgustingly rich' according to the standards of that day." He further states that Bishop Benjamin Eby is the best proof that the early Mennonites were not living "in the isolation of the rural community." Article concludes with a description of the Mennonite community of Waterloo after they founded their own churches. Groh dissents from the mainstream of Church historians working from assumptions of deprivation.

HALE, DOUGLAS
"From Central Asia to America." *ML*, XXV (July, 1970), pp. 133-138.

The historical trek of the Russian Mennonites from Asia to America is the subject of this article.

HAMM, H. H.
Sixty Years of Progress 1884-1944, the Rural Municipality of Rhineland. Altona, Manitoba, 1944.

In describing this municipality in Manitoba, emphasis is placed on the Mennonites, who comprise the bulk of the Rhineland population. Author states that the courage and determination of the Mennonite settlers has made this community one of the most progressive and densely populated rural municipalities in Manitoba. Charts indicate the number of men with Mennonite names who served on municipal councils. Mention is also made of the migrations from the Sommerfelder and Bergthaler Mennonite congregations as a result of government policy on education in 1919.

HAMM, H. H.
"Chortitz Mennonite Church, East Reserve, Manitoba." *ME*, I, pp. 566-567.

This group was formed in 1890 when the conservative members of the Bergthal Mennonite Church separated from the more progressive members in the West Reserve because of the question of higher education.

HAMM, H. H.
"Bergthal Mennonite Church." *ME*, I, pp. 280-281.

The Bergthal Mennonite Church has become one of the largest and most influential of the Mennonite Churches in Manitoba. As a daughter colony of Chortitza, they left Russia in 1874-75 and settled on the east and later the west side of the Red River. They quickly organized as a self-contained church group. Their progressive-minded members aimed for higher education, better qualified teachers, and more active spiritual church life.

HARDER, LELAND

"Mennonites and Contemporary Cultural Change." *The Lordship of Christ; Proceedings of the Seventh Mennonite World Conference.* Edited by Cornelius J. Dyck. Elkhart, Indiana: Mennonite Publishing House, 1962.

This interpretation of cultural change among the Mennonites considers two major factors precipitating the change of any group—external and internal. In his discussion of the influence of the external environment, the writer emphasizes that one of the most obvious areas of culture contact affecting Mennonites is the technological. In the second major discussion of the study, the author concentrates on the language transition in the General Conference Mennonite Church as a good illustration of "the internal dynamics of Mennonite cultural change." An excellent graph of the transition from German to English in the General Conference is provided, as well as a chart listing the inhibiting forces and the catalytic forces accompanying the changes from German to English. Two other indices of social change in the General Conference are examined. They are: change in the proportion of recruited members and change in the proportion of conscientious objectors.

HARDER, LELAND

"The Oberholtzer Division: Reformation or Secularization." *MQR*, XXXVII (October, 1963), pp. 310-334.

The Oberholtzer division explains the origin and development of the General Conference Mennonite Church as a result of liberalizing and secularizing forces at work. This is an analysis of social and historic change. In order to understand change, the concepts of cultural contact, diffusion, and organizational disequilibrium are required. Author states that the same tensions which produced the Oberholtzer division of 1847, are still present today in the Mennonite brotherhood.

HARDER, LELAND

"An Empirical Search for the Key Variable in Mennonite Reality." *MQR*, XLV (October, 1971), pp. 331-351.

This empirical study seeks to find the key variable in Mennonite life. In particular it seeks data to examine John H. Yoder's thesis that "Mennonitism still finds its identity most properly on the ethnic community level." A seventy-two item questionnaire, ranging from religious to secular matters of attitude and behavior, was given to 588 church members belonging to nine Elkhart area congregations. An analysis of the data indicates the relative strength of these commitments: associationalism, communalism, conversionism, devotionalism, doctrinalism, and Mennonitism. One major finding revealed that the strength of the communal bond is only moderate for Elkhart Mennonitism which the author feels is sufficient cause to question the Yoder thesis. It was also found that Mennonitism tends to be a strong commitment in most of these churches and from this the author suggests that "adherence to the norms of the Anabaptist vision is conceptually, if not operationally, a significant commitment."

HARDER, MARVIN
"Mennonite Parochial Schools; Disadvantages of the Parochial School System." *Conference on Mennonite Cultural Problems*, VII (June, 1949), pp. 81-86.

"It is the thesis of this paper that Mennonite education has neglected the political man; that this neglect is at present the Mennonite doctrine; and that this neglect is at present the most serious disadvantage of the Mennonite parochial schools. Mennonite educational weaknesses can be seen in the curriculums of Mennonite colleges which are notably weak in political science, in the uncertainty among Mennonites as to what jobs in government constitute the kind of jobs that they cannot hold without compromising their beliefs, and in the absence in Mennonite journals and magazines of controversial discussions about the problem of Mennonitism and politics. The writer also questions whether Mennonite non-participation is required by reasons of doctrine.

HARDER, M. S.
"The Development of Mennonite Education." *Conference on Mennonite Educational and Cultural Problems*, VIII (June, 1951), pp. 31-39.

Mennonite educational activities in nine countries, including Canada, are described. Mennonite attitudes concerning the German language, higher education, and kind of education are discussed. Article also tells of trends in Mennonite education such as the rise of modern humanism, the establishment of parochial elementary schools, and preservation of Mennonitism.

HARDER, MENNO S.
"Education, Mennonite." *ME*, II, pp. 150-151.

A brief paragraph on Mennonite education in Canada explains that the most serious conflict between the Mennonites and the state in modern times took place over the Manitoba school question. Author concludes that there has been an educational renaissance in the interest of preserving and perpetuating Mennonitism.

HARDER, SARA LEHN
   "Mennonites Along the Peace." *The Canadian Mennonite*, XIII
   (November 9, 1965), p. 8.

   An historical account of the beginning of Mennonite settlements
   in Northern Alberta. The Old Colony, Sommerfelder, and
   Bergthaler groups are the major Mennonite churches in the area.
   Article also discusses their isolationist way of life.

HAYWARD, VICTORIA
   "Mine Host—the Mennonite." *The Canadian Magazine* (November,
   1921), pp. 63-70.

   This pictoral essay privides a simple description of what life was
   once like in a Mennonite village on the Old Reserve in Manitoba.

HEINRICH, ALFRED
   "The Indian and the Canadian Mennonites." *ML*, XXII (January,
   1967), pp. 27-28.

   The author attempts to make the Canadian Mennonite Church
   aware of the Indian problem. He feels it is now time for the
   affluent Mennonite to re-evaluate his position toward the Indian.

HOLDEN, J. L.
   "Pursuit of Utopia: Manitoba Mennonites Leaving for Paraguay."
   The Canadian Forum, XXVIII (August, 1948), pp. 106-107.

   A discussion of the causes and implications of the Mennonite
   migration from Manitoba to Paraguay. Author feels that no
   Mennonite community can leave without loss to the province "for
   they are good citizens, industrious, law-abiding, and thrifty." Also
   questioned is the responsibility of Mennonites who are constantly
   fleeing from change and searching for a better country.

HOSTETLER, JOHN A.
   "The Settlement in the Peace River Country." *Mennonite Community*,
   III (May, 1949), pp. 18-23.

   Hostetler tells the story of the settlement of the Peace River
   district which was begun by Jasper T. Bronson and Peter W.
   Friesen. Included are descriptions of the Peace River country, the
   pioneering experiences, and church life. The writer feels that this
   community demonstrates some striking characteristics. In particular there exists a strong spirit of Christian hospitality and
   unity among the brotherhood as well as a vision for maintaining
   the future welfare of the community. Manifestations of this can
   be seen in the development of a rest home, a co-operative store, a
   bulldozer association, and a co-operative cheese factory.

HOSTETLER, JOHN A.
"Farmers Organizations and the Non-resistant Conscience."
Mennonite Community, VI (February, 1952), pp. 12-17, 32.

The role of the Mennonite in farmers' organizations is the concern of this article. Mennonites have had very little to do with these organizations even though they maintain some of the most productive farming communities. It is the author's intention to discuss Mennonite business ethics which often seem little concerned with justice in the business of agriculture. This can be seen in their capitalistic practices, in Mennonite saturation in the materialistic system, in the lack of church pronouncement against excessive interest rates, and in their unconcern in heated disputes between labour and management. It is necessary, the writer feels, to cultivate a conscience on social justice, to protest vocally against social injustice, and to find ways to maintain the simple life in economic areas. Participation in farmers' organizations if recommended since Mennonites could act as the "conscience" of a larger group.

HOSTETLER, JOHN A.
"The Impact of Contemporary Mennonite Evangelistic Out-reach on the Larger Society." *MQR*, XXVII (October, 1953), pp. 305-330.

Evangelistic outreach is central in the Mennonite belief system. Today its practice depends upon social and situational factors or the degree of religious reawakening. This study shows the impact of Mennonite evangelism on non-Mennonite persons in the American environment. It assumes certain factors attract and repel persons who come in contact with the Mennonite system of values and deals with mobility, the movement of persons in and out of the Mennonite Church.

JANZEN. LESTER
"Profile Shows Similarity." *Gospel Herald*, LXVI (May 1, 1973), p. 382.

A description of research being developed on church membership for the General Conference Mennonite Church, the Mennonite Conference, the Mennonite Brethren Conference, and the Evangelical Mennonite Conference by J. Howard Kauffman and Leland Harder. Some insights are emerging from the data. For example, teaching on Anabaptism has had a significant influence on present-day beliefs and practices, fundamentalism has had a negative influence on maintaining Anabaptist emphasis on peace witness and social concern, and education has had an influence on attitudes and practices in the area of social ethics. This profile will also discuss the effect of urbanization on the Mennonites.

JANZEN, SIEGFRIED
   "From Gronau to Canada." *ML* (October, 1951), pp. 34-36.

   The Canadian immigration procedures were very difficult experiences for many Russian Mennonites. Author describes the
   steps of emigration, the various immigration schemes introduced
   by the Canadian government, and the help of MCC.

JUST, L. ROY
   "An Analysis of the Social Distance Reactions of Students from the
   Three Major American Mennonite Groups." *Conference on Mennon-
   ite Educational and Cultural Problems*, IX (June, 1953), pp. 73-77.

   The purpose of this study was to determine and compare the
   social distance reactions of Mennonite secondary school and college students toward thirty selected ethnic groups, thirty-four
   non-Mennonite groups, and twenty-six Mennonite groups. "The
   problem derives from an inadequate knowledge of the social
   distance attitudes of Mennonite students." Among the hypotheses tested and proven are: Mennonite secondary students show
   more social distance toward the ninety selected groups on the
   three social distance scales than Mennonite college students; Mennonite male students reveal more tolerant attitudes than do
   female students; and Mennonite students show more tolerance
   when a group's ethnic name is used than when its religious name
   is used.

JUST, L. ROY
   "A Study of Mennonite Social Distance Reactions." *MQR*, XXVIII
   (July, 1954), pp. 197-204.

   Mennonites possess strong in-group loyalties fortified by distinctive cultural characteristics. Today they are seeking an adjustment to the world. This study attempts to determine and analyse
   the social distance attitudes of Mennonite young people who have
   grown up in cultural islands resulting from self-imposed segregation and who are undergoing a critical adjustment to the world
   from which they have been taught to remain separate. The three
   main Mennonite branches studied are the General Conference,
   the Old Mennonite, and Mennonite Brethren Churches.

KALBFLEISCH, HERBERT K.
   "German or Canadian?" *Waterloo Historical Society*, XL (1952), pp.
   18-29.

   Article investigates some phases of assimilation as it applies to the
   German settlers of Southwestern Ontario. Author feels that the
   Germans have very strong attachments to Canada but have not
   become assimilated; "they gave as much as they absorbed." Although not specifically on Mennonites, this article is partially
   applicable to them.

KAUFFMAN, J. HOWARD
"The State of the Mennonite Family." *Gospel Herald*, LXVI (May 8, 1973), pp. 393-395.

The rising tide of family problems among American families is also evident in Mennonite families of the United States and Canada. The divorce rate, generation gap, economic affluence, urbanization, changes in status of women, religious life, and family size represent a few situations which Mennonites have to cope with. The article presents statistics for these areas of family change to indicate how Mennonite families compare with families in society as a whole.

KAUFFMAN, J. HOWARD
"Authority and Freedom in Mennonite Families." *Conference on Mennonite Educational and Cultural Problems*, XV (June, 1965), pp. 75-87.

Kauffman presents a study of social relationships within six Mennonite groups. The concept of authority is defined as the power of one person to influence, or control behavior, and freedom is described as the opportunity to make one's own decision and to act upon it. After discussing his research problems, author concludes that the challenge of the Mennonites is not to give up sectarian norms but to produce them within the framework of a democratic atmosphere in family life.

KEENEY, WILLIAM C.
"Mennonite Cooperation with Government Agencies and Programs." *Conference on Mennonite Educational and Cultural Problems*, XV (June, 1965), pp. 62-74.

Article describes the Mennonite position with regard to the state. In the conclusion it notes that if the church cannot participate in the sword-bearing functions of the government, it should be wary in benefiting directly from it. The church must examine itself carefully so that it does not drift into an easy compromise. The state can provide no final answer to man's need for community.

KEHLER, LARRY
"A Profile of Mennonite Personnel Involved in International Experience." *Conference on Mennonite Educational and Cultural Problems*, XVI (June, 1967), pp. 9-39.

Article presents a profile of the international experience of Mennonite and Brethren in Christ overseas workers. Also included are nineteen separate charts indicating the areas of involvement in MCC, Pax, etc.

KEHLER, LARRY

"The Many Activities of the Mennonite Central Committee." *MQR*, XLIV (July, 1970), pp. 298-315.

Article outlines the development and organizational structure of the Mennonite Central Committee. It provides a description of its work abroad, such as the Pax and Tap programs, medical services, material aid, and child sponsorship. On the home front, it has such programs as Voluntary Service, Mental Health Services, Mennonite Disaster Service, Menno Travel Service, aid societies, and Mennonite Indemnity. Mennonite Central Committee demonstrates that Mennonites can work cooperatively in many areas and it is a valuable instrument for giving Mennonite youth a more positive view of the church.

KEHLER, LARRY

"Inter-Church Relationships." *Call to Faithfulness; Essays in Canadian Mennonite Studies*. Edited by Henry Poettcker, and Rudy A. Regehr. Winnipeg: Canadian Mennonite Bible College, 1972.

Kehler highlights some of the instances in the Conference of Mennonites in Canada when its members have moved in an ecumenical direction. Proof of united Mennonite endeavors and of interdenominational efforts is given. It is felt that Mennonite relief and immigration organizations, Mennonite Pioneer Mission, inter-Mennonite communications through newspaper and radio, and the mergers of some Bible schools exemplify a move toward unity among Mennonites. Evidence of broader ecumenical contacts can be seen in joint vacation Bible schools, Holy week services, and evangelistic rallies, and in the representation by Mennonites on national ecumenical bodies such as the Canadian Council of Churches and the Evangelical Fellowship of Canada.

KLAASSEN, WALTER

"The Church's Involvement in Higher Education—A New Venture." *ML*, XX (April, 1965), pp. 83-85.

The origins of Conrad Grebel College, the first Mennonite liberal arts college to be part of a University campus, is the main concern of this study. Of interest is a discussion on the goals and objectives of such an educational venture at the University of Waterloo in Ontario.

KLASSEN, PETER J.

"Mutual Aid Among the Anabaptists: Doctrine and Practice." *MQR*, XXXVII (April, 1963), pp. 78-95.

Anabaptists presented a radical view of property which was a sacred trust existing not only for the possessor but also for the benefit of his fellow men. This completely voluntary expression of love is at the heart of their concept of discipleship. Mutual aid has, therefore, always been a natural and necessary part of the Mennonite fellowship. The author relates the attitudes of some of the Anabaptist founders concerning mutual aid.

KLASSEN, WILLIAM
"Community Mental Health." *ML*, XXI (October, 1966), pp. 153-154.

The development of mental health centres was a major emphasis of North American Mennonites after World War II. In addition to deep encounter with modern psychiatry, these centres thrust the Mennonites into major relationships with the community, a trend which the author urges to higher levels of cooperation.

KLASSEN, WILLIAM
"Eden Mental Health Center." *ML*, XXI (October, 1966), pp. 182-183.

This article describes the reasons why a new Mental Health Center is needed by the Mennonites of Manitoba. It was written after he studied at the Menninger psychiatric hospitals in Topeka, Kansas.

KRAHN, CORNELIUS
"From Bergthal to Manitoba." *ML*, XII (January, 1957), pp. 84-85.

The story of the Mennonites in Manitoba represents one of the most colourful chapters in Mennonite history. This article provides a brief historical outline of the Bergthal Mennonites of Canada.

KRAHN, CORNELIUS
"Old Colony Mennonites." *ME*, IV, pp. 38-42.

A socio-religious group originating in Manitoba whose name was derived from the Chortitza Mennonite settlement in Russia. This account outlines their history in Russia and Manitoba, and describes the Manitoba school question which caused many to leave for Mexico.

KRAHN, CORNELIUS
"West Reserve, Manitoba." *ME*, IV, pp. 926-929.

In 1875, Mennonites of the Chortitza and the Fürstenland settlements in Russia settled in the West Reserve in Manitoba. They were later known as Old Colony Mennonites. A disruptive element occurred when the Bergthal Mennonites who were adapting to the new Canadian environment settled in the area. A description of the village patterns, agriculture, and differences between Mennonites are given as well as a map of the original settlements.

98

KRAHN, CORNELIUS
"Immigration of the Mennonites from Russia." *The Lordship of Christ; Proceedings of the Seventh Mennonite World Conference*. Edited by Cornelius J. Dyck. Elkhart, Indiana: Mennonite Publishing House, 1962.

An appraisal and interpretation of the Mennonite migrations from Russia and their results. Of significance is a discussion on the immigrants who came to Canada after World War I and II. These immigrants, the writer states, contributed to "a revitalization and challenge of the religious, cultural and social life of those who had been in North America since the 1870's." He also feels that the immigrants of Swiss and South German background who had come to Ontario in the eighteenth and nineteenth centuries gained a sense of responsibility from the suffering and persecution of these new immigrants. As Krahn states, "This was the turning point of die Stillen im Lande."

KRAHN, CORNELIUS
"Mennonite Migrations as an Act of Protest." *ML*, XXV (January, 1970), pp. 20-27.

This paper begins by saying that the history of the Christian church has been one of protest and then goes on to describe the "protesting and witnessing radical Anabaptists." Author categorizes the Mennonites into those who took issue with their environment and those who solved their problems by leaving the country. With the use of maps, the author describes how persecutions drove Anabaptists to other communities, including Canada.

KRAHN, CORNELIUS; FRETZ, J. WINFIELD and KREIDER, ROBERT
"Altruism in Mennonite Life." *Forms and Techniques of Altruistic and Spiritual Growth*. Edited by Pitirim A. Sorokin. Boston: The Beacon Press, 1971.

An account of the ways and means of altruistic and spiritual education in the Mennonite community which is marked by notable friendliness and unselfish service both within and without this group. The authors of this article attempt to explain why this group is so altruistic by looking at its background and by studying the underlying principles motivating such action. Mutual aid is discussed as one of the most important aspects of altruism in Mennonite communities "from the standpoint of determining the character and significance of Mennonites as a socio-economic group." The principle of nonresistance is also viewed as a form of altruism which leads to a discussion on alternative service during World War II. Finally the relief services provided by Mennonite Central Committee is discussed as an important factor in Mennonite altruism. In explaining the perpetuation of a tradition of altruism among Mennonites, the authors stress that it is "less the product of conscious cultivation than a derivative from a disciplined brotherhood way of life."

KREIDER, CARL

"An Economic Program for the Mennonite Community of Tomorrow." *MQR*, XIX (April, 1945), pp. 156-170.

Economic factors exert a pronounced influence on the Mennonite community. Article discusses such subjects as the place of economics in Mennonite life, the place of agriculture in the future Mennonite life, and a diversified economic program for this community. Author stresses that efforts should be taken to revitalize agriculture in the Mennonite community but also states that economic and social forces are operating which make it undesirable to base Mennonite community life exclusively upon an agrarian economy.

KREIDER, ROBERT

"Environmental Influences Affecting the Decisions of Mennonite Boys of Draft Age." *MQR*, XVI (October, 1942), pp. 247-259.

The assumption of this paper is that the behavior of an individual is profoundly affected by environmental factors which can be religious, sociological, economic, and psychological. These environmental factors are grouped into the specific categories of the church, the home, the community and other institutions. Article states that the factors which preserve the Mennonite peace testimony are the very same factors which serve to maintain and enrich the entire Mennonite culture: nonresistance, simplicity, mutual aid, and emphasis on the New Testament.

KROEKER, J. A.

"The Crosstown Credit Union." *ML*, IV (July, 1949), p. 32.

A study of the Mennonite credit union movement which began in Europe and spread to Canada and the United States. Author discusses aims of a credit union and the reasons why the Crosstown Credit Union in Manitoba succeeded.

KUROKAWA, M.

"Psycho-social Roles of Mennonite Children in a Changing Society." *Canadian Review of Sociology and Anthropology*, VI (1969), pp. 15-35.

Mennonite children, reared in an isolated world which constantly changes to meet challenges from the outside society, must assume roles which are extremely complex psychologically and sociologically. Observations of children belonging to three different Mennonite groups, traditional, transitional, and progressive, show that the consequences for children varied according to the breadth of difference existing between each Mennonite group and the outside society. The effect of cultural conflict was most clearly seen in the transitional group. Parents of this group were likely to be authoritarian to their children and inconsistent in discipline. Their children in turn tended to show value inconsistencies and a sense of inadequacy.

KUROKAWA, M.
"Beyond Community Integration and Stability—A Comparative Study of Oriental and Mennonite Children." *Journal of Social Issues*, XXV(1) (1969), pp. 195-213.

Comparative data is presented on the process of cultural change, family structure and mental health among Orientals in the United States and Mennonites in Canada. These groups were chosen for study because of the similarities in their traditional collectivity orientation, strong social and familial integration, relative absence of individual initiative and spontaneity, and in their subsequent process of acculturation. It was hypothesized and tested that 1) Traditional Orientals and Mennonites are likely to show covert symptoms of mental disturbances, such as physical symptoms, habit disturbances and psychological stresses and that 2) Orientals and Mennonites who are transitional from traditional to modern orientations are likely to experience conflict and to manifest overt symptoms of maladjustment. Both hypotheses received support from the data.

KUROKAWA, M.
"Individuation Among Orientals and Mennonite Families in California and Waterloo." *International Journal of Compatative Sociology*, II (December, 1970), pp. 292-300.

"In spite of the difference of East and West, Orientals (Chinese and Japanese) and Mennonites have close similarities in their processes of individuation from collectivity orientation. While the former relied on familism and the latter on religiosity, both groups used to place primary importance on social groups rather than on individuals. For children of both groups family served as a socialization agent to internalize the value of collectivity orientation. However, neither group can maintain complete segregation from other culture which stresses individuality. This is a comparative study of the processes and accompanying problems of individuation of Orientals in California and Mennonites in Waterloo County, Ontario. The major focus is placed on the change in family relations and in the behavior of children who are caught in the process of individuation."

KUROKAWA, M.
"Alienation and Mental Health of Mennonites in Waterloo County." *The Canadian Family*. Edited by K. Ishwaran. Toronto: Holt, Rinehart and Winston of Canada Ltd., 1971.

"Mennonites in the contemporary world are at the crossroads of orthodox religiosity and secular materialism." The conflict that arises from being in such a position has had an impact upon the mental health of Mennonites. It is the author's intent to reveal the varying impact of this upon three different Mennonite groups in Waterloo County: the Old Order Mennonites or the traditional group, the Waterloo-Markham Conference or the transitional Mennonites, and the Mennonite Conference of Ontario or the progressives. In its analysis, the article centers on the issue of education since it has caused the greatest value conflict and has been a source of various mental disorders among the Waterloo Mennonites. The major conclusion is that the greatest strain appears to be on the marginal or transitional Mennonites who "suffer from a sense of alienation and exhibit feelings of inadequacy in the changing society."

LAPP, JOHN A.
"The Peace Mission of the Mennonite Central Committee." *MQR*, XLIV (July, 1970), pp. 281-297.

The search to find positive ways of helping mankind while refusing to serve in the military motivated Mennonites to organize service agencies. Their nonresistant peace testimony is at the heart of the Mennonite Central Committee. A brief description of MCC organization, leaders and services is given. The major part of the paper stresses the functions of the Peace Section which are threefold: the nurturing of peace convictions, the search for ways to stay out of military service, and expansion of peacemaking.

LEIBBRANDT, GEORG
"The Emigration of the German Mennonites from Russia to the United States and Canada in 1873-1880." *MQR*, VI (1932), pp. 205-226; VII (1933), pp. 5-41.

The article emphasizes the emigration movement which is revealed in the official government documents of both Russia and America. This event is an important part of internal Russian history and reveals in many ways the working machinery of the Russian government. It also portrays the attitude of the American government, its interest in the settlement of the land, but at the same time, its caution in regard to this matter for political reasons. Article presents a review of the cultural and social life of the colonies, their reasons for leaving and their settlement patterns in Canada and the United States.

LETKEMANN, PETER
"Mennonites in Vancouver—A Survey." *ML*, XXIII (October, 1968), pp. 160-164.

A description of the behavior patterns of urban Mennonites. It also deals with the relationship between religio-ethnic groups and the larger community.

LITTELL, FRANKLIN H.
"The New Shape of the Church-State Issue." *MQR*, XL (July, 1966), pp. 179-189.

The writer takes a new look at the Christian college and the Christian retirement home. He sees no reason why a church agency cannot cooperate with a governmental agency to serve the public good. The only danger, he states, is that the church may be diverted from the essential Christian task to witness where no others have dared to go. Author feels the real purpose of such action would be to provide models of what a college and a retirement home should be like and states that it is the church's mission to provide society with these models.

LOEWEN, JACOB A.
"Missionaries and Anthropologists Cooperate in Research." *Practical Anthropology*, XII, pp. 158-190.

A Mennonite anthropologist who has worked in the Third World, the Mennonite colonies and in North America explains how anthropology stimulates research with the cooperation of missionaries.

LOHRENTZ, JOHN H.
"Religious and Cultural Background of the Mennonite Brethren." *Conference on Mennonite Cultural Problems*, VII (June, 1949), pp. 139-150.

This article provides the historical background of the Mennonite Brethren in Russia and North America, outlining the factors which led to their split from the main branch of the Mennonites in Russia, and revealing their struggles in Canada, where they finally became prosperous due to their "industry, thrift, and economic way of living." Also included are descriptions of the early home life, local congregations and ministry of the Mennonite Brethren, as well as a discussion of their educational efforts.

LOHRENZ, G.
"The Mennonites in Winnipeg." *ML*, VI (January, 1951), pp. 16-25.

Aim of this article is to show how another Mennonite group came to Canada, penniless and not knowing the customs and language, but who succeeded in business, industry and community enterprises in the city of Winnipeg.

LUCE, P. W.
"Unwelcome Mennonites Making Model Farms by the Fraser,"
Saturday Night, February 12, 1944, p. 32.

A description of the Mennonites in the Fraser Valley, particularly
in the town of Yarrow which the author calls the "communal
centre of the sect." Lack of dance hall, theatre, and pool room is
said to indicate the great ambition of Fraser Valley Mennonites to
work hard. Other characteristics, such as application of scientific
principle, a living standard which is often a bare existence, and a
thrifty attitude which might be described as penurious, are said to
be responsible for the profitable farms of the Mennonites. The
resentment of other farmers towards the Mennonites is also discussed and a comparison is made of the Mennonites and the
Doukhobors.

MAGE, J. A.
"Selected Aspects of the Agricultural Economy of Waterloo
County." *The Waterloo County Area Selected Geographical Essays*. Edited
by A. G. McLelland. Waterloo: University of Waterloo, 1971, pp.
83-95.

Mennonites play a major role in the economy of Waterloo
County. A brief case study is used to show the characteristics of
mixed farming in the Mennonite group.

MAGE, JULIUS and MURDIE, ROBERT
"The Mennonites of Waterloo County." *Canadian Geographical
Journal*, LXXX (January, 1970), pp. 10-19.

The main emphasis of this article is on the Old Order Mennonites
of Waterloo County and a clear distinction is made between them
and the more progressive Mennonites. After providing a brief
historical outline, the authors attempt to reveal how the "increasing forces of secularization and urbanization" resulted in the
division of the Mennonites of Waterloo County into a number of
orders. The differences between these groups are based upon
ownership of modern inventions and as a result "a continuum of
modernity can be distinguished amongst Mennonite groups."
The Old Order Mennonite way of life is described with emphasis
on their dress, homes, meeting houses, agricultural practices, and
farming ability. Their attitudes on social assistance and education
are contrasted with the more progressive Mennonites. Authors
believe that Waterloo County Mennonites have helped to create
prosperous villages and towns because of their qualities of "re-
sourcefulness, honesty, and hard work."

MARTENS, HILDEGARD M.
"Accommodation and Withdrawal: The Response of Mennonites in
Canada to World War II." *Histoire sociale, Social History*, VII, No. 14
(November, 1974), pp. 306-327.

A realistic and pessimistic description of the Mennonite peace position in the context of accommodation by the majority and dissent by the minority, a response which the author ascribes to a long history in the past. Broad generalizations are avoided by noting the specific responses of the recent immigrants from Russia who endorsed non-combatant work under the military, the proportion who enlisted in the regular army and the group which opted for civilian alternative service. The author interprets the Conference of Historic Peace Churches as affirming an optimistic view of changing the social order.

McKEGNEY, PATRICIA
"The German Schools of Waterloo County, 1851-1913." *Waterloo Historical Society*, LVIII (1970), pp. 54-67.

A report on the establishment of German Schools in Waterloo County between 1851 and 1913. It deals with conflicts over government legislation on education and with the problems of granting certificates to German teachers and of creating uniform standards of instruction and examination. Author says the period 1851-1900 shows a gradual decline in the number of German Schools in Waterloo County so that by 1900 they had almost ceased to exist.

MEYER, ALBERT J.
"Mennonite Students in Non-Mennonite Schools." *Conference on Mennonite Educational and Cultural Problems*, XIII (June, 1961), pp. 20-42.

Through the years there has been a decrease in attendance at non-Mennonite Bible Institutes in a period of rapidly increasing school attendance. Presently the Mennonite Student Services and Mennonite Graduate Fellowship are organizing Mennonite activities on university campuses. Author sees the university as an opportunity for further Christian growth and as a way of involving the church in the world.

MILLER, ORIE O.
"The Present Mennonite Migration." *MQR*, I (April, 1927), pp. 7-17.

Orie Miller, longtime head of the Mennonite Central Committee, presents an outline and the essential features of the migratory movements of the Mennonites during their past history. After the first World War three movements occurred; the movement from Russia to Canada, U.S. and Mexico, the movement from Canada to Mexico, and the movement from Canada to Paraguay. The background of each movement is given with emphasis on Mennonite aid.

MUMAW, JOHN R.
"Current Forces Adversely Affecting the Life of the Mennonite Community." *MQR*, XIX (April, 1945), pp. 101-116.

The historic Mennonite community is essentially the creation of a group-consciousness rooted in applied Bible teachings. Such forces as materialism, education, urbanization, secularization, and religious tolerance and their effect on the life of this community are discussed.

MUMAW, JOHN R.
"Mennonite Folklore." *Pennsylvania Folklife*, XI (Spring, 1960), pp. 38-39.

A small collection of Mennonite sayings, folk beliefs, riddles, customs and folk tales.

MURDIE, ROBERT A.
"Cultural Differences in Consumer Travel." *Economic Geogrpahy*, XLI (July, 1965), pp. 211-233.

A comparative analysis of the factors affecting distances travelled by two groups of consumers, the Old Order Mennonites, and the "modern" Canadians, living in the same area in Ontario. Such a study affords an opportunity to compare and contrast consumer travel behavior under varying technological conditions. It was found that travel for modern goods and services (doctor, dentist, bank, and appliances) produces patterns showing the greatest similarity between these two groups. But when "traditional" goods and services were required such as food, clothing, and a blacksmith, the two groups display vastly different levels of space preference. "The retention of certain cultural traditions by the Old Order Mennonite plays a much more important role in determining consumer mobility and the level of spatial interaction." In general it is concluded that socio-economic differences influence mobility.

NEUFELD, ELMER
"Christian Responsibility in the Political Situation." *MQR*, XXXII (April, 1958), pp. 141-162.

Author presents two general considerations regarding political involvement: the motivation to act and the form of the expression of concern. In his opinion the Mennonite Church only takes political action when their own interests are at stake. When the political situation involves such issues as foreign aid and civil rights, Mennonites seldom become seriously involved. Examples are given showing the cleavage which exists between the church and the state and between the Christian and government. Author feels that when the Mennonite Church is thoroughly motivated by the love of Christ and when its members take their neighbors' interest as seriously as their own, it will find expression in action that does have political relevance.

NEUFELD, I. G.
"Fraser Valley." *ME*, II, pp. 380-382.

In 1928 this area attracted 12,000 Mennonites from the Prairie Provinces. This article deals with the location, business, politics, and activities of the Mennonites. A map indicates where the Mennonite population is concentrated.

NICKEL, J. W.
"The Canadian Conscientious Objector." *ML*, II (October, 1947), pp. 24-28.

During the two World Wars many Mennonites went to C.O. camps. The life and work at these camps is described in this article. The Canadian camps were civilian but operated without the official cooperation of the churches as in the U.S.A.

PANNABECKER, S. F.
"The Anabaptist Conception of the Church in the American Mennonite Environment." *MQR*, XXV (January, 1951), pp. 34-46.

The author examines how changes in the Anabaptist conception of the church are a result of the social environment, even though it is recognized that the church is also influenced by developments within the church itself. Author divides the development of the Mennonite Church regarding customs and thinking into four periods. Article is valuable for understanding the changes that took place in the church as physical separation of the church from the world became impossible and as secular interests increased.

PEACHEY, PAUL
"Some Trends in Urban Church Studies." *ML*, XIX (January, 1964), pp. 33-35.

Today there is considerable literature related to the American churches' concern with urban problems. This article describes many studies which are taking place, suggesting the way in which Mennonite scholars are reading and absorbing a wide range of current studies of the Church.

PENABAKER, D. N.
"Extending Our Frontiers in Canada West: An Example of Self Reliance and Enterprise 80 Years Ago." *Waterloo Historical Society* (1934), pp. 132-135.

An instance of Mennonite pioneering enterprise in the new section of country opened up between 1850 and 1860 on the shores of Lake Huron.

PENNER, VICTOR
"Altona from Village to City." *ML*, XI (July, 1956), pp. 116-117.

Altona is one of the most rapidly growing Mennonite centres in Manitoba. Author discusses reasons for this growth such as its increased crop diversification, the organization of the Cooperative Vegetable Oils Ltd., and the enlarged school, church, and hospital facilities.

PICKWELL, F. C.
"Mennonite Menace in the West." *Saturday Night*, October 12, 1918, p. 7.

Unrest in western Canada caused by the granting of special privileges to the Mennonites is the concern of this article. One such privilege is exemption from military service and author outlines the objection to American Mennonites coming to Canada in order to avoid the draft. Education is cited as another reason for this unrest since the Mennonites, being permitted to have their own schools, made no effort to become Canadianized. The article is valuable primarily as an expression of attitudes during World War I.

QUIRING, WALTER
"The Canadian Mennonite Immigration into the Paraguayan Chaco 1926-1927." *MQR*, VII (January, 1934), pp. 32-42.

The migration of Canadian Mennonites to Central and South America from 1922 to 1927 was the result of nationalistic legislation in Canada during World War I. The government's policy to "Canadianize" minority groups found expression in the "One Language Law" which forbade the instruction of German and of religion in schools. An account of the journey to the Chaco is also given.

RAMSEYER, ROBERT L.
"The Revitalization Theory Applied to Anabaptists." *MQR*, XLIV (April, 1970), pp. 159-180.

Anthony C. Wallace declares that any attempts at reform are characterized by a uniform process which he calls revitalization. This movement is a deliberate, organized, conscious effort by members of a society to construct a more satisfying culture. The author uses this framework for considering the Anabaptist movement. He sets the movement in a cultural context and offers a basis for comparison of the Anabaptist phenomena with other revitalization movements. The author is a former Mennonite missionary to Japan who did doctoral studies in Anthropology at Michigan.

REDEKOP, CALVIN

"Patterns of Cultural Assimilation Among Mennonites." *Conference on Mennonite Educational and Cultural Problems*, XI (June, 1957), pp. 99-111.

Author distinguishes between acculturation, assimilation, and secularization to provide a framework to look at cultural patterns in such areas as technology, education, occupation, and language. Redekop discusses the relation of acculturation to assimilation and states that Mennonites have been ignorant of the varying influences of cultural traits on the assimilation process. The movement is discussed as one means of avoiding assimilation.

REDEKOP, CALVIN

"The Sect From a New Perspective." *MQR*, XXXIX (July, 1965), pp. 204-217.

Every religious organism shows evidence of resistance to change and attempts to reaffirm the traditional way of life. Article uses the Old Colony Mennonite Church as an example of this sectarian trait. The new perspective shows that there is no pure sectarian character.

REDEKOP, CALVIN

"Toward an Understanding of Religion and Social Solidarity." *Sociological Analysis*, XXVIII (Fall, 1967), pp. 149-161.

"The integrating power in the sociology of religion is a generally accepted fact, but little careful analysis of this 'fact' is available. The creation of a working definition of solidarity (integration) is one of the prerequisites; another is the specification of how religion functions in the integration process. The paper presents a working definition of solidarity which involves dependence and interdependence. The function of religion in an actual minority, the Old Colony Mennonites, is briefly described which indicates the variety of the functions in society in reference to solidarity. Conclusions indicated from this study include the proposition that religion can contribute to disintegration as well as integration, that alternatives to religion are observable, and that solidarity is a multi-faceted variable."

REDEKOP, CALVIN and BASSO, ELLEN B.

"Anthropologists and Anthropological Reporting" and "Reply to Calvin Redekop." *American Anthropologist*, LXXVII (March, 1975), pp. 81-84.

Canadian Mennonites are closely related to the Mennonite Colony in Paraguay by common experiences in the Russian Revolution, kinship, denomination, services and money. Hence, it is
interesting to note the debate between Redekop (Tabor
—Sociology) and Basso (U. of Arizona—Anthropology) regarding the alleged exploitation of Indians by the Paraguayan Mennonites and the old problem of European settlers with greater
resources and more sophisticated economic and educational institutions. The Mennonites do occupy the former lands of the
Indian hunter-gatherers.

Basso charges that the Indians must live in segregated institutions and must work as disenfranchised laborers. Redekop points
to a number of factual errors in the reporting of Chase Sardi, a
Paraguayan anthropologist, errors passed on by Basso in review.

The dilemmas of a unique sub-culture operating with special
privileges from the government are permanent dilemmas. This
debate, at least, takes place between trained social scientists and
will continue in the years ahead.

Redekop writes critically and fairly of the Mennonite missions
in Paraguay in "Mennonite Mission in the Paraguayan Chaco"
published in the *International Review of Missions*, (July, 1973), pp.
302-317.

REGEHR, RUDY A.
"A Century of Private Schools." *Call to Faithfulness; Essays in Cana-
dian Mennonite Studies*. Edited by Henry Poettcker and Rudy A.
Regehr. Winnipeg: Canadian Mennonite Bible College, 1972.

This essay reviews the development of private schools among
Mennonites during the past century and discusses the debate
among Mennonites concerning the need for church schools. The
surge of Mennonites from Russia in the years 1929-1938, and the
Fundamentalist movement are given as reasons for the prolifera-
tion and expansion of Mennonite private schools which lasted
until 1945. It is the author's opinion that the years 1969-1988 will
be an era of cooperative efforts because of financial problems,
recent religious movements, and the pressures of pluralism. The
article ends by questioning the purpose of Mennonite church
schools.

REMPEL, C. J.
"The Waterloo Mennonites." *ML*, XVII (July, 1962), pp. 106-108.

This article includes a very brief historical description and a very
detailed map of the Mennonites in Waterloo County. Author
states that Mennonites continue to be highly regarded in the
county, that they are recognized as outstanding farmers as well as
professional businessmen, and that the county enjoys a good
spirit of inter-Mennonite fellowship.

REMPEL, D. D.
"From Russia to Canada—Twenty-Five Years Ago." *ML*, III (July, 1948), pp. 42-44.

During the 1920's, thousands of Mennonites left Russia for Canada. Author describes the problems and obstacles of these immigrants.

√ ROHMAHN, J.
"Minority Who Don't Want Pensions." *Macleans Magazine* (August, 1967), p. 2.

This is a brief outline of the plea of some 2000 Old Order Amish and Old Order Mennonites in the Kitchener-Waterloo area to be exempt from the new Canadian Pension Plan. Elven Shantz is mentioned as their spokesman.

√ SAWATZKY, H. L.
"Viability of Ethnic Group Settlement, With Reference to Mennonites in Manitoba." *Canadian Ethnic Studies*, II (December, 1970), pp. 147-159.

Mennonites who came to Manitoba from 1870 to World War I formed what the author calls a mosaic of "ethnic islands" throughout southern Manitoba. There were however many factors which altered the character and structure of these "islands." It is the purpose of this article to examine these changes occurring in the major Mennonite settlements in southern Manitoba. The revivalist missionary influence, the rise of modern farm equipment, and government laws over homesteading are considered as disruptive forces in the Mennonite community. But the author feels that most of the forces that tend to cause dissolution of the Mennonite communities have come from within the Mennonite groups. For example, he says the Mennonites themselves tend to regard the Mennonite Low German mother tongue as a dialect deserving of a status well below that of a "language," and to minimize ethnic identity.

SAWATSKY, JOHN C.
"Business and Industry." *ML*, XVII (July, 1962), pp. 113-116.

Eighty percent of Ontario Mennonites are in non-farming vocations. This brief article indicates that Mennonites are moving into the category of proprietors, managers, and officials.

SAWATSKY, RODNEY
"Pacifism and Mennonite Identity." *Call to Faithfulness; Essays in Canadian Mennonite Studies*. Edited by Henry Poettcker and Rudy A. Regehr. Winnipeg: Canadian Mennonite Bible College, 1972.

It is the intention of this essay to indicate the correlation between pacifism and Mennonite identity and to offer some suggestions as to the significance of that correlation for the contemporary situation. The article is divided into four sections representing four stages in the development of Mennonite history in which pacifism has been integral to the definition of Mennonite identity. These stages are: the Biblical, the Anabaptist, the Diaspora, and the Awakening. The writer concludes with a criticism of the present Mennonite pacifist witness which he says is much too weak. This is apparent from the "uncritical support of our militarized societies" and from the unwillingness to speak out against social problems. The ultimate root of all reasons for the weak Mennonite peace witness is the fear of being identified as different. It is concluded that, since the meaning of Mennonite is integrally related to pacifism, Mennonites must deal with their insecurities and restudy their pacifist position.

SCHMIEDEHAUS, WALTER
"Mennonites Again on the Move." *The American-German Review*, XXVII (February-March, 1961), pp. 16-18.

This brief article explains the Mennonite migration from Mexico to British Honduras in 1958. It is emphasized that this migration was for the first time not motivated by spiritual causes. Rather an acute shortage of land was the major motivating factor. Author also believes that some of these Mennonites from Mexico found their way back to Canada.

SEYFERT, A. G.
"Migrations of Lancaster County Mennonites to Waterloo County, Ontario, Canada from 1800 to 1925." Historical papers and addresses of the *Lancaster Historical Society*, XXX (1926), pp. 33-41.

Reasons why American Mennonites became restless and moved on to Canada are discussed in this paper. It states that cheaper land in Canada may have been an important factor. It also describes the purchase of land in Waterloo County by Samuel Bricker and Joseph Shirk as well as the difficult journey of the Mennonites over 500 miles of mountains and swamps.

SHANTZ, ELVEN
"Mennonite Groups in Waterloo County and Adjacent Area." *Waterloo Historical Society*, LV (1967), pp. 19-29.

This is an excellent summary of the various Mennonite groups in Waterloo County. Following a description of the beliefs and practices common to all Mennonite groups, the author then discusses each separate group and its individual practices. Through this the reader can gain an understanding of some of the reasons for the schisms and of their differences, such as between the Amish Mennonites and the Mennonites. A chart indicates the date and direction of each split that occurred among the Mennonites of Waterloo County.

SHELLY, ANDREW R.
"The Mennonites of Ontario Today." *ML*, V (October, 1950), pp.
17-20, 28.

Mennonite vocational life, churches, and church institutions are
described in this article. Author describes Mennonite activity in
industry and business in such areas as Waterloo County,
Leamington, and Toronto. The House of Friendship and Good-
will Crusade Hall are also described.

SHELLY, ANDREW R.
"An Evaluation of Mennonite Social Welfare Institutions."
Conference on Mennonite Educational and Cultural Problems, IX (June,
1953), pp. 42-60.

Sixty-two Mennonite social welfare institutions in the United
States and Canada are studied. Author then discusses the motives
and priorities for Mennonites in these areas of social welfare and
suggests that more responsiblity and leadership are needed,
especially in the mental hospital field.

SHULTZ, HAROLD J.
"Search for Utopia: The Exodus of Russian Mennonites to Canada,
1917-1927." *A Journal of Church and State*, XI, No. 3 (Autumn, 1969),
pp. 487-512.

Mennonites left the Soviet Union for Canada because of religious
and economic solidarity. This article describes the events leading
to the final exodus.

SIDER, E. MORRIS
"Nonresistance in the Early Mennonite Brethren in Christ Church
in Ontario." *MQR*, XXXI (October, 1957), pp. 278-286.

The Brethren in Christ, first known as River Brethren migrated
from Pennsylvania to Canada in 1788. The Mennonite influence
on the early Brethren can be seen in their firm belief in nonresistance. This account relates the story of nonresistance in the Brethren in Christ Church and shows that in Canada they have been,
along with the Mennonite and Quakers, leaders in advocating this
ethical principle.

SIEMENS, J. J.
"Sunflower Rebuilds Community." *ML*, IV (July, 1949), pp. 28-32.

The Cooperative Vegetable Oils Plant Ltd., marked the beginning of the cooperative movement known as the Federation of
Southern Manitoba Cooperatives in an area with a population of
12,000 Mennonites. Article gives descriptions of the Rhineland
Cooperative, the large scale sunflower growing, and the sunflower by-products.

SMUCKER, D. E.
"A Critique of Mennonites at Mid-Century." *Conference on Mennonite Educational and Cultural Problems*, IX (June, 1953), pp. 99-113.

Mennonites are struggling with the transition from a sect type, which sees itself in permanent tension with the world of culture, to a church type, which considers tradition to be highly important. This paper poses the problems of tradition in the Mennonite Church by considering the four basic tasks of the church: the redemptive, communal, prophetic, and relational. Author sees the present church optimistically in the midst of a creative phase.

SMUCKER, D. E.
"Gelassenheit, Entrepreneurs, and Remnants: Socioeconomic Models Among the Mennonites." In C. Redekop and J. R. Burkholder (eds.), *Kingdom, Cross and Community*. Kitchener: Herald Press, 1976, pp. 219-241.

While the Hutterite communal model is very much alive in both a conservative and progressive pattern, Mennonites have lost the original austerity of mutual aid communities and the special versions of them in Russia and the East-West reserves of nineteenth century Manitoba.

What is functioning now is a vast array of creative programs in missions, education, relief, medicine, disaster aid and third world development requiring approximately $100,000,000 per year from Canada and the U.S. These programs require endless funds from business surpluses which tend to certify the burgeoning business, industrial and farming institutions.

Much self-scrutiny is taking place about these developments but there is no inclination to adopt the capitalistic restraint of the Holdeman Mennonites who prefer both limited outreach and limited expansion.

The original version of this paper was presented to the 1976 meeting of the Canadian Sociology and Anthropology Association, Laval University, under the title, "The Twentieth Century Mennonite Experience with Collective Settlements."

STAHLY, DELMAR; REMPEL, C. J.; SCHMIDT, JOHN R. and KRAHN, C.
"Mennonite Programs for Mental Illness." *ML*, IX (July, 1954), pp. 118-126.

The establishment and growth of Mennonite mental health institutions of Canada, Russia, and South America. Author also tells of neglect by these programs of those who need pure custodial care.

STEVENSON, J. A.
"The Mennonite Problem in Canada." *The Nation*, CVII (November, 1918), pp. 551-552.

This article is of value since it was written during World War I at a time when hostility against the Mennonites was beginning to emerge in Canada. It states that the trouble arose after the Mennonites emphasized that their nationality was German. Author believes that this outcry against foreign elements will prevent further American Mennonites from entering Canada. The history and unique traits of the Mennonites are also discussed. Several interesting viewpoints are expressed: the Mennonites are "hardworking and industrious people"; their early religious unity has been broken up by schisms which has permitted a variety of "weird" doctrines to flourish under the shelter of the Mennonite faith; and economically, the Mennonites have been useful assets in the development of the west, but politically and socially, the benefits of their presence are less marked.

SWARTZENTRUBER, DOROTHY
"Education in Ontario." *ML*, XVII (July, 1962), pp. 120-122.

Author discusses the role that Mennonites played in the educational pattern that evolved during the pioneer days. Article is a brief history of Mennonite Sunday schools, Bible schools, and colleges.

TAVES, HARVEY
"Welfare and Missions." *ML*, XVII (July, 1962), pp. 123-125.

Mennonites have many welfare institutions and missions in Ontario. Some of these organizations are the Mennonite Aid Union, Mennonite Benefit Association, mission boards, and the Ailsa Craig Boys Farm. Author says that most Mennonite groups in Ontario have a strong interest in missionary outreach.

TEICHROEW, ALLAN
"World War I and the Mennonite Migration to Canada to Avoid the Draft." *MQR*, XLV (July, 1971), pp. 219-249.

It is the author's intent in this article to bring to light the efforts of Mennonites in both Canada and the United States to protect the rights of nonresistants during World War I. In a very detailed manner, the author describes the determination of Mennonites not to be drafted under any guise and the diversity of their response toward military service when they were drafted. The constant pressuring of the government to grant them forms of labour that were entirely separate from "the military arm" and finally the exodus by Mennonites of all branches to Canada are examples of Mennonite determination to gain freedom from conscription and complete separation from the "feverish wartime environment." Author also notes that the psychological trauma of the American Mennonites, resulting from pressure to buy war bonds, harassment by the press, economic and social ostracism, and generally alienation from the prevailing national mood, was a strong motivating factor among the Mennonites who migrated to Canada during World War I.

THIESSEN, IRMGARD
"Mental Health and the Mennonites." *ML*, XVIII (July, 1963), pp. 114-115.

This paper examines the problems associated with mentally ill Mennonites. A conflict between Mennonite culture and the facts of life cause former values to break down and may result in disorders, behavior problems, or depression.

THIESSEN, IRMGARD
"Values and Personality Characteristics of Mennonites in Manitoba." *MQR*, XL (January, 1966), pp. 48-61.

Mennonite religious teachings do form personality characteristics. This research deals with the relationship between a cultural value system and personality characteristics. It also shows that attitudes are not just inborn habits but are superimposed by cultural variables. Religious teaching has an influence on how the individual interprets problems and is a focal concern for those who become mentally ill.

THIESSEN, I.; WRIGHT, M. W. and SISLER, G. C.
"A Comparison of Personality Characteristics of Mennonites with Non-Mennonites." *Canadian Psychologist*, X (1969), pp. 129-137.

Compared the value system of 204 Mennonite young people with a control group of 200 non-Mennonites using a battery of five psychological tests. Findings suggest that Mennonites are more strongly motivated to interpret behavior in religious terms. Urban M nnonites were found to be more socially dominant and to feel more guilt than rural Mennonites. The greater dominance reflects the result of being exposed to surrounding cultural pressures, which may then increase anxiety as the influence of the primary value system is challenged.
Later published in *Social Psychology: The Canadian Context*. Edited by J. W. Berry and G. J. S. Wilde. Toronto: McClelland and Stewart Limited, 1972.

THIESSEN, JACK
"The Low German of the Canadian Mennonites." *Mennonite Life*, XXII (July, 1967), pp. 110-116.

This study traces the Low German dialect of the Mennonite immigrants who came from Russia to Canada and those who moved on to Mexico.

THIESSEN, JACK
"Arnold Dyck—The Mennonite Artist." *Mennonite Life*, XXIV (April, 1969), pp. 77-83.

Arnold Dyck, a contemporary German-Canadian Mennonite artist, has realized in his work that Low German is more than a dialect. It is a way of life. This article is a critical review of some of his writings.

THIESSEN, J. J.
"Present Mennonite Immigration to Canada." *ML*, IV (July, 1949), pp. 33-36.

This article deals with the Canadian Mennonite Board of Colonization and the part it played in bringing Mennonite immigrants to Canada and in providing material aid to refugees.

TIME
"Pilgrims Return." April 4, 1949, p. 16.

A brief discussion of the return to Manitoba of some Paraguayan Mennonites who had only recently emigrated from Manitoba to Paraguay. The hardships of starting a new life in Paraguay are described and particular reference is made to the case of Jacob Friesen and his family.

TIME
"Exodus in Canada." July 5, 1949, p. 21.

The movement of Canadian Mennonites to Paraguay is the concern of this article. The gradual settling of the prairies ended Mennonite isolation leading to conflict over worldly possessions, to infiltration of new ideas, to inter-marriage, and to the trend away from the soil. But the main reason given for this exodus is the crisis of World War II at which time "50 per cent of the young Mennonites deserted the sect's pacifist principles and joined armed services."

TOEWS, D.
"The Mennonites of Canada." *MQR*, XI (January, 1937), pp. 83-91.

An historical survey of the Mennonite settlements in Ontario and Western Canada. It summarizes fifteen branches of the Mennonites in Canada, their military service, education, and the care of the sick and the aged.

TOEWS, JOHN A.
"Mennonite Colleges in Canada." *The Lordship of Christ; Proceedings of the Seventh Mennonite World Conference*. Edited by Cornelius J. Dyck. Elkhart, Indiana: Mennonite Publishing House, 1962.

Toews stresses the need for a distinctive educational program in the Mennonite Church in order to preserve the distinct spiritual heritage of the Mennonites. Topics discussed in this article are: the role of the Bible colleges, the program of studies of the Bible colleges, the character and classification of students in Mennonite colleges, and the growth and prospects for the Bible Colleges.

TOEWS, JOHN B.
"Russian Mennonites and the Military Question (1921-1927)." *MQR*, XLIII (April, 1969), pp. 153-168.

The Mennonite exodus to Canada in 1923 symbolized a massive protest against the prevailing Soviet economic and religious policies. Although emigration rested on economic and social factors, the military question emerged as the central force which sustained, on a consistently high level, the sentiment favoring emigration. This article traces the problem of participation in military conscription from the 1870's until the 1920's.

TOEWS, JOHN B.
"Russian Mennonites in Canada: Some Background Aspects." ✓ *Canadian Ethnic Studies*, II (December, 1970), pp. 117-146.

Although this study focusses upon the experiences of the Mennonites when they were in Russia, it is useful for providing a better understanding of the Mennonite settlers entering Canada during the 1920's. It shows how "economic adaptation in Russia made no area of the North American economy seem formidable." Author also states that, while these immigrants were not adverse to cultural assimilation, they felt that group structure was a prerequisite for the maintenance of their historic religious values.

TOTTEN, DON EDWARD
"Agriculture of Manitoba Mennonites." *ML*, IV (July, 1949), pp. 24-27.

A description of the pattern of early settlements of the Mennonites on the Red River Plain. Recent developments such as mixedfarming, sunflower production, and the cooperative movement are also discussed.

UNGER, GEORGE
"Religious Education among Mennonites in Manitoba." *ML*, XII (January, 1957), pp. 86-87.

Mennonites of Manitoba established their own schools as soon as they arrived in Manitoba. Their educational views, methods of instruction, and conflict with the government of both Old Colony Mennonites and the Chortitz Church are discussed.

ULRICH, WILFRED
"Mennonite Vocations." *ML*, XVII (July, 1962), pp. 117-119.

Examines the many vocations that Mennonites are in and states that urban development reduced the importance of agriculture. A chart included outlines the various areas of vocational activity and the percentage of those of the Mennonite community who are found in each category.

VOGT, REINHARD H.
"Association of Mennonite University Students." *ML*, XX (April, 1965), pp. 63-64.

The Association of Mennonite University Students (A. M. U. S.) has developed in many centers across Canada. The purpose of this organization is to gather Mennonite students for fellowship and discussion. Author also discusses the limited nature of these student groups.

WAGNER, JONATHAN F.
"Transferred Crisis, German Volkish Thought Among Russian Mennonite Immigrants to Western Canada." *Canadian Review of Studies in Nationalism*, I, No. 1 (Fall-Aut., 1973), 17 pp.

If the Jewish holocaust took place in Germany under Hitler, the Mennonite holocaust found its locus in Russia under Lenin and Stalin. Twenty-two thousand Mennonites fled in despair and anguish to Canada after persecution, confiscation, looting, raping, labour camps, and death had ended a brilliant experiment in a semi-communal existence.

Against that background of anti-Communism, the 1930's saw the German language Canadian Mennonite paper, *Der Bote* succumb to Nazi propaganda after Hitler came to power in 1933. It was Frank Epp, leading historian of Canadian Mennonites, who first analyzed this embarrassing chapter in the history of his people in his University of Minnesota Ph.D. dissertation.

J. F. Wagner has written this article to *explain* what Epp had described by way of emphasis, space and content. Considering Mennonites in terms of *Volkish* ideology, Wagner views his own work as a pioneering study going beyond the past concentration on religious and ethnic themes, an oversimplified summary of themes as the Smucker bibliography makes clear. His explanation is that the "*Volkish* movement became the revolutionary means for many to end their alienation; it became the means for the individual to combat the disruptive forces of modernity by anchoring himself firmly in the *Volk*."

Frank Epp was the son of Russian immigrants in the period studied by Wagner. His emancipation from this tainted ideology and his pioneer work in exposing it are not an isolated development. His views are dominant, typical and regulative among the second generation *Russländers* of Canada today.

WARKENTIN, JOHN
"Time and Place in the Western Interior." *Artscanada*, XXIX (August, 1972), pp. 20-37.

The changing patterns of the landscapes in the Western plains is the subject of this pictorial essay. "The gross patterning of the present cultural, or man-made, landscape is due largely to the way in which man subdivided the land." The Mennonites are part of the discussion since they objected to the section survey and the dispersal of homesteads. They introduced farm-operator villages in the midst of the sectional survey system. This article provides brief descriptions and also photographs of the layout of these villages as well as of a Mennonite trading centre. Author notes that the Mennonites also added a peculiar style of architecture to the landscape since they erected buildings in which the house and barn were attached.

WARKENTIN, JOHN
"Mennonite Agricultural Settlements of Southern Manitoba." *Geographical Review*, XLIX (July, 1959), pp. 342-368.

The Mennonite settlements of southern Manitoba serve as an example of a nucleated agricultural settlement. Author describes the settlement of the East and West Reserves in Manitoba, emphasizing the Mennonite village system which provided for an equitable distribution of a variety of land. Other topics include the rigorous division of the land in order to preserve the pattern of "Gewannflur," and the construction methods of buildings which nearly always connected the house and barn. Writer says the break-up of these villages was inevitable and gives several reasons for this: the peasant way of life was not suited to Canadian commercial wheat growing; the small plots of land were very inefficient; the ambition of some Mennonites drove them to homesteads; the increasing population pressure; and the impatience of competent farmers with their more indifferent neighbors. It is concluded that the Manitoba Mennonites showed to others that agriculture was possible in the Canadian west.

WIEBE, RUDY
"Tombstone Community." *ML*, XIX (October, 1964), pp. 150-153.

The Russian Mennonites were among the first settlers of Saskatchewan. The author describes life in the community of Speedwell as an example of the western homestead idea.

WIENS, B. B.
"Pioneering in British Columbia." *ML*, I (July, 1946), pp. 9-13.

The centre of Mennonite settlements of British Columbia is Yarrow. Also described are the towns of Sardis, Abbotsford, Arnold,

Coughlan, and Vancouver. Author gives reasons why Mennonites have been thronging to British Columbia and also tells of the
cultural life of B. C. Mennonites through such things as school
building programs, newspapers, church choirs, and Bible
schools.

YOUNG, GERTRUDE S.
"A Record Concerning Mennonite Immigration, 1873." *American
Historical Review*, XXIX (April, 1924), pp. 518-522.

"The tradition among Russian-German Mennonites and Hutterische, relating to a certain expectation of freedom from military
service after they became residents of the United States, appears
with such differentiations of intensity that the degree of reason-
ableness of the expection presents an interesting problem." Author presents the record concerning the petitioning of the Presi-
dent by Mennonite delegates and concludes that these immigrants of 1873 and 1874 came with some assurance of privileges
in respect to war duty.

D. Unpublished Sources

BAER, RAYMOND E.
"A Study of Ministerial Support Within the Ontario Mennonite
Conference." Unpublished paper, Goshen College, 1958.

The purpose of this study is to gain an insight within the ministry
of the Ontario Mennonite Conference since the author feels
"there is a need for Spirit-filled, trained ministers" in this conference. The paper is particularly concerned with the problem of
support or full support of the pastor. A questionnaire was sent to
each bishop and minister in the Ontario Mennonite conference in
an attempt to gain an insight into the financial conditions of the
ministers and also to know the attitude of these men on the
subject of a fully supported ministry. Baer attempts to answer
such questions as: Do the ministers receive adequate financial
support so that work of the church need not be hindered? Does
the pastor receive financial support which enables him to maintain socio-economic status equal to his average church member?
There are three parts to the study: 1) a brief historical view of
the Church's attitude toward the support of the ministry; 2) a
review of scriptural teachings on ministerial support; and 3) a
small study of methods of ministerial support used by other
conferences and denominations.

BURKHOLDER, HAROLD L.
"The Mennonite Church in York County, Ontario." Unpublished
manuscript at Conrad Grebel College Archives, 1933.

DRIEDGER, LEO
"Ethnic Self Identity: A Comparison of Ingroup Evaluations."
Paper presented to the 1974 Annual Meetings of the Society for the
Study of Social Problems in Montreal, August 23-25, 18 pp.

Factor analysis of the data suggested that ethnic self identity
could be described in terms of four dimensions: ingroup affirmation, ingroup denial, real self identity and ideal self identity.
Comparison of seven ethnic groups in Manitoba by the self-
identity factors indicated strong French and Jewish ingroup affirmation and low ingroup denial, while the British and Scandinavian groups scored low on both. Ukrainian German and
Polish real and ideal ethnic self identity were most discrepant,
suggesting ethnic marginality. But, the Ukrainians have a greater
ideal affirmation. From this study the reader must conclude that
the German background is a questionable channel for the Mennonite identity.

The author, noting the French-Jewish superiority concludes
that Lewin's thesis is correct that one must maintain ethnic
"ground" to minimize ingroup self hatred.

DRIEDGER, LEO and PETERS, JACOB
"Ethnic Identity and Social Distance: A Test of Sumner's Theory."
Paper presented to the 1974 annual meeting of the Canadian
Sociology and Anthropology Association in Toronto.

In 1906 Sumner of Yale, a pioneer sociologist and neo-
Darwinian, predicted that when ingroup solidarity and identity
are higher there is social distance between the minority group
and other out-groups.

The study reveals that Mennonite students of Winnipeg placed
greater social distance between themselves and the other twenty
ethnic and racial groups of the community than the French,
Jewish, Ukrainian, Polish, British or Scandinavian people. It was
concluded that Sumner was correct: The Mennonite strong sense
of identity tended to create social distance between himself and
others.

DRIEDGER, LEO
"Structural, Social and Individual Factors in Language Maintenance
in Canada." Unpublished paper presented at Canada Council's
Conference on the Individual, Language and Society, Queen's University, 1975.

Another Driedger study of genuine importance relevant to Mennonite groups rapidly losing the use of German language and to

French Canadians who are obsessed with language maintenance; and other ethnic groups with language problems. Driedger concludes that more than one language is functionally and symbolically necessary in a heterogeneous urban society.

Prior in importance is the maintenance of enclavic pluralism (territorial control, institutional completeness, cultural identity, social distance) by rural and urban villagers. After several generations must come regenerating pluralism via ideological mythology, creation of historical symbols, charismatic leaders who bring commitment to the ideology and symbols, and sufficient social status in order to defend and propagate the ideology. Recommended for government policy makers in Ottawa, Quebec City and Winnipeg.

DRIEDGER, LEO

"Attitudes of Students Towards Immigrants of European and Non-European Origin." Unpublished paper presented to Multiculturalism and Third World Immigrants Conference, the University of Alberta, 1975.

Until recently the typical Canadian immigrants were "industrialized Caucasian Europeans." The author undertook research to discover if there is prejudice against Mongoloid and Negroid people who practice a variety of religions and tend to be less industrialized than the earlier immigrants.

The research failed to locate prejudice toward the non-Europeans. This work of Driedger's suggests the importance of applying his methodologies in other parts of Canada—Quebec and southern Ontario for example—where recent incidents towards dark-skinned people are on the increase, and, therefore, raise questions about the optimism of his conclusions. Moreover, the application of Driedger's methodology to native people from the Prairie cities may shed more light on the nature of prejudice and discrimination.

DRIEDGER, LEO

"Continuity and Identification: Plain and Urbane." Unpublished paper presented to 1976 annual meeting of the American Sociological Association, New York City.

Do the Mennonites, Amish and Hutterites relate to each other?

In one of his most original and creative articles Driedger answers the question affirmatively. First, he argues that the mini-local studies of static communities by the Structuralist-functionalists cannot answer this question. He proposes a new approach "which reveals that there is an identification *ladder* which is functional to the survival of the modern Anabaptists. There is a great deal of continuity between these groups, something we tend to ignore when we study only the mini-structure and a community of one plain group. The identification ladder is anchored by the Hutterites at the one end, and the urban Mennonites at the other. The identification change tends to flow from the plain to the urban. Plain groups with their high fertility rates, contribute many who move (up or down?) the Anabaptist Urbanization ladder." The crucial point of Driedger is that this identification ladder permits urbanization and mobility without assimilation. Highly recommended.

EPP, FRANK H.
"The Problems of Mennonite Identity: A Historical Case Study of One Canadian Minority." Unpublished paper presented to a national conference on the Canadian ethnic mosaic and the ethnic quest for identity sponsored by the Canadian Ethnic Studies Association, Winnipeg, October 15, 1975, 14 pp.

A brief summary of the basic approach by one of Canada's most indefatigable students of the Mennonites. The search for identity is the key motif but the author concedes that the experience of separatism and the struggle for survival are also legitmate motifs, frequently used by scholars. Accommodation without assimilation is the basic device which Canadian Mennonites are now pursuing, "though to varying degrees and at various speeds." The author concludes with eight observations concerning Mennonite fragmentation and differentiation. This is the best brief introduction to the Canadian Mennonites now available, deserving publication for a wider audience.

FRETZ, J. WINFIELD
"The Pilgrimage of a People." Unpublished paper written for Sesquicentennial of the Amish Mennonites in Canada, 1972 (Conrad Grebel College Archives).

The paper traces the Amish Mennonite pilgrimage through their changing patterns of thought, behavior, life style, and value system. In order to understand the Amish, one must view them as a religio-social group and evaluate changes in the light of the group's professed aims and goals. The author makes three evaluations: as a group they demonstrate the inability of a social group to resist social and cultural change; in Ontario the social interactions and community relations have been friendly; and the Amish Mennonites demonstrate the final stage of what sociologists call the sect cycle. Today they still emphasize separation from the world but imply this to mean a spiritual separation rather than a cultural or social separation.

FRETZ, J. WINFIELD
"Emerging Communes and Mennonite Communities." Unpublished paper delivered to Conference on Communes, Northern Illinois State University, April 18, 1975.

In Canada and the United States Mennonite young people are forming intentional communities with Christian foundations, a common treasury, scaled to smallness and which reject conventional congregational life but are not wholly alienated from the mainstream of the church. It is a Protestant equivalent of Catholic monasticism which opted out of conventional living under the blessing of the church. For a number of professionals the new communes provide an opportunity to become artisans living the simple life.

GRAY, ELMA E.
"Threads of Mennonite History." Unpublished manuscript, London, Ontario, 1971.

The purpose of this study is to give Canadians a picture of the Pennsylvania background of the Ontario Mennonites. It deals with the arts, crafts, and everyday life of Mennonites in Pennsylvania, as well as their relationships to their neighbors, and to other religious groups. The thread running throughout the book is that of *Fraktur* of folk art as revealed by singing books, birth certificates, family records, and marriage records. This is a folk art brought to Canada by a very limited number from Pennsylvania. It is also a relatively unknown art. Examples of it are found mainly in private homes.

HORST, J. ALTON
"Lay Participation in the History of the Mennonite Church." Unpublished paper, Mennonite Historical Library, Goshen, Indiana, 1951.

In this study on laity in the Mennonite Church, Horst begins with a discussion of early Anabaptist concepts and shows how Anabaptism emerged with the conviction that the laity was the vital significance of the church. He then proceeds to reveal how, with the beginning of religious toleration, Mennonites became content to live as the "quiet in the land," and to depend on their ministers for all spiritual action. But once again the need for more democratic participation in church life was realized at the turn of the twentieth century which led to the rise of the Sunday school movement, evangelism through missions, and interest in higher education. Author also notes differences with regard to lay participation between the Amish and the Mennonites. He concludes that the practice of using ordained men to perform all church functions must be changed. There is a need to return to the original Anabaptist concept of the Church.

HURST, ROBERT L. and KLASSEN, WALDEMAR
"A Comparative Study of Divorce and Remarriage in the Mennonite Church of North America and the General Conference Mennonite

Church of North America." Unpublished paper, Goshen College, 1970.

The major hypothesis of this study is that "change and inconsistency have caused the two conferences and their congregations to react differently when confronted with decisions about divorce and remarriage." Therefore, finding interrelated elements and statistics which show inconsistency and change in two North American Mennonite Conferences is the basic research problem of this study. The paper begins with an historical survey which reveals divorce and remarriage issues which occurred at various times in conference histories. Following this, present-day research is analysed for a comparative analysis of statistics on divorce and remarriage. It is clearly seen that Mennonites have acted differently when encountering problems of divorce and remarriage, and that present-day roles in divorce and remarriage situations offer a clear contrast with roles played in the past.

KAUFFMAN, J. HOWARD
"Community Factors in Mental Health With Implications for the Mennonite Community." Unpublished paper presented at the Mennonite Mental Health Service Conference, Goshen, Indiana, 1957.

This paper considers the role of the community in the mental health of individuals as it applies to the Mennonites. In the first part of the study, the author notes comparisons between urban and rural communities, and between ecological areas within the large city. Secondly, he examines writings of those who have studied the relation between culture and mental health. Particular consideration is given to the study of the Hutterites done by J. Eaton and R. J. Weil from 1949-1953 and the value of group unity and social cohesion as a supportive to the individual is emphasized. Finally the strong and weak points of the Mennonite community are discussed as they relate to mental health. They are: 1) tension between cultures; 2) tension between Christian ideas and actual behavior; 3) the Christian faith as a resource; and 4) the expressson of brotherhood.

LAURENCE, HUGH
"Communication of Formal Ideology Through Particulars." Unpublished paper presented to Temple University Conference on Culture and Communications, March, 1977, 17 pp.

Utilizing symbolic interaction concepts from Bateson, Watalwick and Rose; and power concepts from Burridge and Festinger, the author researched a progressive Mennonite group of Amish background in southwestern Ontario concerning the controversy over the coming of television. The Mennonite lay-people tested the limits of old contexts of power and then established new contexts in which individuals and not Bishops drew the boundaries. Laurence has opened a new methodology for researching the movement of Mennonites away from traditional community patterns.

MARTIN, MARY
"The Church of Christ and Old Order Mennonites in Waterloo County." Unpublished term paper, University of Waterloo (CGC), 1970.

This paper compares the beliefs of the Old Order Mennonites with those proclaimed by the early Anabaptists. It discusses such topics as the concept of the church, the doctrinal beliefs of the church, the ordinances practiced, and the ethical implications of their concept of the church. Author continually questions whether they have managed to retain the essential message of Christ preached by the Anabaptists.

REDEKOP, CALVIN W.
"Social Service vs. Social Revolution: An Anabaptist Option?" Association of Mennonite Social Workers, Bluffton, Ohio, April 11, 1970.

This article is divided into three parts. The first, entitled Mennonites and social service, considers a service ethic as based on the Sermon on the Mount, and effective expression of it. The second part, Mennonites and social revolution, shows how the Anabaptist stance regarding involvement in the world was revolutionary. Finally, author proposes the "Anabaptist option" in which violence is excluded, which demands confrontation and says that coercion is different from violence, and is an option based on brotherhood and on reconciliation.

REDEKOP, CALVIN and CHESEBRO, SCOTT
"Contemporary Anabaptist Communes: Free Churches or New Ethnic Retreats?" Unpublished paper presented to annual meeting of the American Academy of Religion, 1976, available at Tabor College, Hillsboro, Kansas, 33 pp.

Assessing the significance of many urban, Mennonite communes the authors conclude that "the urban commune has psychologized the Kingdom by concentrating their energies on therapeutic groups restoring wholeness to broken relationships and atomized personalities. This contrasts sharply with the socio-political character of the Kingdom envisioned by their early leaders in their emphases upon separation from state-church authority and influence."
The communes are addressing themselves to the loss of community, not the loss of freedom, the latter being the classic Mennonite problem.

An original contribution of substance which amplifies J. W.
Fretz's paper on Mennonite communes.
Lengthy bibliography.

RIDDICK, ED
"Mennonites and Community Organization: A Possibility." Urban
Pastors Seminar, Kitchener, Mennonite Board of Missions and
Charities, 1966, pp. 31-34.

An attempt to deal with the meaning of community organization
and why it should be of interest to Mennonites. Mennonites have
lagged behind in community organization for several reasons:
Mennonite understanding of modern community organization is
blunted by a history of a built-in concept of community; Mennonites "over adapt to authority"; and tactics of direct action employed by many community organizations would be considered a
clear breach of the ethic of nonresistance. The writer feels it is
necessary to become involved in community organizations since it
is a viable approach to urban problems. He feels the Mennonites
most often become involved in fields of education and social work
which are often fields of irrelevance, and he accuses the Mennonites of accepting a middle-class orientation that reflects their
affluence.

RUDY, JAMES S.
"Mennonite Family in Its Cultural Milieu: Trends from the 1920's to
the 1960's." Unpublished paper, Goshen College, 1971.

An examination of the trends in the Mennonite family evident
from the 1920's to the 1960's and of the factors responsible for
these changes. Author believes that in this period of time "a
transition from theological belief to a rational pragmatic formulation of ideas" took place. The two most important factors causing
this trend are communication and education. Rudy then applies
Margaret Mead's typology of three ideal types of cultures: post-
figurative, co-figurative, and pre-figurative. The conclusion is
made that the Mennonite family is losing its distinctive identity
and that the indispensable functions which the church per-
formed in past eras for the family have now been taken over by
other social systems. Author believes that Mennonite traditional
institutions may be proving ineffectual in dealing with rapid
change and, if so, they should not be preserved.

UNGER, GEORGE
"The Social Thought of the Early Manitoba Mennonites:
1874-1924." Unpublished paper, Mennonite Historical Library,
1954.

Unger deals with the problem of the relationship of the Christian
to the national political state as it specifically applies to the "Old

Colony", "Sommerfelder" and "Chortitza" Mennonites. A few years after these groups arrived in Canada, the pressure of change was thrust upon them and neither group was unified and adequately prepared to face it squarely. Three areas of confrontation in the Canadian environment are discussed: 1) their concept of the state; 2) their philosophy of education; and 3) their idea of progress. In each of these areas, all three Mennonite groups were concerned about keeping what they had rather than to seek any change. Such confrontations were often answered by migrations and the article provides a number of reasons for the frequency of migration. In general, the author states, there are three solutions to the problem: rejection of all cooperation; full cooperation; or a passive attitude. He concludes that "the existence of an Anabaptist religious group within a national political state, is faced with a continual problem of assimilation and loss of its vitality."

YODER, MERVIN
  "A Study of the Church Status of Mennonites Who Accepted Military Service." Unpublished seminar paper, Mennonite Historical Library, Goshen, Indiana, 1951.

A study of the present church status of Mennonites who accepted military service and the relative methods used by the different conferences in dealing with the men upon their return. Its scope is the Old Mennonite Conference in the United States. Two purposes of the study are: 1) to determine how many men were restored to the church and how many were not; and 2) to get a general idea of how different conferences and congregations dealt with their men who entered military service. From a 1948 report, it was found that over 40 per cent of Mennonite men who were drafted accepted military service. More than two-thirds of this group have been lost to the Mennonite Church. Of the one-third who have been restored only half have been indicated as in good standing. A much higher percentage of drafted Mennonites were in good standing with the church when they accepted noncombatant service.

III. Hutterites

A. Books and Pamphlets

ALBERTA (PROVINCE OF)
Report on Communal Property 1972. Select Committee of the Alberta Legislature. Edmonton, 1972.
Communal Property in Alberta. Department of Municipal Affairs, Special Advisory Service, Edmonton, 1974, 35 pp.

As a result of the information and new perspective contained in the report of the Select Committee of the Legislature in 1972 the Communal Property Act was repealed on March 1, 1973. The second of the above publications summarizes the key provisions of the new approach which replaces legal sanctions against expansion with a structured consultation. The new plan now in effect (1977) is that the Hutterite Council of Elders agrees to discuss proposed land transactions with a government-appointed liaison officer. This officer is chairperson of an Advisory Committee which establishes guidelines for expansion. Saskatchewan has a less structured advisory approach while Manitoba and the U. S. states have no provisions of any kind. For the moment this signalizes the end of repressive measures aimed at the Hutterites. *Communal Property in Alberta* not only summarizes the new approach but is a valuable compendium of research in its own right.

ARNOLD, EBERHARD (ED.)
Children in Community: A Survey of the Educational Work of the Bruderhof Communities. London: Plough Publishing House, 1939.

131

The purpose of this collection of articles is to give an impression of Hutterite children's work and "to reveal the child-like characteristics that lead to the community of the Church." It begins with an introduction by the editor outlining the fundamental principles of Hutterite educational work and is followed by accounts of men and women taking part in Hutterite educational work as well as essays, poems, and drawings by Hutterite children.

ARNOLD, EBERHARD
The Hutterite Brothers: Four Centuries of Common Life and Work. Aston, Keynes, Wiltshire, England: Plough Publishing House, 1940.

This booklet is a review of the history of the Hutterian movement. Its purpose is to make known some of the fundamental facts about this movement which started in the early sixteenth century and to show the relationship between the Hutterites and the Mennonites. Contents include: the origin, life, activities and literature of the early Hutterian Brothers; struggle of the church: persecution, growth, decline and rebirth during the years 1536-1877; the Hutterian Brothers in America and the rise of a new community in Europe.

BACH, MARCUS
Strange Sects and Curious Cults. New York: Dodd, Mead and Co., 1961.

One chapter in this book provides a descriptive account of the Hutterites and their way of life. Several questions are raised which the author attempts to answer. For example, he is interested in discovering whether the claims can be justified that the Hutterite communal system is a dictatorship where few liberties are enjoyed. Author also questions whether Hutterites are really as dedicated to their quest for utopia as they claim and whether they will be able to hold out much longer against the forces of change.

BENNETT, JOHN W.
The Hutterian Brethren: The Agricultural Economy and Social Organization of a Communal People. Stanford, California: Stanford University Press, 1967.

This book is based on an extensive study made by the author in 1964 and 1965 of six Hutterian colonies in the Jasper region of Saskatchewan. The main interest in this study arose out of the relative economic success of the Hutterites in a specialized region and also out of the fact that the colonies are the most enduring form of cooperative-collective agriculture. The book places particular emphasis on the economy and the formal organization of the colony. In a very detailed manner the author shows how one group of colonies found their land, established their economy, and managed their enterprises. The author believes that the conventional view of Hutterite society as an anachronistic system that resists any change is a limited one. He says that Hutterite society is what it is: "a Christian body practicing communal living." He shows how thay have done this within the agricultural mode, and how they have accommodated change when it was necessary for the continuity of the colony system.

BENNETT, JOHN W.
Northern Plainsmen; Adaptive Strategy and Agrarian Life. Chicago: Aldine Publishing Company, 1969.

This socio-economic study of a sample region in Western Canada was designed "as an exercise in the analysis of a modern agricultural community from an ecological point of view." Four main social groups in the region, called Jasper by the author, are studied in detail: Indians, cattle ranchers, farmers, and Hutterites. These groups live side by side and share political and many social institutions, but essentially they remain distinct cultural units, engaging in separate kinds of economic activities. Author describes the process of adaptive adjustment for each group and shows how each one must take into account the existence of the other three as a significant element in their adaptation. The section on the Hutterites provides a valuable description of their history, beliefs, family and marriage, colony organization, economic adaptations, and relations with the Jasper community and indicates how the theocratic social system of the Hutterites led to a dramatic pattern of adjustment for the other groups. (Reprinted in *Immigrant Groups*, edited by J. L. Elliot. Scarborough: Prentice-Hall, 1971.)

CALGARY BOARD OF EDUCATION
The People Called Hutterites. Calgary: Calgary Board of Education, 1974.

For an immediate or instant collection of materials on the Hutterites the Calgary materials are without a rival. The kit includes four casettes, three filmstrips, a laminated map of Alberta showing the Hutterite colonies, ten laminated photographs of Hutterite life, legend and location list, eight binders, four government reports and Hostetler's major work, *Hutterite Society* (1974). The binders include several hundred articles, letters and newspaper clippings on the following topics: Relations with Society, Filmstrip Scripts, Teaching Strategies and Related Information, Communal Economy, Hutterite Land Purchases and Government Policy, Life on a Hutterite Colony and "The Hutterite," a chapter from *Faith and My Friends* by Marcus Bach. Although focused on Alberta colonies and Alberta responses to these colonies the kit is still the finest collection of materials for teachers anywhere; and it provides quick access to many crucial items for researchers.

CANADA
Laws, Statutes, etc. 15 George VI. Chapter 77 (1951), "An Act to Incorporate the Hutterian Brethren Church," pp. 61-65.

CANADIAN MENTAL HEALTH ASSOCIATION
The Hutterites and Saskatchewan: A Study in Inter-Group Relations. A study conducted at the request of Government of Saskatchewan. Regina, Saskatchewan, 1953.

This is a report of a study of Hutterites and their relations with larger societies in which they have lived. The study, carried out by the Canadian Mental Health Association at the request of the Government of Saskatchewan, focuses its attention upon two Saskatchewan communities where Hutterites had recently settled, Maple Creek and Shaunavon areas. Findings are based on a field study which involved a comparison of attitudes toward the two Hutterite communities and the communities near which they had settled. Several conclusions are significant: the Hutterites are quickly identified as different; when a "different" group is seen as an obvious threat by another group, conditions are most conducive to misconceptions, rumors and scapegoating; economic insecurities and particularly conducive to scapegoating of the Hutterites; and the problems of inter-group relations identified in Maple Creek or Shaunavon can be solved by planning and by making use of factual data.

CONKIN, PAUL K.
Two Paths to Utopia: the Hutterites and the Llano Colony. Lincoln: University of Nebraska Press, 1964, 212 pp.

In this book, the Hutterites, whose communal way of life is based strictly on religion, are contrasted with the Llano Colony, an attempt at secular communal living. The section on Hutterites includes four chapters with emphasis on their period in North America. One chapter, of particular value, is entitled, "The Community Way—1963." It emphasizes the strengths and stresses in Hutterite life. Author says the point of greatest stress in Hutterite life is "probably the desire for luxuries, entertainment, or a better standard of living," but he also predicts that the Hutterites' separate religious identity and their more distinctive customs and rituals will "remain for endless centuries."

DAVID, MORRIS and KRAUTER, JOSEPH F.
The Other Canadians. Toronto: Methuen Publications, 1971.

Presentation of the social conditions and the political problems of six Canadian groups, including the Hutterian Brethren. The chapter on the Hutterites begins with some general background information concerning population size, geographical location, degree of heterogeneity, and leadership structure, and proceeds

to a discussion of specific socio-political problems such as immigration restrictions, harassment by the press and farm organizations, and the Land Sales Prohibition Act. Author draws attention
to the fact that the Hutterites deliberately chose to preserve their
distinctive way of life and also that, aside from the Chinese and
Japanese, only the Hutterites, whose goals are strictly preserva-
tional, have generated within themselves the means sufficient for
the self-development of their communities.

DEETS, LEE EMERSON
The Hutterites: A Study of Social Cohesion. Gettysburg, Pennsylvania:
Time and News Publishing Co., 1939.

The social cohesion of a communal, religious order is the concern
of this investigation of the Hutterites of South Dakota, Manitoba,
and Alberta. "How have the Hutterites cohered?" Topics of discussion include the collective security of a cohesive order, the
economic and physical environment, the central beliefs, the pattern of government, and technology. Some of the factors discussed as relating to Hutterite community cohesion are: an ideology
which defines the objectives, self-discipline, a system ordered
around clearly established central beliefs, homogeneity of the
Hutterites, isolation, and a high birth rate.

EATON, JOSEPH W.
*Exploring Tomorrow's Agriculture: Cooperative Group Farming—A Prac-
tical Program of Rural Rehabilitation*. New York: Harper and Brothers
Publishers, 1943.

A study of the cooperative group farm, "an association of a
number of family farms who operate jointly a large-scale farming
enterprise and who equitably share the returns of their group
effort," based on surveys of several such farms including the
communal villages of the Hutterian Brethren in South Dakota. A
discussion on pages 218-230 deals with Hutterite administration,
economic structure, history, future, communism, and work relations. The author is interested in the Hutterites because they are a
society which practices cooperative group farming and has
achieved many desirable characteristics. They are: uniformity
and classlessness; certainty or no conflicting goals; isolation and
protection from disrupting influences of other cultures; and a
well-developed system of education to perpetuate goals.

EATON, JOSEPH W. and WEIL, ROBERT J.
*Culture and Mental Disorders; a Comparative Study of Hutterites and Other
Populations*. Glencoe, Illinois: The Free Press, 1955.

The aim of this book is to discover the relationship, if there is any,
between culture and mental illness. To do this, an extensive study
was made of the Hutterites so that the authors could examine

what happens to the adjustment of people who grow up in this peculiar cultural mold. Part of the study looks at certain features of the social system of the Hutterites, such as the degree of homogeneity within the group and the high degree of stability in membership, to find out whether the Hutterites have found a "social system of high contentment." The authors also employed an epidemiological study of which the incidence and prevalence rates of mental disorders are compared with nine other populations.

EATON, JOSEPH
"Folk Obstetrics and Pediatrics Meet the M.D.: A Case Study of Social Anthropology and Medicine." *Patients, Physicians and Illness*. Edited by E. Gartly Jaco. Glencoe, Illinois: The Free Press, 1958.

Author examines Hutterite attitudes, beliefs, and practices regarding sex, reproduction, preparation for motherhood, prenatal care, childbirth, infant feeding, and family relationships.

FLINT, DAVID
The Hutterites, a Study in Prejudice. Toronto: Oxford University Press, 1975.

"This study has been motivated by the desire to produce a text that would be interdisciplinary, useful in more than one course at different levels of reading skill, and that would give a viewpoint on Hutterites and on the problems of minority groups that would enable students not only to achieve understanding but to debate and analyse issues..."
Flint's experience as a Toronto secondary teacher is reflected in searching questions, a glossary, a good bibliography and a remarkable collection of photographs. Field work for the book was done in the Hutterite colony at Pincher Creek, Alberta. With this book Hutterite scholarship is now focused to the high school classroom, auguring well for better understanding of the "Leut" as a test case of Canadian acceptance of minorities.

FRIEDMANN, ROBERT
"The Hutterian Brethren and Community of Goods." *The Recovery of the Anabaptist Vision*. Edited by Guy Franklin Hershberger. Scottdale, Pennsylvania: The Herald Press, 1957.

Author interprets the underlying principles which motivated the Hutterites and made their survival possible. He believes that social scientists in interpreting this group sociologically, economically, and genetically, have missed the central point, "the deep Christian foundation upon which the Hutterites have built and still continue to derive their strength and courage." Author concludes that there are three major motives of the Hutterites: the longing of Christians for brotherly love and sharing; Gelassenheit or yielding absolutely to the will of God while forsaking one's own will; and obedience to the divine commandments. These motives are shown to reveal that the Hutterites "represent a most original type of theocratic society or theocratic communism."

FRIEDMANN, ROBERT
Hutterite Studies. Edited by Harold S. Bender. Goshen, Indiana: Mennonite Historical Society, 1961.

A series of essays by Robert Friedmann collected and published in honour of his seventieth anniversary. Many of the articles are taken from such periodicals as the *Mennonite Quarterly Review*, and *Mennonite Encyclopedia*. It concerns a detailed account of Hutterite history, doctrines, way of life, writings, bibliographies, and a comprehensive review of research. The book begins with a good explanation of Anabaptism which is useful as a basis for a study on Hutterites. Of more importance from a sociological point of view are the chapters on Hutterite economics, marriage practices, medicine, education, and pottery.

GROSS, PAUL S.
Hutterian Brethren: Life and Religion. Pincher Creek, Alberta, 1954.

A pamphlet tracing the events leading to the basis, foundation, and religion of the Hutterite Colonies. It also provides a definition of the Church of Christ and the procedures to follow for joining it. Biblical quotations are used to support their way of life.

GROSS, PAUL S.
Who are the Hutterites? Scottdale, Pennsylvania: Mennonite Publishing House, 1959.

A brief pamphlet written by a Hutterian minister. It contains information on their origins, Anabaptist background, basic principles, and articles of faith as well as a short list of other studies on the Hutterites.

GROSS, PAUL S.
The Hutterite Way. Saskatoon: Freeman Publishing Company Limited, 1965.

As a Hutterite himself, the author gives a very accurate, lively picture of Hutterite life, customs, religion, and traditions. The book is a straightforward account of such things as their education, worship, dress, menu, and holiday celebrations. The description of the community life which creates similarity of spirit and mind, and the chapter on the impact of technology are important sections of the book. The book is filled with photographs and concludes with Jakob Hutter's Last Epistle to the Church of Moravia in 1535.

HOEPPNER, K. and GILL, J.
Communal Property in Alberta, Technical Report No. 6-C. Edmonton:
Alberta Land Use Forum, 1974, 19 pp.

Established by the legislature in 1973, the Alberta Land Use
Forum considers public policy for land in the province which
leads North America with ninety-one Hutterite colonies compared with fifty-seven in Manitoba and thirty in South Dakota
and Saskatchewan. The ninety-one colonies held 712,793 acres by
ownership and 94,613 through rental. This is 1.63 per cent of the
land farmed in the province or 1.15 per cent of the arable land. "It
would be difficult," the report notes, "to consider such a small
percentage as significant in determining patterns of ownership.
The real concern is couched in the projection of existing trends
which indicate that while the number of farms and the farm
population is declining, the number of communal holdings and
the Hutterite population is increasing. Such trends continued
indefinitely, some projectors would postulate, that communal
farm ownership will be the predominant form of agricultural
land tenure in some future time."

After this grim picture, the Forum embraces the conservative
trust in natural forces which will inhibit the Hutterite growth:
High costs for financial resources such as land, buildings,
machinery, operations and credit; the quest by the Hutterites for
inside plumbing and central heating driving up the standard of
living and a statistical correction of Eaton's forecast of a four per
cent annual population increase made in 1951. It is now three per
cent, doubling the population in 25.3 years, not seventeen years.
The report concludes with a salute to diversity including the
communal along with individual, family and corporate farm operations as a healthy characteristic of Alberta agriculture. "It is a
heritage enriched by variety rather than uniformity." The Forum
concludes in a well researched, enlightened statement of public
policy by conservatives who now accept pluralism.

HOFER, ARNOLD M. and WALTER, KENNETH J.
History of the Hutterite Mennonites. Freeman, South Dakota: Pine Hill
Press, 1974.

An uneven but valuable source book containing diaries, ship lists,
chronologies, recipes, dialect vocabularies and photographs of
South Dakota Hutterites during the past century. All North
American Hutterites originated in South Dakota. For sociologists
the most valuable aspect of this publication is a picture of what
happens when Hutterites leave the communal life for a more
individualistic existence. There are thirteen churches in South
Dakota formed by defecting Hutterites. These churches appear
to be intensely fundamentalistic with few distinctive expressions
of communal or semi-communal programs or institutions.

HOFER, PETER
The Hutterian Brethren and Their Beliefs. Starbuck, Manitoba: The
Hutterian Brethren of Manitoba. Approved by the Committee of
Elders, 1955.

This booklet prepared by the Committee of Elders of the Hutterian Brethren of Manitoba is an attempt to dispel popular
misconceptions regarding their beliefs and communal way of life.
It defends the Hutterites against arguments used by those who
want to restrict Hutterite expansion and states that they are
entitled to tolerance and unrestricted exercise of their religious
tenets and objectives. Reference to the Scriptures is used as their
defense.

HORSCH, JOHN
The Hutterian Brethren, 1528-1931: A Story of Martyrdom and Loyalty.
Goshen, Indiana: Mennonite Historical Society, 1931.

Horsch describes the communistic organization of the Hutterian
Brotherhood as based on Christian principle; the "religious faith
of the Hutterite group has been the normative factor in its life."
The book is largely an historical account of the Hutterites. The
author traces the history of the Hutterites from origin in 1525
through their "ideal period" in Moravia, their persecutions and
wanderings, to settlement in Russia and then in America. A
section of the book is also devoted to the faith and principles of
the Hutterian Brethren.

HOSTETLER, JOHN A.
Hutterite Life. Scottdale, Pennsylvania: Herald Press, 1965.

A very brief description of Hutterite history, survival and growth,
education, family, women, marriage, art and humour, and the
'Bruderhof.' It serves as an introductory study on Hutterites and
provides a basic understanding of the Hutterite pattern of communal living and their non-conformist way of life.

HOSTETLER, JOHN A.
Education and Marginality in the Communal Society of the Hutterites.
University Park, Pennsylvania: The Pennsylvania State University,
1965.

The purpose of this book is to "advance basic knowledge of
learning processes through observing a cultural setting very different from the typical American one." Its aim is to study the
goals, methods, and educational processes of the Hutterite system in order to learn about motivation, personality, and culture.
The Hutterites were chosen for the study because this society was
reputed to be successful in relation to its professed goals. The
objectives are as follows: 1) to formulate the moral postulates of

the society; 2) to observe the socialization methods in the community and to describe and classify them objectively; 3) to discover the social and personal characteristics of persons who defect from the communal society through in-depth interviews with those who have left the group; and 4) to state the findings in the form of inductive generalizations. The study is supplemented by empirical data, maps, and charts.

HOSTETLER, JOHN A. and HUNTINGTON, GERTRUDE ENDERS
The Hutterites in North America. New York: Holt, Rinehart and Winston, 1967.

This one hundred page book provides an understanding why the Hutterite communal way of life has worked and continues to work. The material is presented in a personal manner with detailed descriptions of the day-to-day living patterns of the Hutterites. In this way the reader can see what happens to a Hutterite child at each stage of his socialization and how, between birth and death, each member loses his individual identity and surrenders to the "communal will." The authors effectively reveal this process and also the total life-style of the Hutterites by dividing the book into these four chapters: Colony Life Patterns, Technology and Economic Patterns, Socialization and Family Patterns, and Disruption Patterns. Through these chapters, it can be seen that the authors view the principle of order as a key concept underlying the Hutterite way of life.

HOSTETLER, JOHN A.
Hutterite Society. Baltimore: The Johns Hopkins University Press, 1974, 403 pp.

For years to come this will be the definitive work on the Hutterites of Canada and the U. S. Based on research started at the University of Alberta in Edmonton in 1959, Hostetler has completed a fifteen-year search in Europe and North America for an accurate and comprehensive description of the Western world's oldest communal societies. It supercedes his work with Gertrude Huntington, *The Hutterites of North America* published seven years earlier.

In addition to the basic analysis in the main text of the book Hostetler has, in effect, created a source book for Hutterite studies with sixteen appendices, five maps, seven charts and ten statistical tables. Add to this forty-two photographs and a definitive bibliography and the reader has a book of major importance.

Because Hostetler combines objectivity with sensitivity to the genius of the Hutterites, he concludes that he is not studying a Utopia but a functionally effective answer to poverty, inequality, work, education, meaning and security. At the end of his preface he concludes: "A small society that comes under the scrutiny of scientific investigation exposes itself to the risks of disclosure of its weaknesses and strengths. I found the Hutterite people fully knowledgeable of this fact, yet admirably open and fearless of anything science might uncover about them. I acknowledge not only the courage and help of many Hutterite men and women who were my informants but also my gratitude to them for acquainting me with communities of people who live a satisfying, stable and rewarding life."

HOSTETLER, JOHN A.
Communitarian Societies. Toronto: Holt, Rinehart and Winston Co., 1976.

The latest book from the prolific pen of John Hostetler places the Hutterites in the context of communitarianism rather than utopianism. The communitarian society is essentially a counter-culture which rejects the reformist universalism of the utopians. Hostetler affirms an ethnographic approach whose aim is to understand the social and cultural context of each community. Hutterites are compared with Oneida and The Family, a group marriage community. The book is excellent for courses in utopian societies, bringing a solid corrective to much fuzzy thinking concerning the neo-romantic precariously-constructed hippie communes of the 60's which overlooked the insights from the 400 years of Hutterite experience.

As always, Hostetler's extensive bibliography is priceless.

HUTTERIAN BRETHREN
Constitution of the Hutterian Brethren Church and Rules as to Community of Property. Winnipeg, Manitoba: E. A. Fletcher, Barrister, Solicitor, 1950. (Amended 1951 and 1952.)

A document containing the articles of association of the Hutterian Brethren Church as adopted by the Darius-Leut, the Lehrer-Leut, and the Schmeidt-Leut Colonies. The articles of association listed are the name, objects and powers of organization, board of managers, organization of conferences and of congregations, membership, holding of property, rights and duties of members, expulsion of members, officers given certain powers, admission of further congregations, and amendments.

INFIELD, HENRIK F.
Cooperative Communities at Work. New York: The Dryden Press, 1945.

Aim of this book is to sum up the lessons offered by cooperative communities of the past and present. The Hutterites are, therefore, an important element of this study. In the chapter concerning this group, the author considers several aspects: the motives behind the Hutterite community, their cooperative spirit, customs, patriarchal government, division of labour, and a consideration of the advantages and disadvantages of the pathology in a number of forms exists among the Hutterites.

KAPLAN, BERT and PLAUT, THOMAS F.
Personality in a Communal Society: An Analysis of the Mental Health of the Hutterites. Lawrence, Kansas: University of Kansas Publications, 1965.

This book reports on one part of the investigation carried out by J. W. Eaton. Its purpose is to lay the foundations for a mental health evaluation by describing and analysing the personalities of a large sample of more or less "normal" Hutterites. The study first describes the most prevalent personality characteristics of the Hutterites and then provides an evaluation of the mental health of the group. It was found that psychopathology in a number of forms exist among the Hutterites and the authors conclude that "the Hutterites have not developed personality characteristics which harmonize with the social pattern to such an extent that mental health problems are either minimal or eliminated."

KLASSEN, PETER JAMES
The Economics of Anabaptism, 1525-1560. The Hague: Monton and Co., 1964.

This book makes available in English much material previously limited to the German studies of Correll and Peachey. While documenting the centrality of the religious motivation of the Anabaptist the book underscores the unique contributions of the mainline Anabaptists to the economics of mutual aid which permitted a highly qualified acceptance of private property as a sacred trust in a communal context.

The Hutterites were the minority who successfully and permanently adopted Christian communism. Two excellent chapters and four appendices set forth the Hutterite view.

The twelve pages of bibliography add to the value of this crucial book which provides the starting point for any comparison between past and present economic patterns of the communal and semi-communal Anabaptists and forerunners of today's Mennonites, Amish and Hutterites.

LOOMIS, CHARLES P. and BEEGLE, J. ALLAN
Rural Sociology: The Strategy of Change. Englewood Cliffs, New Jersey: Prentice Hall, Inc., 1957.

Elements of the Hutterite social system and the social process in the Hutterite communities are described in order to reveal how the structure and value orientations of this system differ from those in capitalistic economies. Norms, status-roles, communication, decision-making, and boundary maintenance are some of the topics discussed. The Gemeinschaft-like structure of the Hutterite communities is shown to contrast sharply with the more Gesellschaft-like structure of the plantation, corporation farm, or large estate. The family farm is described as occupying a position between these two extremes.

MONTANA AGRICULTURAL EXPERIMENT STATION
The Hutterites in Montana: An Economic Description. Bozeman: Montana State University, 1971.

Although this study is specifically on the Hutterites in Montana, it is useful for dispelling certain myths about the Hutterites in general. It is an investigation of three aspects of economic influence of Hutterite life in Montana. The three aspects are concerned with 1) marketing of output; 2) the purchase of household goods and agricultural inputs; and 3) the payment of taxes. The study is largely concerned with presenting factual information. The bulletin shows that Hutterites do market their goods locally; they do buy locally and make a conscious effort to patronize local merchants who price competitively and give good service; the Hutterites do pay taxes—both property and income taxes; and the Hutterites have shown a remarkable ability to adjust to scientific agricultural and have become an integral part of the Montana economy.

PALMER, HOWARD
Land of the Second Chance: A History of Ethnic Groups in Southern Alberta. Lethbridge: The Lethbridge Herald, 1972.

 A chapter (pp. 39-53) in this book, entitled "Hutterites", discusses two forces within Hutterite society which continue to counter assimilative forces: one is the isolation of the colonies in rural areas, and the other is their systematic education. In Southern Alberta the colonies have been confronted with much hostility since their arrival from South Dakota in 1919. Article briefly discusses the anti-Hutterite sentiment and the values, authority patterns, family life, education and economic organization of the Hutterites.

PETER, KARL
"The Hutterite Problem in Alberta." *Social Problems: A Canadian Profile*. Edited by R. Laskin. Toronto: McGraw Hill Company of Canada Ltd., 1964.

This work considers the arguments and solutions brought forward by two groups for the "Hutterite problem." One group is the patriotic-minded segment of population which emphasizes the apparent lack of interest by the Hutterites in Canadian patriotism. The other group which reflects the sentiments of certain parts of the Alberta farm population is concerned with the spread of Hutterite colonies. The effects of both arguments upon the Hutterites are discussed. First it is emphasized that, in terms of their beliefs, to be a Canadian patriot would mean for the Hutterites to lose everything that is of any value to them. The second argument, the writer feels, is best understood by looking at one aspect of Hutterite culture—its organization of labor. Through specialization of jobs, a pool of manpower, and elaborate repair and construction facilities, the Hutterites have found a security which is almost impossible for the family farm to achieve. As a result hostility to the Hutterites is expressed by those who haven't found security of operation and outlook into the future. The conclusion is reached that once the threat of assimilation is removed, the strong ties of the Hutterites to Canada will create an atmosphere of cooperation and understanding.

PETERS, VICTOR

All Things Common; the Hutterian Way of Life. Minneapolis: University of Minnesota Press, 1965, 233 pp.

This book on the Hutterites is both an historical study and a sociological field report, primarily concerned with the colonies of Manitoba. Historically the author provides a brief account of their persecutions, migrations, and settlements in North America, as well as a discussion on the opposition in Canada to Hutterite expansion. In his field research, the author visited all Manitoba colonies and participated in the work, meals, and religious services of the Hutterites. As a result he provides a complete story of the Hutterite way of life. This includes descriptions of the 'Bruderhof,' the administration of the colony, family relationships, the division of a colony, and the education of members. He concludes that the Hutterite colonies show remarkable stability, cohesion, and vitality, and that in the absense of legislation to drive out the communities, the Hutterites will remain a noticeable ingredient of ethnic diversity in the province they live in.

RIEDEMANN, PETER

Account of Our Religion, Doctrine, and Faith. Rifton, New York: Plough Publishing House, 1970.

This account represents the official position of the Hutterites in matters both of doctrine and practice. It also serves as a basic source for the knowledge of Anabaptist doctrine and theology. The appendix includes a brief history of the Hutterites and the Society of Brethren.

Riedemann (1506-1556) is considered the second founder of the Hutterites after Hans Hut. He was born in Silesia, Germany.

RILEY, MARVIN P. and STEWART, JAMES R.

The Hutterian Brethren: South Dakota's Communal Farmers. Brookings,

South Dakota: South Dakota State University Agricultural Experiment Station, 1965.

Although this bulletin deals specifically with South Dakotan Hutterites, it is useful for any study on Hutterites since it provides information of the agricultural aspects of Hutterite life. The first part attempts to answer such questions as who are the Hutterites, what they believe, and where they are located. The second part of the paper reports on the census of the communal farms and summarizes the sect's agricultural enterprises and changes in farm operations. In this section the author shows how Hutterite principles of "self-sufficiency," "simplicity of living" and "efficiency" serve as rules for everyday life and help the outsider to gain a better understanding of the farming and production practices of the Hutterites. Detailed descriptions are provided of Hutterite farming practices, diversification of enterprises, major livestock enterprises, and major crops.

RILEY, MARVIN P. and JOHNSON, DARRYLL
South Dakota's Hutterite Colonies, 1876-1969. Brookings, South Dakota: Agricultural Experiment Station, South Dakota State University, 1970.

An updating of Riley's earlier survey of the South Dakota colonies in the state with the largest number of colonies in the United States; and, in a university with long history of research in Hutterite culture.

SERL, VERNON C.
"Stability and Change in Hutterite Society." *Research in Progress: A Report on Field Work and Research in the Departments of Psychology and Sociology-Anthropology of Western Washington College of Education.* Edited by Herbert C. Taylor. Bellingham, Washington: Graphic Arts Press, 1960, pp. 1-6.

Stability and continuity of the Hutterite value system "is one of the most striking characteristics of Hutterite life." The aim of this study is to provide an explanation and interpretation of this continuity. Author concludes that "small population size, isolationism, and above all the maintenance of 'primary-group' contacts and interactions, have been remarkably successful in perpetuating the Hutterite value structure and religious belief." But the author also questions whether this stability will continue in view of some recent developments such as wide dispersal of colonies, continued mechanization, and increasing involvement in local affairs.

SOCIETY OF BROTHERS
Children in Community. Rifton, New York: Plough Publishing Company, 1975, 175 pp.

Three hundred enchanting photographs *of* the children and eighty drawings *by* the children in the progressive Hutterite community near Poughkeepsie, New York provide the most appealing picture of communal life ever published. For scholars who have not visited a commune with joyful collectivity this is the place to start prior to Zablocki's more critical analysis or the abrasive description of children in the hippie communes presented by Mary Higgins Clark in *Where are the Children?* (Dell, 1976). Added to the photographic and textual materials of the Rifton book are six articles on childhood by Aberhard Arnold, the founder of the original communities in Germany.

ZABLOCKI, BENJAMIN DAVID
  The Joyful Community. Baltimore: Penguin Books, 1971.

This intimate, realistic analysis of the Woodcrest, New York Bruderhof was written as a doctoral dissertation at Johns Hopkins using participant observer methodology of four months' duration, supplemented by twenty interviews of ex-members. The Bruderhof recreates the old Hutterite pattern with more educational and cultural sophistication. Hence, its importance as an adaptation of the oldest pattern of Christian communism in the world.

The Bruderhof is not a libertine love-in. It operates with an assault on the self through severe discipline which leads the novitiate into a steady movement towards a genuine collectivity. But it is harshness based on love, not on retribution. The central problem of the Bruderhof is to cope with tension without destroying community. Recommended for a realistic view of the price which must be paid in sacrificing freedom for an intentional community.

B. Graduate Theses

BADEN, JOHN A.
  "The Management of Social Stability; A Political Ethnography of the Hutterites of North America." Unpublished Ph.D. dissertation, Indiana University, 1967.

It is the author's aim in this study to provide an understanding of the Hutterites' largely successful effort to "accommodate the demands of traditionalism and modernity without violating traditional norms or jeopardizing systematic viability." Hutterite social organization is maintained on the basis of ascriptive qualities justified by tradition. Yet, the author states, the aggregated behavior under this set of proscriptions must be consistent with viability in an alien setting. He shows how successful accommodation is arrived at through the political organization of the Hutterite system and how their policy decisions are often "relevant to accommodational propensities." Another central concern for the viability of a society, which the author examines, is the degree to which externally determined political issues receive attention roughly to their import. Also, because of the concern of this study for the maintenance of traditional patterns, author deals in depth with deviance and defection among the Hutterites.

BLEIBTREU, HERMAN K.
"Marriage and Residence Patterns in a Genetic Isolate." Unpublished Ph.D. dissertation, Harvard University, 1964.

This study of a Hutterite colony describes some of the social regularities involving marriage and residence which determine the passage of genes in the population and reveals how these social regulatory methods developed and how they are maintained. It was found that the human social behavior in the Lehrerleut Colony is so regular that it readily lends itself to the kind of analysis generally reserved for natural phenomena. For the geneticist it provided an opportunity to measure genetic drift, gene flow, and selective mating—phenomena known to cause change in the gene. For the anthropologist it provided the opportunity to discover if, or how, each genetic phenomenon is influenced by social-cultural factors. Analyses were made of different kinds of data including the history of migrations and social groupings, genealogies, a census of all living people, and a record of residence before and after marriage. Charts indicate the direction of clan exogamy, the source of females for marriage, and the pathways to second cousin relationships.

BOLDT, EDWARD D.
"Conformity and Deviance; the Hutterites of Alberta." Unpublished M.A. thesis, University of Alberta, 1966.

This study tests the sociological tradition that views "total communities," such as the Hutterites, as immune to "deviance." This resistance to deviance is produced through a sociological process that produces "conformist personality." Sixty Hutterite children reared in five colonies were compared with sixty "worldly" children to test the assumption that children from a "total community" will conform more to the decisions of their peers than children reared in a more "open" society. Contrary to common belief, Hutterite children were found to be significantly less conformist than their non-Hutterite peers. Once this was discovered, the author felt compelled to "test the power of religious commitment as a defense against defection." Ten intensive interviews with defectors from Alberta gave evidence "that defection is better explained as a function of perceived opportunity in the "world" than as a function of commitment to Hutterite values."

BOLDT, EDWARD D.
"Acquiescence and Conventionality in a Communal Society." Unpublished Ph.D. dissertation, University of Alberta, 1968.

It is a common assumption that acquiescence (i.e. yielding to group pressure) becomes a personality feature of individuals reared in *gemeinschaftlich* societies and that this process then accounts for the marked conventionality (i.e., behavior in accordance with group norms) characteristic of such societies. Using a revised acquiescence-including technique, the study tests this assumption experimentally.

CHALMERS, LESLIE EDWIN
"A Comparison to Determine the Effect of Hutterite Culture Upon Educational Achievement." Unpublished M.Ed. thesis, Montana State College, 1964.

This study was undertaken to determine whether there is a difference in achievement in the grade eight Hutterite pupil and the grade eight pupil of a comparable rural school in Montana.

Based on data derived from the Stanford achievement test administered in Teton County, Montana, over a three-year period, Chalmers discovered the following: On the average the non-Hutterite pupils achieved better scores except in spelling and arithmetic reasoning. The score in language and arithmetic computation were very close together. The greatest average difference was in science where the non-Hutterite pupils were considerably better.

CLARK, PETER G.
"Dynasty Formation in the Communal Society of the Hutterites." Unpublished Ph.D. dissertation, University of British Columbia, 1974. This dissertation provided the basis for a paper, "Political Mobility Patterns Within Canadian Hutterite Communities" presented to the Canadian Sociology and Anthropology Association, Toronto, 1974.

Contrary to claims of pure equality, Clark's study demonstrates "that political mobility patterns on Hutterite colonies are largely determined by labor market conditions. In colonies with labor surplus, leadership success tends to be based upon the principles of ascriptive family status; and in colonies with a labor shortage, succession to leadership positions proceeds independently of family status." He also cites Mackie, Peter and Frideres to show that out-migration rates from Hutterite colonies can be seen as a response to labor market conditions as well.

EVANS, SIMON M.
"The Dispersal of Hutterite Colonies in Alberta, 1918-1971." Unpublished M.A. thesis, University of Calgary, 1973.

Some new ground is broken in colony research by showing that the Hutterite settlement pattern in Alberta and neighboring provinces is a product of the locational decisions made by the leadership of the colonies. This research reveals the consistent and overwhelming importance of the core areas as centres of primary colonization where the Hutterites comprise 10 per cent of the rural population. From the core areas new colonies are established where they constitute only 1 or 2 per cent of the population.

Evans makes a number of predictions for the future. The key prediction is a move toward labor-intensifying production such as horticulture in the core areas. The reason is the need of the Hutterites to support themselves with less land.

Another inference of the study is the absence of a monolithic pattern for the colonies with variations of wealth, land, experience and orthodoxy bringing varying responses to land limitations.

HARDER, D. E.
"The Hutterite Church." Unpublished M.A. thesis, Bethel College, North Newton, Kansas, 1930.

In the history of four centuries, it is shown that the Hutterian organization has continued to exist. As individuals and as a social group they are often evaluated according to the contributions they made, such as in their military, economic, civil, and moral values. But the author feels that their prosperity has been gained at a great price: loss of individual initiative, loss of social responsibility, and ignorance of the world around them. Their social viewpoint, influenced by their group isolationism, is often provincial and narrow. But their citizenship value is very high since they are enthusiastic, thrifty, and industrious. He says their merits outweigh their weaknesses.

HOLTZMAN, JEROME J.
"An Inquiry Into the Hutterian German Dialect." Unpublished M.A. thesis, University of South Dakota, 1960.

This linguistic examination of the Hutterian dialect begins with an historical outline and with the author's first impressions of the Hutterites. The author has intended this study to be the first step in the research of tracing the speech development process of the Hutterite language and to be a synchronic record of the Hutterian dialect spoken by the Hutterites of Bon Homme Colony, South Dakota. The stress of the work is on the phonological aspect although it does take into consideration the diachronic aspect. One section of the study is devoted to Anglicisms since the Hutterian Brethren have been exposed to many non-German environments. Also, since the Hutterian dialect is an offshoot of the Tirolean dialect, a comparison was made of these two dialects.

KANTER, ROSABETH MOSS
"Utopias; A Study in Comparative Organization." Unpublished Ph.D. dissertation, University of Michigan, 1967.

This thesis, although not specifically on the Hutterites, provides a broad theoretical framework with which to study them. The study defines commitment as the central problem of a communal system. On the basis of this conceptualization of commitment, it is proposed that particular organizational strategies should be more effective than others for generating commitment, and, hence, communities that employ them should be more successful. Three types of commitment that bind the actors' orientations to areas of a social system are continuance, cohesion, and control.

KNILL, WILLIAM DOUGLAS
"Hutterite Education: A Descriptive Study Based on the Hutterian Colonies Within Warner County No. 5, Alberta, Canada." Unpublished M.A. thesis, Montana State University, 1958.

The technique of controlled acculturation is tested in this study of Hutterites in one small area of Alberta. While Knill's data finds the technique successful he sees the end products as assimilation in the larger culture—a pessimistic conclusion not shared in other studies. The greatest threat, he finds, is the public school system. His data also shows that the achievement levels of Hutterite students are above the national level in grade four and below the national level in grade five.

Knill suggests future studies should deal with a longitudinal analysis of student achievement and the psychological impact of Hutterian culture on the intergroup dynamics of the colony, especially the adolescent group.

KRAUTER, JOSEPH FRANCIS
"Civil Liberties and the Canadian Minorities." Unpublished Ph.D. dissertation, University of Illinois, 1965.

A survey of civil liberties among the Canadian Doukhobors, Indians, Negroes, Orientals, Eskimos and Hutterites with a special section dealing with the Canadian bill of rights and courts. Original data analysis is confined to voting restrictions by provinces, the role of organized labor, sources of opposition and the role of public opinion by pressure groups. The conclusion covers voting, employment, immigration, land restrictions, housing, public accommodations, medical and social welfare benefits, education, liquor, citizenship, arbitrary search and seizure, and taxation.

Chapter on Hutterites brings together current data with emphasis on the problem of land use. Author sees "little likelihood of Hutterites assimilating into the Canadian community, but there is reason to hope for accommodation." This dissertation is the best single study of the subject of civil liberties among six key minorities in Canada.

MACKIE, MARLENE
"The Defector from the Hutterite Colony." Unpublished M.A. thesis, University of Alberta, 1965.

Thirty-seven defectors were interviewed from Hutterite colonies to determine their motivation for leaving and their success in adjusting to the outside world. Author found that "defection was related to the cohesion of the colony of origin and the status held in its stratification system." She says three-quarters of the defectors left a disorganized colony and their desertion was a reaction to both the deviant atmosphere and their low position in the status hierarchy. A second group of defectors are the sons of those in leadership roles and author states that "this behavior stemmed from their social-psychological response to the high status positions enjoyed by their families." From these findings, author concludes that non-conformity is a symptom of breakdown in some segments of the Hutterite system.

MACKIE, MARLENE
"The Accuracy of Folk Knowledge Concerning Alberta Indians, Hutterites and Ukrainians: an Available Data Stereotype Validation Technique." Unpublished Ph.D. dissertation, University of Alberta, 1971. Part of dissertation is summarized under the title "Outsiders' Perception of the Hutterites," in *MQR*, LI (Jan., 1976), pp. 58-65.

Using two indicators of stereotyping, an open-ended questionnaire and a semantic differential, Mackie's instruments were randomly distributed in such a way that half the subjects from each sample organization received each instrument. Both indicators measured impressions of Hutterites, Indians, Ukrainians, Jews, lawyers, teachers, lower class, women and old people. The challenge of the methodology is to answer the questions: How is a sacred community perceived by members of the containing society? Do outsiders withhold acceptance of people which refuse to be integrated; i.e., is the emotional detachment reciprocal?
"Aside from reference to the Brethren's self-imposed cultural and physical isolation, the rationale for the social distance that sample members placed between themselves and the Hutterites did not find expression in the stereotyping imagery they provided. These findings suggest that stereotypes should not be viewed simply as the cognitive dimension of prejudice. Folk impressions contain neutral 'factual' and flattering traits as well."

Mackie's dissertation is the best study of stereotyping among Hutterites to date.

MANGE, ARTHUR P.
"The Population Structure of a Human Isolate." Unpublished Ph.D. dissertation, University of Wisconsin, 1963.

One of the three original Hutterite colonies called the S-leut is studied for several reasons. First it provides an understanding of the growth of a colony from 1874 to 1961 and reveals how the original colony consisting of 200 members has branched out into fifty-one colonies with a population of 5,450 located in South Dakota, Minnesota, and Manitoba. Secondly it reveals the in-breeding changes over time and the inbreeding effects on fertil-ity, height, and weight, and lastly, this study allows for an analysis of the curious shifts in sex ratios within families and between generations. Some of the characteristics that were revealed from this study are: a growing population with a considerable degree of homogeneity; interesting marriage patterns with respect to age, surname sessions and dependence on marriage choices of parents and sibs; a stable and a high level of inbreeding with no significant effects on fertility but with an effect on height; and a low sex ratio at birth, a high shift in sex ratios with families dependent on birth order, and a shift in sex ratios in alternative generations.

MANN, GEORGE ADOLPH
"Functional Autonomy Among English School Teachers in the Hutterite Colonies of Southern Alberta: A Study of Social Control." Unpublished Ph.D. dissertation, University of Colorado, 1974.

The research studies the social control process as it applies to the English school teacher in the colonies of southern Alberta based on personal interviews with forty-one teachers in thirty-seven colonies supplemented by data from divisional county superin-tendents. Utilizing concepts from Alvin Gouldner, the author hypothesized that some parts of a social system have less inter-dependence and thus may be said to possess high functional autonomy. The data supported the hypothesis. The teachers with high functional autonomy conformed less to Hutterite expecta-tions and sought to improve teaching facilities and to be innova-tive.

MARTENS, HELEN
"Hutterite Songs; the Origins and Oral Transmission of Their Melodies from the Sixteenth Century." Unpublished Ph.D. disserta-tion, Columbia University, 1968.

"Today in North America some seventeen thousand persons, bearing the name of Hutterite, are singing songs to the melodies

of sixteenth century German folk songs which they have orally
transmitted from that time." This dissertation is primarily a study
of the melodies which serve as vehicles for the Hutterite songs. It
is also a study of their relationship to the era and milieu from
which they sprang. Part of the study is concerned with determining how old and direct the oral singing of the Hutterites was,
while another major section of this work consisted of taping and
transcribing the Hutterite melodies from seven different colonies. Through this the author is able to disprove the "assertions
of several musical scholars that the sixteenth century German
folk melodies are no longer being sung."

PETER, KARL ANDREAS
"Factors of Social Change and Social Dynamics in the Communal
Settlements of Hutterites 1527-1967." Unpublished Ph.D. disserta-
tion, University of Alberta, 1967.

The analysis of this study is concerned with the structural fluctua-
tions of the Hutterite socio-cultural system during the last 440
years. Author shows how the social and cultural system of the
Hutterites has moved through five social phases and these fluctu-
ations have been between "community of goods" and "community of love." Included are graphs and tables concerning the vol-
umes of Hutterite songs, number of composers, the Hutterite
population from 1535-1965, a distribution of Hutterite population by age and sex, and a comparison of 1880 and 1950 age
distribution of the Hutterites.

PETERS, VICTOR J.
"All Things Common: The Hutterites of Manitoba." Unpublished
M.A. thesis, University of Manitoba, 1958.

This study is an attempt to present not only an account of the
history of the Manitoba Hutterites but also an analysis of the
group's institutions. "The thesis tries to portray 'total community
life' as practiced by the Hutterians. Structurally, the Hutterian
colonies function as Gemeinschaft societies. As such they provide
intrinsic interest for the historian and the sociologist. Beyond
that, the Hutterian colonies, because they have resisted assimilation to a greater degree than any other religious or ethnic group
of European stock, pose a problem: Will their members in time
integrate into the larger Canadian society, sharing all its duties
and privileges, or will they continue to perpetuate their introverted life?" The chapters of the study include such topics as the
communal economy, education, spiritual and cultural heritage,
health and community stability, Hutterites and the public school,
and the Hutterites and the outside world.

PITT, EDWIN L.
"The Hutterian Brethren in Alberta." Unpublished M.A. thesis,
University of Alberta, 1949.

Author attempts to provide an understanding of the belief, basic
in Hutterite doctrine, by which the Hutterite Church places itself
apart from all other societies and "out of the world." The aspects
of Hutterite life that are dealt with are their European background, their dispersal to Western Canada, Paraguay, and Ontario, Hutterite faith, Hutterite Organization, Hutterite controversy in Western Canada, and their growth and expansion. Of
particular interest is a description of the sociological aspects of the
Hutterite way of life. Author notes such characteristics as satisfac-
tion with life, spirit of friendly cooperation, sense of security,
self-confidence, and dignity. In a very detailed discussion of the
Hutterite controversy in Western Canada, the author presents
opinion both for and against Hutterite expansion. Also included
are maps, charts, and a list of each colony in Alberta with its
address, acreage, and population.

PRIESTLY, DAVID T.
"A Study of Selected Factors Related to Attitudes Toward the Hut-
terites of South Dakota." Unpublished M.Sc. thesis, South Dakota
State University, 1959.

An empirical study exploring two commonly made assumptions
regarding the relationship of contact and knowledge to inter-
group attitudes. The first assumption is that "contact brings
friendliness" especially if it is "basic and intimate." The second
assumption is "give people the facts and prejudice will disap-
pear."

The data collected by Priestly did not support either of these
assumptions. The data, on the other hand, established a low but
significant relationship between attitude and *inaccurate* knowledge.

Priestly suggests further clarification of theoretical
frameworks for Hutterite studies. He affirms that Merton's
theory of relative deprivation is viable even though needing
further scrutiny.

A valuable work for both theory and methodology because it is
an empirical study in search of a sounder theory, hence, a focus
fully aware of the two dimensions of social science research.

RILEY, MARVIN P.
"Farmers' Attitudes Toward the Hutterite Brethren: A Study in
Intergroup Relations." Unpublished Ph.D. dissertation, University
of Missouri, Columbia, 1968.

The central problem of the study focuses on the attitudes held
toward a rural religious sect by nonsectarians and the social and

economic factors associated with those attitudes. The study makes a contribution to knowledge in the field of sociology in four areas: 1) the theory of intergroup relations; 2) attitude research; 3) the sociology of religion; and 4) problems of practical concern. From the findings it is suggested that the resolution of value conflicts is necessary for tolerance and understanding of the ethnic group, that the social organization of the Hutterites tends to generate negative attitudes toward them, but that these attitudes are necessary for the maintenance of the social cohesion of the Hutterites.

RYAN, JOHN
"The Agricultural Operations of Manitoba Hutterites." Unpublished Ph.D. dissertation, McGill University, 1972.

Going beyond Hutterite studies in demography, history, religion, psychology and sociology, Ryan has made the definitive study of Hutterite agriculture compared with the non-colony, commercial agriculture of Manitoba. The study is based on the first detailed census of agricultural operation (hogs, chickens and grain, for example) in forty-three Manitoba colonies.

If scholars of Hutterite social patterns want specificity on the economics of Hutterites this is the best source. Hutterites are more productive than their neighbors but they have lower returns. Their total assets in forty-three colonies are $39,000,000 with gross sales in hogs alone (1969) of nearly $5,000,000. Thus, Ryan deals with both micro and macro-economics—a brilliant achievement all in all.

This dissertation is also unique in its astute comments on similarities and differences between Hutterite colonies and commercial farms in socialist countries.

The dissertation is recommended to experts in Ottawa, Peking, Moscow and Washington!

SERL, VERNON
"Stability and Change in Hutterite Society." Unpublished Ph.D. dissertation, University of Oregon, 1964.

A delineation of the colony as an unusually efficient socialization milieu in which there are no sub-groups to provide support to alternative perceptions of social reality since dissenters are excluded from the colony. Serl's most original contribution in the study is to underscore the efficiency of the "fission" pattern of expansion by dividing the colony in half insuring that the primary group is reestablished with all age proportions represented in the new colony unit, thus duplicating the old organized unit without altering its character. The author utilizes Redfield's "little community" concept in characterizing the Hutterites.

SHEER, HERFRIED W.
"Studien zum Wortschatz der Mundart der Hutterischen Brüder."*
Unpublished Ph.D. dissertation, McGill University, 1972.

A study of the German dialect and vocabulary of North American
Hutterites which transcends the focus on linguistics by revealing
the social context of the dialect by locating the various streams of
influence from Austria (the South Bairische mixed dialect), Russia (only forty Slavic loan words survive), and English America (10
per cent).
In the Bairische dialect there are three times as many Carin-
thian words as Tyrolean. The phonology of the dialect is Carin-
thian.
Thus the Hutterites speak a dialect which still reflects the early
origins on Tyrol and Carinthia as their homelands, the brief stay
in Russia and the hundred years in English America.
Sheer's study is another painstaking addition to the large array
of empirical studies which permit social scientists to understand
the Hutterites better than any minority in North America.

* English title: "A Lexicological Analysis of the Hutterian German Dialect."

THOMAS, KENNETH C.
"A Survey of the Hutterite Groups in Montana and Canada." Unpublished M.A. thesis, Montana State University, 1949.

It is believed that much of the opposition to the Hutterites is a
result of ignorance of their way of life. "Ignorance causes fear
and fear causes persecution of minority groups." This study,
which seeks to provide a better understanding of the Hutterites,
presents a survey of Hutterites in Montana and Canada. The
contents include Hutterite history, their beliefs, the communal,
agricultural, and educational life of the people, their problems in
Canada and Montana, and the future of the Hutterites in Mexico
and Paraguay. The section specifically on Canada reveals the
reasons for opposition to them. Economically, they are bad for
merchants' business; morally, they believe in nonresistance; and
socially their communal living destroys the community life of the
remaining citizens. It is felt that many of these arguments are
unsound. The thesis also describes internal conflicts which are
probably the greatest source of worry for Hutterite leaders. They
include inbreeding, enmity between family and community, increasing conflict with the outside culture, and outmoded folkways.

WILLIAMS, JULIA E.
"An Analytical Tabulation of the North American Utopian Communities by Type, Longevity, and Location." Unpublished M.A.
thesis, University of South Dakota, 1939.

The objective of this study is to determine the number of known communities which have existed on the North American continent and to ascertain certain quantitative data regarding them concerning types into which they may be classified, comparatively how long such types have continued to exist, and where, by geographical divisions, they have been located. Utopian communities are defined as communities of people seeking to establish relatively autonomous, more perfect systems of order. The Hutterites of South Dakota, Montana, and Alberta are included in the statistics. It was found that the religious communities lived much longer than the non-religious.

C. Articles

ALBERTA (PROVINCE OF)
Report of the Hutterite Investigation Committee. Edmonton, Alberta, September, 1959.

A report based on a study by a Provincial committee to enquire into certain matters concerning acquisition of lands by the Hutterites and establishment of Hutterian colonies. Included in the report are chapters on some economic aspects of the Hutterites, an outline of the Communal Property Act, recommended changes in administrative procedure, education, and a summary of recommendations.

ALLARD, WILLIAM ALBERT
"The Hutterites, Plain People of the West." *National Geographic,* CXXXVIII (July, 1970), pp. 98-125.

A descriptive, popular article concerning the Hutterites in Canada and the United States which emphasizes the humiliation they suffered as conscientious objectors, their abundance of up-to-date equipment, and the prejudices against the Hutterites. Problems of education and defection are discussed and the author concludes that the strength and future of the colonies must rest with their children. A detailed map of the Hutterites is provided which indicates the branching out of the three original colonies. Superb photography.

ARNDT, KARL J.
"The Harmonists and the Hutterites." *American-German Review,* X (August, 1944), pp. 24-27.

The important early connection between the Hutterites and the Harmonists is the subject of this article. The Harmonists, who were dedicated to celibacy, felt that the Hutterites were fellow believers and thus, began to share some of their wealth with them. The writer discusses the many loans made to the Hutterites as well as the advice given by the Harmonists concerning business matters and feels that the Hutterites practically became a part of the Harmony Society.

BACH, MARCUS
  Faith and My Friends. Indianapolis: The Bobbs-Merrill Co. Inc., 1951.

  A chapter in this book entitled "The Hutterite" is a description of how the author defended the Hutterites before the Manitoba legislature where a bill was proposed to curtail land purchases. Both sides of the conflict are weighed. On the one hand he enjoys the peacefulness of living in a Hutterite colony, understands how communal living is totally based on scripture for the Hutterites, and appreciates the cultural contributions of the Hutterites in plain songs, and Gregorian chants, antiphonal music and a capella singing. But he also sees the other side and feels that the complaints about the lack of Hutterite co-operation in civic affairs are justified. Four suggestions that Bach makes before the legislature are: 1) an improved school curriculum; 2) tolerance of the Hutterite religion; 3) participation of the Hutterites in elections; and 4) rejection of the proposed land act.

BARCLAY, HAROLD B.
  "Plain and Peculiar People." *Alberta Anthropologist*, I (December, 1967), pp. 4-14.

  The ideal type of Plain People, as described in this article, are characterized by the rigid enforcement of their particular prohibitions. The author indicates how the Plain People typology might be applied as a device for comparing different sects and a way of indicating change among the sects. The terms used to show change are subjectivists (e.g., Molokans and Friends) and objectivists (e.g., Mennonites and Hutterites).

BARKIN, DAVID and BENNETT, JOHN W.
  "Kibbutz and Colony: Collective Economies and the Outside World." *Comparative Studies in Society and History*, 14, No. 1 (Jan., 1972), pp. 456-483.

  A fascinating comparison by two researchers who have specialized in one of the community patterns under consideration. The article essentially asks the question: How will the Kibbutz and Hutterite colonies withstand the forces of social change? They predict the Kibbutz will drop its utopian-agrarian frontier character as it takes the approach to economic development which preserves traditional institutions of moral and social value.

They see many changes ahead for the Hutterites but see them adamant on one point; that the search for profit and pleasure is the road to evil; and that economics is a means to life and not an end in itself.

Excellent bibliography for comparative analysis of Hutterites and Kibbutz.

BENNETT, JOHN W.
"Communal Brethren of the Great Plains." *Trans-Action*, IV (December, 1966), pp. 42-47.

The Hutterites of the Great Plains are of interest to the writer because they are one group which has deliberately and successfully defied the "consumer culture rat race." This article is, thus, a consideration of the principles on which this unique society operates. They include a managed democracy, rewards and incentives to keep morale high, toleration of those who desire personal property, early social conditioning, and a culture of austerity. A portion of the article is also devoted to a summary of the Anabaptists in North America listing the similarities and differences of the Mennonites, Amish, and Hutterites.

CANADA. LAWS, STATUTES, ETC.
15 George VI. Chapter 77 (1951), "An Act to Incorporate the Hutterian Brethren Church," pp. 61-65.

This act of Parliament describes the different facets of the incorporation of the Hutterian Brethren Church. They include the objects of the corporation, the management, the power to make by-laws, the power to acquire and hold property, investment in and disposal of real property, execution of documents, borrowing powers, and investment of funds.

CANADIAN HOUSE OF COMMONS DEBATE
Session 1951. Vol. II, pp. 1590-1594.

A discussion concerning a bill to incorporate the Hutterite Brethren Church. A Member of Parliament warns of problems which could arise out of the present rate of Hutterite expansion. He states that residents of the same communities as the Hutterites are irritated at their method of living and of doing business, and would regret "to see these people who have not assumed the full rights of citizenship secure any advantage at this stage."

CANADIAN HOUSE OF COMMONS DEBATES
Session 1969. Vol. II, pp. 2335-2339.

The grievance of this Member of Parliament is that the Hutterite farms in western Canada are not subject to income tax in the same manner as are all other farms in western Canada. He questions

whether or not the Hutterian sect and their farms come within
the definition of a religious organization and thus, whether it is a
charitable society free from certain taxes. Also the Hutterites are
criticized for contributing little to well-being of the community as
a whole and for "actually retarding education." The MP demands
that action be taken to prevent Hutterites from earning money
untaxed and from purchasing more and more land.

CLARK, BERTHA
"The Hutterian Communities" (Part I). *Journal of Political Economy*,
XXXII (June, 1924), pp. 357-374.

This is Part I of a two-part article in which the Hutterite communities of South Dakota and Canada are described in a vivid
manner. Author recreates a Hutterite community, discussing the
style of architecture, the layout of the entire community, the
clothing, and the daily religious services. Hutterite organization,
community work, and the Hutterite system of education constitute major topics of discussion. The article has particular value
since it reveals how each day is organized to the minutest detail,
how co-operative housekeeping allows the women to alternate
outdoor work with work indoors, and how the profits of the
community are used only for the purchase of more land and for
the furnishings of a new Bruderhof.

CLARK, BERTHA
"The Hutterian Communities" (Part II). *Journal of Political Economy*,
XXXII (August, 1924), pp. 468-486.

This is the second part of a two-part article on the Hutterite
communities of South Dakota and Canada. This essay is divided
into two sections. The first sketches the historical background of
the Hutterites, and the second emphasizes their group characteristics listed for this group are extreme bluntness of speech,
marked conservatism in clinging to the ways of their fathers, and
dogged perseverance in maintaining any principle which they
have decided is right. Factors such as religion, language, good
leadership and great talent for organization, are given as reasons
for the longevity of the Hutterites as an organized group.

COMMUNITY (THE) WELFARE ASSOCIATION OF CARTIER AND PORTAGE
MUNICIPALITIES
Beware of Manitoba's Cold War. Oakville, Manitoba. Community Welfare Association of Cartier and Portage Municipalities, January 11,
1956.

An account of a public meeting held by the Community Welfare
Association of Cartier and Portage municipalities in which fears
of a "communal country within a country" are expressed. It urges
Provincial government to control Hutterite expansion. Negative
views towards the Hutterites are clearly presented.

CONVERSE, T. A., BUKER, R. S. and LEE, R. V.
"Hutterite Midwifery." *American Journal of Obstetrics and Gynecology*, Vol. 116, 1973.

Once renowned for their medical skills, the Montana Lehrerleut colonies still practice midwifery extensively. In Canada where government health insurance provides low-cost hospitalization midwifery practice is on the wane. The three physicians who have written this article believe that the Hutterite midwives are "responsible, careful workers capable of safely handling routine deliveries." They suggest more collaboration with local physicians but believe Hutterite midwifery could serve as a model for other rural areas. This model is particularly recommended for sparsely populated rural communities. It is a good model and not merely a remnant of the past. Hence, another example of Hutterite creativity.

COOK, ROBERT C.
"The North American Hutterites: A Study in Human Multiplication." *Population Bulletin*, X (December, 1954), pp. 98-107.

This demographic study is concerned with the rapid multiplication of the Hutterites. Charts are provided which compare the birth rates, deaths, and age distribution of the United States and the Hutterite populations in the period from 1926 to 1950. It is concluded that the phenomenal increase of the Hutterites is due almost entirely to the combination of high fertility and low mortality. Author feels that the Hutterite population is a "demographic museum piece" since it closely follows the theoretical model of a stable population: one growing or declining at the same rate through time. A major reason given for this is the communal organization of the Hutterite colonies which eliminates the economic and financial stresses which usually accompany the raising of a family. Article concludes by questioning whether this unlimited reproduction can continue without causing declining living standards or leading to assimilation.

COOPERSTOCK, HENRY
"Prior Socialization and Co-operative Farming." *Canadian Society: Sociological Perspectives*. Edited by B. R. Blishen; F. E. Jones; K. D. Naegele; and John Porter. Toronto: Macmillian of Canada, 1968.

This article compares the co-operative farms of Saskatchewan, established just after World War II, with the Hutterite settlements. Strong ideological underpinnings distinguish the Hutterites from the Saskatchewan communities. "They are sacred or utopian communities in contrast to the secular co-operative farms." Identification is made of three characteristics found in the Hutterite communities: 1) the ideal of co-operation is invested with sacred meaning; 2) the co-operative community may insist upon a more or less firm separation, physical or moral, or

both, from the surrounding society; and 3) the early socialization
of the members to cooperative values. In general, this comparison reveals that the Hutterite communities differ from the Saskatchewan cooperative farms not only according to their position
on the sacred-secular continuum, but also on the basis of where
the locus of sacred values is to be found.

DAVIES, PERCY G.
"Submission to the Agricultural Committee of the Legislature of the
Province of Alberta on Behalf of Alberta's Fifty-one Hutterite Col-
onies of the Darius-Leut and Lehrer-Leut Groups." Edmonton,
March 29, 1960.

This report brings forth arguments in defense of the Hutterites
and reveals what would be the effects of the Alberta legislation
upon them. It emphasizes that "to be legislated out of the right to
own property in common is tantamount to being legislated out of
their faith as they interpret God's word." It attempts to answer all
arguments against them such as: the Hutterites delay rural elec-
trification; and the Hutterites do not vote or accept the responsibilities of citzenship. As defense it presents world concepts in
respect to human rights, and the United Nations Convention on
Crime of Genocide. Charts indicate the social service benefits
utilized by the Hutterites, the farm lands owned or leased, the
acres of land per person, persons displaced by the Hutterites
acquiring land, and the income tax provisions and exemptions of
Hutterites and others.

DEETS, LEE EMERSON
"The Origins of Conflict in the Hutterische Communities."
Publications of the Sociological Society of America, XXV (1931), pp.
125-135.

"The Hutterian Brüder are a sectarian communistic society com-
prising thirty-two colonies, four in South Dakota and twenty-
eight in Manitoba and Alberta, which trace their origin in 1528 to
the Anabaptist movement in Moravia. Their history and culture
formation is a record of crisis, persecution, and frequent migration into isolation. The community life is greatly restricted in
contact and is on a simple cultural level. It is a primary group par
excellence but without the control of gossip. It is controlled by a
religious oligarchy at times verging on autocracy. Adult quarrel-
ing is almost unknown in recent years. The individual member is
submerged in the community. The extreme solidarity of the
community, together with its isolation, provides a good set-up for
the study of community conflict origins. Conflicts in the Hutterische communities may be divided into two major types, outside and internal. They are caused by the enmity of the family and
the community, the desire for money operation as a beginning

point for the introduction of individualism into communism, and lastly, the breakdown of isolation."

DEETS, LEE EMERSON
"What Can We Learn from the Hutterites Regarding the Potentialities of Human Nature for Lasting Peace?" *Human Nature and Enduring Peace*. Edited by Gardener Murphy, New York: Houghton-Mifflin Co., 1945.

The title of this article is posed as a question and then answered with information illustrative of the Hutterian way. Insights concerning Hutterite history, as well as social, political and economic organization are provided.

DRUMHELLER (CITY OF), ALBERTA, CANADA.
"A report concerning the spending habits of a typical colony of Hutterites as compared to those of the individual farmers that would be displaced in the founding of a colony on their land, and an evaluation of the economic impact this colony is expected to have on the City of Drumheller." Report prepared by Bogehold, Jensen and Lefebvre Consultants Chartered Accountants. Calgary, Alberta, Canada. August 24, 1960. (Mimeographed).

This report is the result of a study carried out in 1960 by a firm of consultants and two chartered accountants for the City of Drumheller, Alberta, to determine the effects of expansion of land holdings of the Springvale Hutterite Colony, Rockyford, Alberta, upon Drumheller. The report applies statistical data and analysis and provides information on expenditures in the areas of capital outlays for the establishment of farming, establishment of domestic requirements, current expenses of farm operation, and of household operation. A comparison was made between the patterns of expenditures for a typical farm family and that of a typical Hutterite colony residing in the same area.

EATON, JOSEPH W.
"Canada's Scapegoats." *The Nation*, CLXIX (September 10, 1949), pp. 253-254.

Author discusses reasons for, and prejudice of, Alberta's Communal Property Act which, he states, is carefully worded to affect only the Hutterites. This law is justified as a form of protective custody because of threats made against the Hutterites. But Eaton believes that this discriminatory law is best understood against the background of the war. The hardships of war and the insecurity of a world wheat market required a scapegoat and the Hutterites were chosen.

EATON, JOSEPH W.
"Controlled Acculturation: A Survival Technique of the Hutterites." *American Sociological Review*, XVII (June, 1952), pp. 331-340.

Author is interested in the factors related to the survival of ethnic minorities and feels that the Hutterites offer an opportunity for a more direct study of this problem. Article begins with an outline of a few facets of the Hutterite folk culture such as the communal system of sharing property, high degree of security, primary group type of social relationships, and integration around an absolute value system. The pressures for change from both inside the Hutterite community and the outside world are then described. Author states that what is unique about social change in the Hutterite culture is its gradual nature and the institutionalized techniques that have been developed to deal with pressure for change in an organized fashion. This process of change or "controlled acculturation," whereby the Hutterites tend to accept innovations before the pressure of them becomes so great as to threaten the basic cohesiveness of the social system, is revealed in the areas of communal property, austere simplicity, and self-sufficiency.

EATON, JOSEPH W.
"Folk Psychiatry." *New Society*, August 29, 1963, pp. 9-11.

The mental patients of Hutterites are primarily cared for at home. If medical treatments fail, the Hutterites will try their own folk methods. This article divides their techniques between secular and religious methods. The secular methods are: family nursing care, protection from social-psychological stress, occupational therapy, chiropractic, visiting, and travel. The religious methods described are: prayer, confession, tolerance for deviance, and "culture and salvation." The general finding arrived at is that Hutterite "psychiatry" is helpful to those who accept the value system of the culture, but it gives little consideration to the specific and unique psychic problems of individuals. As the author states, "Hutterites treat patients by fitting them into a cultural straitjacket."

EATON, JOSEPH W.
"Adolescence in a Communal Society." *Mental Hygiene*, XLVIII (January, 1964), pp. 66-73.

The hypothesis that adolescence is not universally a period of strain and stress, that the degree of anxiety, as well as the areas in which it occurs are culturally conditioned, is supported by evidence from this study concerning Hutterites during their adolescence. Factors which contribute to the lack of stress during Hutterite adolescence are: no disparity between expectations and reality in education goals; an increase in toleration of deviant behavior after children leave school; and a partial amnesty on "sin" during adolescence. In general the Hutterite culture "encourages children to participate meaningfully in the life of the adult community. There is a gradual ascent into the adult world, beginning with the kindergarten." As a result, at the end of the adolescent period, there is considerable adherence to Hutterite expectations and, thus, deviancy is not a threat to the group's survival.

EATON, JOSEPH W. and WEIL, ROBERT J.
"Psychotherapeutic Principles in Social Research: An Interdisciplinary Study of the Hutterites." *Psychiatry*, XIV (November, 1951), pp. 439-452.

This paper reports a process of interdisciplinary co-operation in which the barrier between psychiatrists and social scientists was broken down. This was done in a study of the "cultural and psychiatric factors in the mental health of the Hutterites" for which the writers collected social-anthropological, psychological, and psychiatric data in Hutterite colonies. Some of the main features of the Hutterites are sketched such as their strong common religious and cultural tradition, close family ties, belief in economic communalism, the cohesive force of religion, and their high degree of individual and group security. All parts of this investigation of the possible relationships between culture and mental health are discussed in detail including the methods of research, the establishment of a research relationship, motivations for co-operation, resistances to co-operation, the data-getting process, and the termination of the working relationship.

EATON, JOSEPH W. and WEIL, ROBERT J.
"The Mental Health of the Hutterites." *Scientific American*, CLXXXIX (December, 1953), pp. 27-31.

A report on the findings from one phase of the authors' larger study on culture and mental disorders. The Hutterites provided an ideal social laboratory for determining whether such a unique cultural background affected the occurrence of neuroses and psychoses among its people. The authors conclude that although culture is important to mental health it is not the only criteria. The existence of illnesses in Hutterite society suggests that there may be genetic, organic, or constitutional predispositions to psychoses. The article outlines how the Hutterites deal with mental illness and the author's conclusion is significant: "Their culture is therapeutic only for conformists." Information is also provided on religious beliefs and practices and on social and cultural change.

EATON, JOSEPH W.; WEIL, ROBERT J. and KAPLAN, BERT
"The Hutterite Mental Health Study." *MQR*, XXV (January, 1951), pp. 47-65.

Author says the Hutterites seem to have an immunity against mental illnesses. Article is a study of the Hutterite culture to see what implications it has on achieving a good mental balance.

Beliefs, values, community cooperation, discipline, etc., are discussed. Author says this stable community reduces areas of conflict and, therefore, cultural factors are important for mental health. But genetic factors also have an effect on mental health. Author also includes a summary of the Hutterite Population Census in Canada.

EVANS, SIMON
"Spatial Bias in the Incidence of Nativism—Opposition to Hutterite Expansion in Alberta." *Canadian Ethnic Studies*, VI (1974), pp. 1-16.

This article is based on the unpublished M.A. thesis at the University of Calgary, 1973, "The Dispersal of Hutterite Colonies in Alberta, 1918-1971." See the annotation under Hutterites III, Part B, Graduate Theses.

FABER, JAMES
"Prolific People." *New York Times Magazine*, April 17, 1955, pp. 36, 39.

This article discusses the study of Drs. J. W. Eaton and A. J. Meyer who set out to determine the relationship between culture and mental disorder, and who, at the same time, discovered many new things about the Hutterites. For example, they found that the Hutterites have a population increase that is unmatched elsewhere in the world, that their communal villages are mushrooming, and that they will not accept welfare or social security. The article also provides reasons why the Hutterites are disliked in South Dakota despite the record of manifesting no violent crime, no divorce or suicide, and follow a life of austerity.

FINANCIAL POST (THE)
"Have the Hutterites Run out of Cheeks." August 10, 1963, p. 19.

A brief article outlining the controversy over Alberta's Communal Property Act. It tends to be sympathetic towards the Hutterites and underlines the opinion that this is intolerant, cruel legislation. One effect of this legislation which restricts expansion of the colonies is that it is threatening to set off wholesale defections among the Hutterite youth. Of significance the article states that the merchant complaints against the Hutterites are not well-founded.

FRETZ, J. W.
"An Evaluation of the Hutterian Way of Life from the Sociological point of View." *Conference on Mennonite Cultural Problems*, V (August, 1946), pp. 89-93.

Article begins by saying that the family as a unit and the physical organization of the church are less important to Hutterites than to Mennonite communities or to society as a whole. Author feels the positive side of the Hutterite way of life can be seen in the high degree of social organization, in the minimization of materialism, and in the development of a group mind. On the negative side, author discusses the failure to develop a well rounded personality, the complacency of the Hutterites, and their lack of any missionary zeal for their way of life. "Community of goods" is also discussed.

FRIDERES, JAMES S.
"Termination of Migration: The Hutterites—A Case Study." *Canadian Ethnic Studies*, III (June, 1971), pp. 17-24.

The central thesis of this paper is to show that "selected Canadian provincial governments are bringing about the death of the Hutterite culture." Author describes legislation enacted by the provincial governments of Alberta and Manitoba for the purpose of hindering Hutterite expansion. The social structure and the value system of the Hutterites is then examined to show how such legislation, that forces the colonies to reside a certain distance apart and that delays the decision affecting the division of colonies, is causing the disintegration of the Hutterite colonies. Author concludes that the "controlled acculturation" used by Hutterites to maintain their way of life is being destroyed at the same time that the possibility of moving out is becoming more remote. The result, he states, will be to "transfer the Hutterite people from an ethnic group into a religious one."

FRIEDMANN, ROBERT
"Community of Goods." *ME*, I, pp. 659-662.

Article begins with a description of community of goods as based on the teachings of Jesus and as supported by certain Anabaptist leaders. Author goes on to indicate that, while the Christian idea of fellowship works toward sharing and caring, but not necessarily for full community of goods, the Hutterites are emphatic that community of goods is the direct outgrowth of Christian love. Because of this belief and because their life-style is not a retreat from secular temptations, author says, it becomes clear that the Hutterite Bruderhofs cannot be compared with Catholic monasteries. He goes on to say that "the most interesting fact of the Hutterite way is the unique compromise between community and family living, thus overcoming the pitfalls of monastic asceticism."

FRIEDMANN, ROBERT
  "Hutterite Education." *ME*, II, pp. 149-150.

  A brief description of the standards, organization and emphases of
  Hutterite education. It describes what guidelines have been laid
  down by preserved Hutterite documents concerning the entire
  upbringing of Hutterite children. Of interest is the type of discipline required so that each child learns to conform with the
  Hutterite principle of community living.

FRIEDMANN, ROBERT
  "Hutterian Brethren." *ME*, II, pp. 854-866.

  An historical account of the Hutterites, including maps and lists
  of Hutterite colonies in Canada and a list of Hutterite family
  names.

FRIEDMANN, ROBERT
  "Christian Love in Action—The Hutterites." *ML*, I (July, 1946), pp.
  38-43.

  This article provides a brief historical background and a simple
  description of Hutterite life. It is useful only for a very general
  understanding of such things as the "Bruderhoefe," the covenant
  of baptism, and the Hutterites in Slovakia, Germany, and
  Paraguay.

FRIEDMANN, ROBERT
  "Fifty Years Society of Brothers (1920-1970). Their Story and Their
  Books." *ML*, XXV (October, 1970), pp. 159-164.

  Eberhard and Emmy Arnold began a new form of communal
  living in the 1920's. After Hitler came to power they started
  several new Bruderhofs in other countries and continued close
  contact with Mennonites and Hutterites in Canada, the United
  States and Paraguay.

FRIEDMANN, ROBERT
  "Economic Aspects of Early Hutterite Life." *MQR*, XXX (October,
  1956), pp. 259-266.

  The economic aspects of the Hutterites must be considered in the
  context of their entire history, their spiritual and social outlook,
  or simply what may be called their basic motivations. Their history reveals considerable change and variation in the details of
  their economic life, according to the degree of freedom experienced. But the underlying principles have remained fairly uniform since their beginnings under Jacob Hutter. Article describes the social status, crafts, large-scale production, and work
  ethics of the Hutterites.

FRIEDMANN, ROBERT

"An Epistle Concerning Communal Life: A Hutterite Manifesto of 1650 and Its Modern Paraphrase." *MQR*, XXXIV (October, 1960), pp. 249-274.

Andreas Ehrenpreis, a Hutterite theologian and leader, revived the old brotherhood along strict lines of community of goods, discipline, nonresistance, and the spirit of brotherly love and discipleship. His most famous document, "Sendbrief," was the only one of three printed books ever published by the Hutterites. In 1920 it was printed again by Elias Walter, a bishop in Canada. The modern paraphrase, which is presented in this article, was written by Eberhard Arnold, founder of the Society of Brothers.

FRIEDMANN, ROBERT

"Report on Haban Pottery." *MQR*, XXXVII (July, 1963), pp. 195-202.

Hutterites developed a remarkable skill and artistry in a craft known as Haban pottery. Although little is known about it, this art of pottery making has helped historians gain more information about the Hutterites. This article deals with a description of the pottery, where it comes from and traces its style and development from its earliest work.

FRIEDMANN, ROBERT

"Recent Hutterite Studies." *MQR*, XLII (October, 1968), pp. 318-322.

Author reviews six books on the Hutterites and underlines the sociological elements of them. He feels this sociological research is inadequate since it does not take into consideration the importance of the religious and spiritual dimensions in the Hutterian way of life.

FRIEDMANN, ROBERT

"A Hutterite Census for 1969: Hutterite Growth in One Century." *MQR*, XLIV (January, 1970), pp. 100-105.

Author presents a census of population and settlement growth of the 180 Hutterite colonies in the United States and Canada. A census of three kinship groups, their locations, distribution of places, and demography of growth are presented in chart form. This study of growth is taken from a span of one century during which they have multiplied sixtyfold. One table indicates that baptized members constitute only 37.5 per cent of the Hutterite groups.

GIFFEN, DOROTHY
"The Hutterites and Civil Liberties." *The Canadian Forum*, XXVII (June, 1947), pp. 55-57.

The restriction of Hutterite expansion by the Alberta and Manitoba governments is considered, in this article, to be "an invasion of civil liberties which by implication threatens the rights of all minority groups." As a background to understanding the situation, the Hutterite way of life is briefly described. Author feels that opposition to the Hutterites comes from those who "are alarmed at their economic success." These opponents overlook the fact that Hutterites are law-abiding, that they are not a burden on the state, and that they look after their own aged and disabled.

GOERZ, H.
"A Day with the Hutterites." *ML*, VIII (January, 1953), pp. 14-16.

A brief description of life in a Hutterite colony. Author feels that the Hutterites still have the earnest wish to uphold the old traditions of simplicity, moral integrity, and godliness.

GOODHOPE, NANNA
"Must the Hutterites Flee Again?" *The Christian Century*, LVII (November 13, 1940), pp. 1415-1417.

This is a description of the persecution suffered by the Jamesville Hutterites in South Dakota during the war. It reveals how a spirit of friendliness had been established between the colonists and the neighboring farmers until war broke out. The malicious rumours, suspicions, torture, and sabotage that the Hutterites went through forced them to flee to Canada. Author feels that they will soon be swept away completely by hatred and persecution.

HOFER, J. M.
"The Historical Background of the Hutterite Colonies—1528-1946." *Conference on Mennonite Cultural Problems*, V (August, 1946), pp. 25-43.

A brief resume of the historical background of the seventy-two Hutterite colonies located in South Dakota, Montana, Alberta, and Manitoba.

HOSTETLER, JOHN A.
"Total Socialization: Modern Hutterite Educational Practices." *MQR*, XLIV (January, 1970), pp. 72-84.

The general aim of this study is to enlarge understanding of the learning processes and to broaden knowledge of socialization in a cross-cultural perspective. The research is directed toward investigating personality development and motivation in a society where the goals are communally rather than individually oriented. In his conclusion the author says Hutterite child-rearing and socialization practices at all ages are remarkably successful in preparing the individual for communal life, and also that individuals are thoroughly trained to meet clearly defined roles.

HOSTETLER, JOHN A. and HUNTINGTON, GERTRUDE E.
"A Note on Nursing Practices in an American Isolate with a High Birth Rate." *Population Studies*, XIX (March, 1966), pp. 321-324.

See annotation under HUNTINGTON, G.E.

HOSTETLER, JOHN A. and HUNGTINGTON, GERTRUDE E.
"Communal Socialization Patterns in Hutterite Society." *Ethnology*, VIII (October, 1969), pp. 331-355.

"The Hutterites' notable ability to train their young for adult responsibility and for living within the confines of their communal society was the impetus for a research project on socialization in Hutterite society." With the aim of understanding socialization in a cross-cultural perspective, this study is primarily concerned with personality development and motivations in a society where the goals were communally rather than individualistically oriented. It attempts to do four things: to formulate the charter or moral postulates of the Hutterite society; to observe the socialization practices in the context of the charter and of the community; and to discover the nature and extent of deviancy patterns. The research is based upon participant observation of life in three specific colonies. The article describes the major characteristics of each Hutterite life-stage and also draws conclusions which relate Hutterite socialization practices to the culture as a whole.

HOSTETLER, JOHN A.
"The Communal Property Act of Alberta." *University of Toronto Law Journal*, XIV (1961), pp. 125-129.

A discussion of the Communal Property Act as it applies to the Hutterite colonies. Author also discusses the history of the Act, the implications of the Act for the Hutterites, and the problems associated with the uses of legal processes in the assimilation of ethnic minorities. Attitudes of others toward Hutterites is also brought out.

HOSTETLER, JOHN A.
"Hutterite Separation and Public Tolerance." *The Canadian Forum*, XLI (April, 1961), pp. 11-13.

There exists in Canada a false assumption that the Hutterites are Marxists, that they do hostile acts, that they pay no taxes, and that they have a high rate of mental illness. This view and the resulting law which restricts Hutterite expansion is viewed as a reflection of three dislikes, other than religious prejudice of the Hutterites: they are prolific, they are efficient, and they are different. Author views such intolerance in a country like Canada as ironical and believes that the pressures to assimilate have only intensified the distance between the Hutterites and the predominant society. He suggests "voluntary participation of sect members in the wider society" so that ethnic groups will be able to borrow that which is best from the surrounding culture while still maintaining their traditional values.

HOSTETLER, JOHN A.
"Amish and Hutterite Socialization: Social Structure and Contrasting Modes of Adaptation to Public Schooling." *Report on the Conference of Child Socialization*. Washington, D. C.: Health, Education, and Welfare, 1969.

"The success of marginal groups," the author notes, "in evading the pervasive educational values of the great society, or of integrating the values of public schooling into their own social system, varies greatly and takes many forms. Over a period of several years the writer has observed a number of significant contrasts in the attitudes of the Amish and the Hutterites toward borrowing from the outer-world, specifically in the areas of education. In this paper I shall describe the effect of non-indigenous schooling upon these two societies. Basic to the analysis is the difference in social structure of the two: The Hutterites are a communal society while the Amish are individual farm operators. I will describe the world view and internal social structure of the two societies in the context of the educational conflicts in the past, the degree of control over the socialization patterns by the two groups, and the assimilation and disruption patterns in the two subcultures."

HOWARD, JOSEPH KINSEY
"The Hutterites: Puzzle for Patriots." *The Pacific Spectator,* II (Winter, 1948), pp. 30-41.

The major theme of this article is inter-group relations. Author examines areas of dissension between the Hutterites and the outside world, land expansion and pacifism being the major areas. A history of the Hutterites particularly in Europe and Canada is provided. The problem of this article is dealt with by giving specific attention to the problems of the Milford Colony near Augusta, Montana.

HOWSE, ERNEST MARSHALL
"Manitoba Seeks to Curb Minority." *The Christian Century*, LXIV (May, 1947), p. 268.

The Hutterites, as objects of farmer-led drives to ban their purchase of land, are the concern of this brief article. Author tells of action by the Civil Liberties Association to aid this religious minority.

HUNTINGTON, GERTRUDE ENDERS
"Freedom and the Hutterite Communal Family Pattern." *Conference on Mennonite Educational and Cultural Problems*, XV (June, 1965), pp. 88-111.

The Hutterite nuclear family of parents and their young children does not form a social unit. Rather, the author feels it forms one essential aspect of an indivisible unit, the colony. Individual freedom is not valued by the Hutterites since they renounce it in favour of the "narrow path" that leads to salvation.

HUNTINGTON, G. E. and HOSTETLER, J. A.
"A Note on Nursing Practices in an American Isolate with a High Birth Rate." *Population Studies*, XIX, Part 3 (March, 1966), pp. 321-324.

Observing 271 nursing mothers in thirty-eight families in three communities revealed that they have a diet high in calories and rich in protein, that the babies spend a relatively short time at the breast because rigid community schedules give a mother little time for relaxed nursing and that women do not find nursing particularly enjoyable or rewarding. Supplementary feeding is introduced into the babies' diet at increasingly early ages; and, healthy women wean their infants between four months and three years for an average of one year.

KELLS, EDNA
"Hutterite Commune." *Maclean's Magazine*, March 15, 1937, pp. 50-54.

A general description of many aspects of Hutterite life. It is of significance in that it gives an account of the conditions and opinions prevalent about the time of the writing, 1937. The description of colony life is based on a visit by the author to the Standoff Colony in Alberta.

LAATSCH, WILLIAM G.
"Hutterite Colonization in Alberta." *Journal of Geography*, LXXX (September, 1971), pp. 347-359.

"This paper discusses the impact of Hutterian migration to Alberta in regards to the Communal Property Act and the evolution of the Hutterian Settlement pattern. The Hutterites arrived in Alberta in 1918 and by 1940 had established thirty-one colonies, clustered primarily in the Lethbridge area. The sect's political and economic beliefs have been unpopular. Legislative action in the form of the Communal Property Act, and the establishment of the Communal Property Control Board has resulted in a dispersed settlement pattern. The legislative action initiated in the 1940's has had the perverse function of causing a hardship on the individual farmer of southern Alberta."

LEE, S. C. and BRATTRUD, A.
"Marriage Under a Monastic Mode of Life: A Preliminary Report on the Hutterite Family in South Dakota." *Journal of Marriage and the Family*, August, 1967, pp. 512-520.

Despite claims by some family sociologists on the universality of the nuclear family, we find in Hutterite colonies a pattern of family life which defies classification. Though the husband is the recognized head of the household, each marriage forms an auxiliary unit of the colony, not a full-fledged conjugal family. The family, being subservient to the church, loses its economic functions and part of authority, training, and discipline over children, all of which weaken its influence. Through religious sanction, however, the family tends to have successful and stable relationships. This is postulated as the way to maintain the colony's cohesion and stability.

Lee and Brattrud conclude their article with a crucial key variable: the rise of the conjugal family in collectivist societies as the eclipse of a once closely knit "cosmos." "Such a change," they conclude, "has happened to bring about decline of China's patriarchal family, and perhaps is also happening in the Kibbutz system, but it is not found to have taken place in the Hutterite colony."

MACDONALD, R. J.
"Hutterite Education in Alberta: A Test Case in Assimilation, 1920-1970." *Canadian Ethnic Studies*, VIII, No. 1 (1976), pp. 9-21. It is also available in A. W. Rasporich (ed.), *Western Canada: Past and Present* (Calgary: McClelland and Stewart West, 1975), pp. 133-149.

Macdonald reviews one of Alberta's oldest controversies—the conflict between the Hutterites and the larger society of Alberta. Urbanization has moderated the controversy as rural political power has waned and as the present government has accepted integration in place of assimilation as a goal. Thus, the culture of communalism and German language are not keys but the economic threat of expansion persists as a permanent irritant. The focus of the controversy is the public schools, the locus of the battle is land, the center of the larger ideology is in the rural areas (including the Farmers' Union) and the possibility of crushing the Hutterites very small.

MACKIE, MARLENE
"Ethnic Stereotypes and Prejudice—Alberta Indians, Hutterites and Ukrainians." *Canadian Ethnic Studies*, VI No. 1-2 (1974), pp. 39-52.

This article is based on Mackie's unpublished Ph.D. dissertation, University of Alberta, 1971. See the annotation under Hutterites II, Part B, Graduate theses.

MANGE, ARTHUR P.
"Growth and Inbreeding of a Human Isolate." *Human Biology*, XXXVI (May, 1964), pp. 104-133.

This study is concerned exclusively with the Hutterite colonies called the S-leut, whose initial colony was established in South Dakota. Topics in the report include a description of the S-leut growth from which an estimate is made of the maximum number of independent genomes present in the contemporary population; a description of some marriage patterns with an analysis of inbreeding changes over time; and the effects of inbreeding on fertility and adult height. It was found that the complete ancestry of 5,450 could be traced back to sixty-eight individuals and that each of the genomes among these "basic" individuals was represented on the average eighty-eight times among contemporary individuals. The findings also indicated that the effect of the branching away from the original colony was to increase the relatedness among the married men within a colony, but to cause little change in relatedness among the married women.

MARTENS, HELEN
"Hutterite Songs: Aural Transmission from Sixteenth Century." *Ars Nova* (Pretoria), VI (May, 1974), pp. 5-15.

This is an explanation of Hutterite music as an expression of their resolute goal to continue 400 years of unbroken tradition. The text of the hymn, "Ich Stund," reveals the borrowing from secular sources of the sixteenth century and the canonization by the Hutterites since that time. Music historians had thought that the melodies of early German folk songs had disappeared until the textual and historical criticism of Martens and other scholars. A theory of Hutterite social development can thus be derived from a study of their music.

M. C. L. A.
"The Hutterite Issue in Manitoba." *The Bulletin of the Manitoba Civil Liberties Association*. Vol. 1 (Winter 1947-1948), pp. 1-3.

The threats to civil liberties caused by possible discriminatory legislation restricting the expansion of Hutterite colonies is the subject of this article. Such topics as the legal status of the Hutterites, anti-Hutterite feeling, and democratic practice are discussed with emphasis placed on the negative unfounded attitude of others toward the Hutterites and on the Hutterite side of the situation.

MATHER, G. B.

"Hutterites." *The Christian Century*, LXXVIII (January 25, 1961), p. 125.

A brief explanation of government legislation which reversed a 1959 ruling and ordered Hutterites to start paying income tax. It states that this case, which centred on the profits from Hutterite farm operations, brought commercial operations of all religious groups under scrutiny.

THE NATIONAL OBSERVER

"Communal Colonies: Why Neighbours Wince When Hutterites Move In." October 21, 1963.

A discussion of attitudes toward the Hutterites, and of opinions and problems in such areas as South Dakota, Minnesota, Montana, and Canada.

NEWSWEEK

"Canada: Heat on the Hutterites." LV (April 11, 1960), p. 67.

A brief statement on the attitudes towards the government's treatment of them.

PALMER, HOWARD

"The Hutterite Land Expansion Controversy in Alberta." *Western Canada Journal of Anthropology*, II, No. 2 (July, 1971), pp. 18-46.

This is one of the finest summaries of the Hutterite land controversy in Alberta. The opposition to the Hutterite communal farms is not exclusively an expression of nativism among veterans and patriotic groups but also a remnant of Alberta's tradition of agrarian radicalism and an expression of its egalitarian and individualistic values. The Farmers' Union, for example, rejects both corporate and communal farms, viewing the Hutterites like the agri-businesses as a trust or monopoly.

After painstaking documentation of the strange mixture of right and left wing opposition to land expansion Palmer forecasts the decrease of opposition in the future because of urbanism, education, pluralism and changing rural patterns.

PETER, KARL

"The Hutterites: Values, Status, and Organizational Systems." *The Journal of the Sociology Club* (University of Alberta), II (February, 1963), pp. 55-59; III (February, 1964), pp. 7-8.

In the first part of this article, Hutterite religious sentiments are divided into four main classes and the author contends that the religio-economic system of the Hutterites has incorporated and integrated these religious sentiments. The locus of authority, the hierarchy of status, the division of labor, and the position of the family are examined in light of the concepts of structure and function.

The second part of the article considers the importance of the Hutterian community to the individual Hutterite, his relationship to that community, and the satisfactions received from such association. It is pointed out that rejection of the Hutterite by the outside world results in increased feelings of identity with the community. Also discussed is the Hutterite's need for rule and authority in order to function adequately.

PETER, KARL

"The Hutterite Family." *The Canadian Family*. Edited by K. Ishwaran. Toronto: Holt, Rinehart and Winston of Canada, Ltd., 1971.

An excellent analysis of Hutterite family relations. Such elements of the Hutterite system as its hierarchical structure, the organization involving four levels of male authority, the extended family, and the patrilineal pattern of kinship are listed as important for understanding the Hutterite family. Author places particular significance upon the fact that, since only 60 to 140 members are required to keep the community functioning, "competition for positions becomes so intense that it threatens the unity of the community." He also emphasizes that the main feature of the child socialization process is suppression of the individual, that peer group behavior is competitive and aggressive, and that Hutterite socialization inhibits the ability to form secondary relations. Other topics discussed are adolescence, courtship, engagement, marriage, husband-wife relations, and old age.

PETER, KARL

"Toward a Demographic Theory of Hutterite Population Growth." *Variables*, V (Spring, 1966), pp. 28-37.

Peter has constructed a synchronized theory of Hutterite life: The fertility cycle of the Hutterite group coincides with a motivational cycle, a structural cycle and a financial cycle. In cases where all these cycles are co-ordinated the system functions smoothly.

This synchronization is now threatened by the gap between their financial power and their reproductive power. Peter rejects calls for increased efficiency (already high) or postponing expansion to new colonies. Postponing marriage four or five years he affirms. He considers postponed marriage the most likely option for well organized colonies with contraception very possible in disorganized colonies.

PETER, KARL

"The Dynamics of Open Social Systems." In James E. Gallagher and Ronald D. Lambert, *Social Process and Institutions: The Canadian Case.* Toronto: Holt, Rinehart and Winston, 1971, pp. 164-172.

Since his doctoral dissertation on the Hutterites ten years ago Karl Peter continues to be amazed at the success of Hutterites in selecting what they want to receive from the local society while locating all meaning, values and norms inside the Hutterite system.

In this minor masterpiece of sociological writing Peter sets forth the social dynamics of the Hutterites with the concluding word "that the relations in the paper allow one to marvel at the creativity of human groups."

PETERS, VICTOR J.

"The Hutterians—History and Communal Organization of a Rural Group in Manitoba." *Historical and Scientific Society of Manitoba* (Season 1960-1961), pp. 6-14.

Article begins with a brief summary of the historical background of the Hutterites and of their reception by Canadians. But the main discussion centers around a description of a Hutterite colony and of colony life in general. Author states that a Hutterian 'Bruderhof,' or colony, is "an organic whole in which it is difficult to segregate the part played by such accepted institutions as the church, the family, the schools, or the industrial enterprises." The topics considered in this discussion are administration, women, marriage, clothes, and the economic basis for the colony. It is concluded that Hutterite communities on the whole indicate remarkable vitality.

PRATT, WILLIAM F.

"The Anabaptist Explosion." *Natural History,* LXXVIII (February, 1969), pp. 8-23.

In today's rapidly changing urban-industrial environment, the Amish and Hutterites still maintain their medieval faith and life-style. Their high level of fertility reflects their rigid theocratic culture, which has managed to survive in an alien environment. This article shows the impact of an uncontrolled population on the social organization of these two groups. For both the Hutterites and Amish, their high rates of population increase has intensified competition with the larger society and has heightened intergroup conflict. Despite the rigid character of their doctrines, these two groups have experienced fundamental changes in their social organization. But they fail to see that their uncontrolled fertility is a cause of many of their problems. Article also contrasts and compares their life-styles and beliefs.

REDEKOP, CALVIN and HOSTETLER, JOHN A.
"Education and Boundary Maintenance in Three Ethnic Groups."
Review of Religious Research, V (Winter, 1964), pp. 81-91. Previously
published as "Education and Assimilation in Three Ethnic Groups."
Alberta Journal of Educational Research, VIII (December, 1962), pp.
189-203.

> The educational efforts of the ethnic group is a "boundary
> maintenance" activity, intended to preserve the social system and
> its traditional interaction patterns. This automatically leads to
> tension with the larger society. This paper relates the value sys-
> tems of three ethnic groups, the Old Order Amish, Old Colony
> Mennonites, and Hutterites, with the value system of the
> "great society; indicates the nature of the conflict; and develops
> several hypotheses on the nature of ethnic extinction." The major
> hypothesis states that "the type of control of the educational
> offensive of the great society will best predict the dissolution of an
> ethnic group." In light of this, the authors reach the conclusion
> that the Amish will lose their identity first, that the Old Colony
> will follow suit, and that the Hutterites could go on forever.

REDEKOP, CALVIN
"The State of the Communion: Contemporary Religious Communes." *Communal Studies Newsletter*, III (January, 1976), pp. 3-9.

> Redekop's article is a literary statement of his approach to com-
> munes: 1) Human beings were meant to be in community (de-
> fined as social of which communes are one expression); and
> community produces communion; 2) The key to communal sur-
> vival is the degree of commitment to common goals and disci-
> plines, an objective met most frequently by religious communes;
> 3) The dynamic of communes is placing community above self,
> and 4) Communes meet many basic human needs.
>
> The *Communal Studies Newsletter* is issued by the Centre for the
> Study of Communal Societies, Temple University, Philadelphia,
> with John Hostetler as director of the centre and editor of the
> newsletter.

SANDERS, DOUGLAS E.
"The Hutterites: A Case Study in Minority Rights." *Canadian Bar
Review*, XLII (May, 1964), pp. 225-242.

> The opposition in the Prairie Provinces to the Hutterites is the
> central concern of this article. Three reasons for this opposition
> are outlined: 1) Hutterite colonies have economic advantages
> which make them unfair competitors to the average farmer; 2)
> Hutterites have detrimental effects on any community of which
> they become a part; and 3) they threaten to take over vast rural
> areas if allowed to expand at all. Other topics of discussion in-
> clude the history of legislation dealing with the Hutterites, the

constitutionality of Alberta legislation, and approaches to the Hutterite problem. In this last section the writer states that three types of relationships that could occur between the Hutterites and non-Hutterites are co-existence, accommodation, and assimilation. He then proceeds to question which relationship is in existence and which relationship is most desirable. It is concluded that the proper goal seems to be a relationship of accommodation which can be promoted in regard to education and the location of new colonies.

SAWKA, PATRICIA
"The Hutterite Way of Life." *Candian Geographical Journal*, LXXVII (October, 1968), pp. 127-131.

A brief description of the Hutterite way of life with emphasis on the historical background, the hostility of the Prairie Provinces for the Hutterites, and the organization of day-to-day activities in the colonies. Of significance, the author notes that unmarried life is considered abnormal, that death is believed to be a transition from life to eternal life and therefore excessive grief is regarded as lack of faith in God, and that the most common form of recreation is visiting.

SCHLUDEMAN, S. and SCHLUDEMAN, E.
"Social Role Perception of Children in Hutterite Communal Society." *Journal of Psychology*, LXXII (1969), pp. 183-188.
"Developmental Study of Social Role Perception Among Hutterite Adolescents." *Journal of Psychology*, LXXII (1969), pp. 243-246.
"Scale Checking Style as a Function of Age and Sex in Indian and Hutterite Children." *Journal of Psychology*, LXXII (1969), pp. 253-261.
"Factoral Analysis of Semantic Structures in Hutterite Adults." *Journal of Psychology*, LXXIII (1969), pp. 267-273.
"Maternal Child Rearing Attitudes in Hutterite Communal Society." *Journal of Psychology*, LXXIX (1971), pp. 169-177.
"Paternal Attitudes in Hutterite Command Society." *Journal of Psychology*, LXXIX (1971), pp. 41-48.
"Adolescent Perception of Parent Behaviour in Hutterite Communal Society." *Journal of Psychology*, LXXIX (1971), pp. 29-39.

In the *Journal of Psychology* (1969-1971) the Edward and Shirin Schludeman research team of the University of Manitoba published six important articles based on solid empirical data from Manitoba colonies to delineate three main problems: social role perception, semantic structures and child rearing attitudes of parents and adolescents.

What emerges from these six articles is a statistically-supported set of generalizations concerning the generational differences among children, adolescents and adults, a set of generalizations providing solid ground for understanding the manner in which the two key ideologies (the Anabaptist and the collectivist) are translated into action. The Schludemans call this "the principle of realization" or "collective education" which requires the collective upbringing of children.

Failing to find developmental differentiation among Hutterite children or adolescents because high achievement is not rewarded by any visible status symbols, the researchers concluded the same would be true among adults. This proved to be incorrect.

In cognitive differentiation the Hutterite children are similar to East Indian children in reaching the impact age but the Hutterites are unlike East Indian children in showing little differentiation based on sex.

Among male and female adults there is a different perception of social roles which exists in contrast to children and adolescents which is due to the delaying effects of the powerful social influences on the development of cognitive differentiation among young respondents.

The Hutterite children perceive their parents along the same dimensions (acceptance, psychological control and firm control) as American and Belgian children and Canadian adolescents. The many peculiarities of Hutterite child-rearing practices did not affect the structure of the CRPBI (Children's Reports of Parental Behavior Inventory).

Child rearing attitudes are authoritarian and patriarchal, and there is no generation gap with little difference between young and old fathers.

Hutterite women have internalized the maternal role assigned to them, yet they had more democratic approaches to children than their husbands. Crucial is the highly stable maternal attitudes across the generations.

In sum, Hutterite society as delineated through the rigorous research of the Schludemans is one of the most radically undifferentiated and equalitarian societies in the world. Although their research was done with the theoretical constructs of developmental psychology it is a major contribution for all social science disciplines studying the Hutterites.

SERL, VERNON C.
"Final Report on the Saskatchewan Hutterite Program." A Report for the Saskatchewan, Canada Government Committee on Minority Groups, Saskatchewan, 1958. (Mimeographed.)

A study which is concerned with the implementation of a program to improve the relationship between the Hutterites and other Canadians. Report describes work of "Provincial Committee on Hutterite Settlement" formed to study intensively Hutterite-Community relations, and to establish local joint committees. Work also contains information on religion, education, legal, social, political, economic organization and agriculture.

SHELLY, PAUL
"Implications of the Hutterian Way of Life for other Mennonite Groups." *Conference on Mennonite Cultural Problems*, V (August, 1946), pp. 83-87.

Discussion of nine emphases of the Hutterites which the author feels the Mennonites should emulate. They include the need to determine basic beliefs, to make their beliefs a total way of life, to realize the importance of fellowship, to set up a system of discipline, and to work out a practical system of mutual aid.

SIEGEL, B. J.
"High Anxiety Levels and Cultural Integration: Notes on a Psycho-Cultural Hypothesis." *Social Forces*, XXXIV (October, 1955), pp. 42-48.

The hypothesis of this article is that severe constricting environmental pressures upon an individual causes a state of comparatively intense anxiety which makes it necessary to seek channels to reduce high tension. To study the dimensions of this problem and to investigate the correlation between these variables, three groups were analysed. The Hutterites constituted one of the case studies and in his discussion of them, the writer describes the rigid prescription of activities and symbols of group indentity, the systematic indoctrination of values with each generation, and the punishment of every indiscreet occurrence of non-permitted variations. It is expressed that Hutterites are not completely free from mental conflicts and tensions and this, the author believes, "would seem to imply that these people also maintain a high anxiety plateau by prohibiting psychologically 'normal' tendencies to drain tension through culturally available channels."

STEELE, C. FRANK
"Canada's Hutterite Settlements." *Candian Geographical Journal*, XXII (June, 1941), pp. 308-314.

A descriptive, popular account of the Hutterites, describing the leadership, their large scale grain farms, the strong religious tie binding the various communities, and daily living in a Hutterite colony. Author describes the Hutterites as "peaceful, plodding, land-loving people" and he says there are "no loafers" and "no hangers-on." Also it is felt that disintegration of the Hutterite colonies will not take place in the near future.

SWAN, JON
"The 400-Year-Old Commune." *The Atlantic* (November, 1972), pp. 90-100.

The author describes his observations and reactions as an out-sider to colony life. Hospitality and kindness are presented as very positive aspects of the Hutterites but the author sees the process of assimilation as a negative force. Most of the colonies visited were in South Dakota but there is mention of the different migrations from Canada.

The title of the article underscores the durability of Hutterite communes in contrast to the short life span of youth communes.

THIELMAN, GEORGE C.
"The Hutterites in Contemporary Society." *ML*, XXV (January, 1970), pp. 42-46.

The aim of this article is to describe the Hutterites as distinct from Mennonites. A discussion of their unconditional nonresistance, and their communistic society indicates that the practices and beliefs of Hutterites have caused friction between Canadianism and Hutterianism. This resulted in discriminatory legislation to prohibit the Hutterites from purchasing more land.

THOMAS, NORMAN
"Hutterite Brethren." *South Dakota Historical Collections*, Vol. 25 (1951).

A study of the history, emigration and settlement in the United States, persecution, social and cultural life, religion and philosophy, social processes of the Hutterites, as well as an ac-count of their colonies in South Dakota as of 1950.

√ TIERNEY, BEN
"Hutterites Uneasy: Alberta May Provoke Exodus." *Critical Issues in Canadian Society*. Edited by Craig Boydell; Carl Grindstaff; and Paul Whitehead. Toronto: Holt, Rinehart, and Winston, 1971.

A brief discussion of the effects of Alberta's Communal Property Act upon the Hutterites. Reasons for resentment of the Hutter-ites are presented. Author feels that most of this hostility has its roots in economics since the Hutterite purchasing pattern affects local businesses. Also discussed are the economic problems facing the Hutterites, whose population doubles every 17.3 years, as they search for new land. It is concluded that economics rather than dissatisfaction among the young might be the major factor affecting Hutterite growth.

TIME
"Homes for the Hutterites." February 10, 1947, p. 13.

Article describes the dislike of Albertans for the Hutterites be-cause of Hutterite aloofness, and because of their pacifism. At-tempts to stop Hutterite expansion and the reactions of the Hut-terites are discussed.

TIME
   "All Things Common." June 4, 1956, pp. 74, 76.

   The protest of the South Dakotan Hutterites towards a law that
   prohibits them from buying more land is the subject of this brief
   article. The background of the Hutterites is discussed and the
   author states that "with their austere habits and considerable
   talents they prospered." Also presented is the attitude that says
   the Hutterites are nothing more or nothing less than a communistic set-up which "isn't the American way."

UNRUH, JOHN D.
   "What About the Hutterites?" *The Christian Century*, LXXVI (July 8,
   1959), pp. 801-803.

   This article discusses why South Dakota, after welcoming the
   Hutterites back in 1935, brought into effect in 1955 legislation to
   prevent Hutterite expansion, and what kind of future the Hutterites have in this state. The rapidity of Hutterite expansion is
   analyzed revealing that the acreage per Hutterite is less than that
   held by non-Hutterites. Other anti-Hutterite arguments are
   studied and it appears that the Hutterites have been singled out as
   a scapegoat. They are also victims of religious discrimination:
   "The experience of the Hutterites in the United States illustrates
   that society continues to be inhospitable to any religious group
   organized along communal lines." Three alternatives for the
   Hutterites are presented: 1) disintegration; 2) abandonment of
   the agrarian for the industrial way of life; and 3) another trek in
   search of peace and freedom.

WALDNER, MARIE
   "The Present Day Social Customs and Cultural Patterns of the
   Hutterites in North America." *Conference on Mennonite Educational
   and Cultural Problems*, V (August, 1946), pp. 45-59.

   A general study of Bruderhof life and beliefs of the Hutterites.
   Factors contributing to the gradual process of assimilation are
   modern technology, outside teachers in their schools, decreasing
   isolation and the cultural influence from the outside world. Hutterite leaders are becoming increasingly aware of these problems.

WILLMS, A. M.
   "The Brethren Known as Hutterians." *Canadian Journal of Economics
   and Political Science*, XXIV (August, 1958), pp. 391-405.

   Covering familiar ground thoroughly and carefully, the article is
   notable as one of the first to reaffirm the approach of the Canadian Mental Health Association abandoning punitive action in
   favor of consultation, accurate press reports and joint committees. The author in 1958 nullified the relevance of these suggestions by the continued acceptance of assimilation as the goal with

consultation as the method. The reader should compare this as an enlightened article of twenty years ago with controlling assumptions in today's climate of pluralism as seen in the Alberta provincial reports.

ZIEGLSCHMID, A. J. F.
"The Hutterites on the American Continent." *The American-German Review*, VIII (February, 1942), pp. 20-24.

This article points out that the Hutterite Colonies are the oldest communal organization—based on apostolic principles—in the world; that the Hutterite collection of hymns is the oldest one in America; that the Hutterites have a unique and old manuscript literature; and that they have been operating a sort of kindergarten since 1568. Descriptions are provided of their origins, the "Little School," and the Bruderhof. The Hutterites themselves are characterized as being "keen-witted, acutely observing, charming practitioners of the art of conversation, tolerant and intelligent of things outside their principal interests, industrious, and tenaciously true to the German language."

ZIEGLSCHMID, A. J. F.
"Must the Hutterites Leave Canada?" *The Christian Century*, LXIV (October 22, 1947), pp. 1269-1271.

Alberta legislation to restrict Hutterite expansion is forcing the Hutterites on another migration in pursuit of religious liberty. "The odious thing about it is that it singles out the Hutterites for discrimination." The article questions the truth of the accusations made against the Hutterites that they are hindering the war effort, that they are buying up all the land, and that they are causing the price of Alberta farmland to rise. It stresses that the right to buy land is one of the fundamental privileges in a democracy.

D. Unpublished Sources

BADEN, JOHN A. and HOVEY-BADEN, MARY ANNA
"Education, Employability and Role Taking Among North American Hutterites." Paper delivered at the Conference on Child Socialization, Philadelphia: Temple University, 1969.

"In each of the three Hutterite *Leut*, a substantial minority of persons, especially young males, defect from their colony. After a trial on the outside, the majority of these defectors return to their colony. This paper will attempt to account for the high proportion of return. An explanation common to natives of the region holds that due to their poor formal education, the Hutterites lack talent, skills, and/or appropriate attitudes sufficient to enable them to obtain and hold satisfactory jobs. This paper will attempt to establish that the above explanation is insufficient to account for the data. We will introduce an estimate of the "employability" of Hutterite males between the ages of eighteen and twenty-two. We shall then introduce data relating to available employment in the region. This material suggests that; 1) Hutterites are regarded as highly employable; and that 2) employment for these people is indeed available."

CLARK, PETER G.

See section on graduate theses for the annotation on his essay, "Political Mobility Patterns Within Canadian Hutterite Communities."

HOSTETLER, JOHN A.

"The Hutterites in Perspective." Unpublished paper based on an address to the Humanities Association of Canada, University of Alberta, Edmonton, Alberta, October 20, and to the University of Alberta, Clagary, Alberta on November 29, 1960.

In this paper, Hostetler is particularly concerned with the conflict and tension that exists between the Hutterites and the main Canadian society. He feels the Hutterites have displayed an unusual record of cultural maintenance survival. A major portion of the paper is devoted to a discussion of the Hutterites in terms of the elements of the social system. The elements considered are beliefs, sentiments, norms, the status role pattern, power, rank end or goals, and sanctions. In his conclusion, Hostetler states that there are many misconceptions about the Hutterites, that not all resistance to the Hutterites may be dismissed as religious prejudice, that the more the majority resists the Hutterites, the more the Hutterites will maintain their separatism, and that the antagonism is probably a function of social distance.

LEWIS, RUSSELL E.

"Controlled Acculturation Revisited: An Examination of Differential Acculturation and Assimilation Between Hutterian Brethren and the Old Order Amish." Paper presented at the Seminar on Communes, Northern Illinois University, April 7-9, 1975.

Author hypothesized six independent variables as being related to a culture's success in controlled acculturation. Comparative data from the Old Order Amish and the Hutterian Brethren were used to test the validity of these relationships. The results of this study suggest that there is a direct relationship between the independent variables and successful controlled acculturation occuring in any given culture.

The Hutterites' success in controlled acculturation indicates that their chances for survival as a distinct cultural group in North America are greater than that of the Old Order Amish.

MACDONALD, R. J.
"A Study of the Conflict Between Hutterian and Non-Hutterian Communities and the Educational System." Unpublished paper, Education Department, University of Clagary, 1971.

This paper concentrates on the land acquisition policy of the Hutterites and opposition from rural areas mainly 1950's and 1960's in Alberta. There is also a brief description of Hutterite education in Manitoba, Saskatchewan, and the United States. The author obtained most of his information from Alberta Teacher's Association briefs and also reports prepared by Alberta government on Hutterites during 1958.

MANITOBA LEGISLATURE
"Report to the Honourable the Legislative Assembly of Manitoba of the Select Special Committee appointed to obtain information regarding colonies or societies of Hutterites or Hutterian Brethren and to report and make recommendations upon the same." Winnipeg, Manitoba, February 2, 1948. (Mimeographed.)

In 1947 the Legislative Assembly appointed a committee to investigate Hutterite colonies in Manitoba. This report includes testimony before the committee and recommendations made, such as the appointment of another committee by the next legislature to consider legislation affecting the colonies. It also includes information on inter-group relations.

MANITOBA LEGISLATURE, SELECT SPECIAL COMMITTEE
"Meeting of Select Special Committee of Manitoba Legislature on Hutterite Legislature." Winnipeg, Manitoba, July 23, 1948. (Mimeographed.)

This select committee considers whether or not appropriate legislation should be enacted to establish a procedure whereby any man, woman, or child may leave a Hutterite colony at any time he or she chooses and may take with him or her his equitable share of colony assets. It includes testimony of interested parties and also contains information on social, political, and economic organization.

IV. Amish, Holdeman,* Old Order and Old Colony Mennonites

* The official name of the Holdeman group is Church of God in Christ Mennonite.

A. Books and Pamphlets

BYLER, URIA R.
School Bells Ringing: A Manual for Amish Teachers and Parents. Aylmer,
Ontario: Pathway Publishing Corporation, 1969.

A discussion of the lessons learned from the strong movement
among the Amish toward parochial schools between 1958 and
1968. Purposes of the book are: to acquaint the reader with the
problems, duties, and responsibilities of a teacher; to outline different methods found to be effective in conducting classes and
maintaining discipline; to help the new teacher prepare for the
field he is entering; and to make suggestions on board-parent-
teacher problems.

GINGERICH, ORLAND
The Amish of Canada. Waterloo: Conrad Press, 1972.

The Amish of Canada exist as an organized and separate group
only in the province of Ontario. This book has a broad grasp of
the historical events and the localized settlements of the Amish
people. It encompasses the most conservative group, the Old
Order Amish as well as the progressive Western Ontario Conference which has abandoned all traditional Amish practices. It also
includes two chapters on the sociological view of the community.
Their adaption to technology, urbanization and acculturation is
described as a slow and painful process. Change in ideas and

religious beliefs took a very long time. The chapter on congregational expansion and development includes a description of nineteen churches, their leaders, and their constitutions.

HISTORICAL COMMITTEE OF THE NEW HAMBURG-WILMOT TOWNSHIP
CENTENNIAL COMMITTEE
More than a Century in Wilmot Township. New Hamburg, Ontario:
Historical Committee of the New Hamburg-Wilmot Township Cen-
tennial Committee, 1967.

This booklet on Wilmot Township contains descriptions of the
Amish and Mennonite pioneers, settlements, and churches. According to the 1960 statistics, the Mennonites and Amish account
for 31.7 per cent of the township's population. The work ethic of
the Mennonites is analyzed briefly.

HORST, MARY ANN
My Old Order Mennonite Heritage. Kitchener, Ontario: Pennsylvania
Dutch Craft Shop, 1970.

This popular booklet attempts to answer questions that many
people have concerning the Old Order Mennonites. The author,
who is of Old Order Mennonite parentage, gives a personal,
inside description of the everyday life of this Mennonite group.
As she tells of their worship experience, Sunday visiting and
recreation, and life as a child and then as an adolescent in this
community, it is possible to gain an understanding about the
beliefs and customs of the Old Order Mennonites.

HOSTETLER, JOHN A.
Amish Society. Baltimore: The Johns Hopkins Press, 1963.

Hostetler's book is the best sociological study of the Amish. Although it deals specifically with the Old Order Amish of America,
it is relevant for a study of any Amish group. The first part of the
book examines the structures and strengths of Amish social institutions, the origins of a sectarian movement, the Amish charter, and family life and personal relations from infancy to childhood. A large part of the book is concerned with the Amish
community is affected by culture contact and by "the ethos of an
expanding technologically oriented civilization." The effects of
change on the American society can be seen through the author's
interviews with those who broke with the community, and
through discussions on defection, excommunication, "meidung,"
mental illness, and suicides. In the last chapter, reorganization
and the future of the Amish community is discussed. Excellent
bibliography.

HOSTETLER, JOHN A.

Educational Achievement and Life Styles in a Traditional Society, the Old Order Amish. Washington, D. C., U. S. Dept. of Health, Education, and Welfare, 1969.

"This investigation is a depth study of socialization in a Gemeinschaft society, the Old Order Amish, with four specific objectives: 1) the formulation of the charter with respect to the view of child nature and the education of children; 2) the construction of the age categories as defined by the culture with a description of the socialization practices; 3) the discovery of the achievement levels of school children on standardized tests, and 4) the development of generalizations with respect to changes in the social patterns affecting the education of children in "traditional" and "emergent" life styles. It is the intention of this investigation to understand socialization on a life participation level and value orientation in the context of culture. How do the Amish children perform in the light of their own cultural goals and values? In what ways do they differ from other children in their capabilities and learning patterns?"

HOSTETLER, JOHN A.

Anabaptist Conceptions of Child Nurture and Schooling. A Collection of Source Materials Used by the Old Order Amish. Temple University, Philadelphia, 1968.

This is a collection of sources compiled as part of a research project in order to establish the value orientations and basic beliefs of the group studies as background material for the research. Hostetler has attempted to collect sufficient material to be representative of the concept of the child rearing among the Old Order Amish through time. Some of the writings are concerned with child disobedience, influence of mothers and grandmothers, the meaning of a good education, and the supreme court ruling of 1963 which stated that the recitation of the Lord's Prayer in public school is unconstitutional.

HOSTETLER, JOHN A.

Report on the Conference on Child Socialization. Washington, D. C.: Health, Education, and Welfare, 1969.

"The design of the conference was to focus on a single cultural system, the Old Order Amish, in the belief that the holistic approach for understanding interconnected patterns of culture and behavior has proven fruitful for interdisciplinary studies and particularly for the study of child development and socialization patterns." Broad aspects of socialization in the context of culture were considered: Is there a "design for living" in Amish culture? How are the young prepared to live by the values of the culture? How are the basic needs of personality met? Are the schools within the Amish culture capable of preparing the young for a way of life? What is an adequate education in a subculture that makes agrarian simplicity the norm for its offspring?

HOSTETLER, JOHN A. and HUNTINGTON, GERTRUDE ENDERS
Children in Amish Society. Socialization and Community Education. New York: Holt, Rinehart and Winston, Inc., 1971.

The Amish school system is integrated with their own life style. "The school supports the family and the traditions and economy of the Amish community and enables the child to learn both the facts and the roles he needs to function as an Amish person in twentieth-century America." This study concentrates on the processes of nurture and socialization as well as on the formal schooling in the context of the Amish culture. Almost every aspect of socialization patterns and of Amish schools is dealt with in this small book: curriculum, teaching methods, discipline, schedules, the problem school, etc. The conflict with the public schools and the struggle to keep the school under their own control is another important aspect of this study. The authors believe that this careful nurture of their children has allowed the Amish to remain a minority true to their "vision of the good life." Along with Hostetler's *Amish Society* (1963) this study is crucial for understanding North American Amish.

PATHWAY PUBLISHERS
Tips for Teachers, A Handbook for Amish Teachers. Aylmer, Ontario and Lagrange, Indiana: Pathway Publishers, 1970.

This teachers' aid manual was compiled especially for Amish parochial school teachers. It contains ideas, suggestions, and opinions on such topics as discipline, compositions, games, free period, and art.

REDEKOP, CALVIN WALL
The Old Colony Mennonites: Dilemmas of Ethnic Minority Life. Baltimore: Johns Hopkins Press, 1969.

This vivid account of almost every facet of Old Colony Mennonite life is presented from several different perspectives. First as an historical account, it outlines the background of the Old Colony, its emergence in Manitoba, and the migrations to Mexico, Alberta, British Honduras, and Bolivia as a means of survival. Author also gives a sociological-anthropological description of the Old Colony Mennonites. For example the Old Colony social system is described in full detail with emphasis on the beliefs, values, and norms. This book is also useful for a general study on sects. The author gives a thorough review of literature concerning sects and he defines certain concepts about religious ethnic groups. The book concludes with some propositions regarding the causes of cultural and structural assimilation, based on Old Colony evidence. It is a book that should, as Everett C. Hughes says in the foreword, "add to our insights concerning the struggle to be different."

SCHREIBER, WILLIAM I.

Our Amish Neighbors. Chicago: University of Chicago Press, 1962, 227 pp.

Although this book is specifically a description of the Old Order Amish in Ohio, it serves as a general study on Amish background, way of life, and community life and organization. A chapter is also included defining the "meidung" and how it is applied today.

SMITH, ELMER L.

Studies in Amish Demography. Harrisonburg, Virginia: The Research Council, Eastern Mennonite College, 1960.

Although a study of the Amish in rural southeastern Pennsylvania, this book provides an adequate understanding of the Amish in general through a thorough analysis of some recent quantitative research findings. The study is divided into three main classifications: "The Demography of Amish Marriage and Family Life"; "The Amish Population, Its Structure and Composition"; and "The Amish Family Cycle." Some interesting conclusions are reached concerning Amish family size, remarriage, pre-marital pregnancy, Amish nicknames, bundling, and age of marriage. Statistics are presented in such a way that comparisons are easily made between the Amish and the major society.

SMITH, ELMER L.

The Amish Today: An Analysis of Their Beliefs, Behavior and Contemporary Problems. Allentown, Pa.: Pennsylvania German Folklore Society, 1961.

The central theme of this book is contemporary Amish life. The author believes that many fallacies about the Amish result from the use of materials from the distant past and he hopes to establish material for more realistic and adequate generalizations about the Amish. Some of the data presented are the results of statistical analysis from adequate samples, while in some of the work only limited samples were obtained and the conclusions can be accepted only on a tentative basis. The book is divided into four parts: 1) the geographic location, the population structure and composition, and the makeup of the community; 2) the sources of Amish beliefs; 3) the Amish family system; and 4) the problems faced by the sect today. It is explained that the focus of attention on the Amish family results from the belief that the family is the main force perpetuating Amish culture today. The book refers primarily to the Old Order Amish of Lancaster County, Pennsylvania but is applicable to the Amish in Canada.

SMITH, ELMER L.
Bundling Among the Amish. Akron, Pennsylvania: Applied Arts, 1961.

This pamphlet outlines the controversy concerning whether the Amish practiced bundling; gives reasons why bundling is practiced; and shows that bundling was widespread in rural America.

STOLL, JOSEPH
Who Shall Educate Our Children? Aylmer, Ontario: Pathway Publishing Corp., 1965, 80 pp.

The purpose of this booklet is to present the case for church schools and to hold up the Christian ideal in child training, teaching, and management of schools. The areas discussed are the duties of Christian parents, what is wrong with public schools, what church schools offer, the curriculum, textbooks and supplies, teachers, and general administration. Through these discussions, the author hopes to awaken interest in church schools among the Amish and to provide an understanding of the need and role of the church school.

B. Graduate Theses

BILLINGS, THOMAS A.
"Old Order Amish vs. the Compulsory School Attendance Laws: An Analysis of Conflict." Unpublished Ph.D. dissertation, University of Oregon, 1961.

In general terms this is a study of Protestant resistance to any transformation of the educative function of the church to the state. More specifically, this research attempts to clarify the fundamental points of the conflict between the Old Order Amish and the state of Ohio, a conflict which centers around the state's compulsory school attendance laws. To do this the author focuses on an analysis of several questions which attempt to discover the differences between public school education and the education provided in Amish parochial schools, the areas of parental jurisdiction with which the government may not interfere, the intentions of the compulsory attendance laws, and the basic liberties and rights of minority groups. The author is particularly adamant in stressing that the rights of the Amish, or of any religious minority, must be more than "those rights which majority opinion tolerates or defines as rights at any given moment."

BURKHART, CHARLES
"The Music of the Old Order Amish and the Old Colony Mennonites: A Contemporary Monodic Practice." Unpublished M.A. thesis, Colorado College, 1952.

The Old Order Amish and the Old Colony Mennonites have developed a very similar type of music even though they have had no cultural inter-relations since their emergence as separate entities. They both perpetuate specific tunes by oral tradition. Their original tunes have become completely obscure and forgotten and today they are much slower and more ornamented. This phenomenon is a reproduction in miniature of what happened over a longer period of time to the Gregorian chant. It exhibits a monody unusual in this era of harmony and is also one of the few examples of nasal singing in contemporary Western culture. The thesis gives a detailed analysis of the musical style in question and also accounts for its origin and development.

CROSS, HAROLD E.
"Genetic Studies in an Amish Isolate." Unpublished Ph.D. dissertation, The Johns Hopkins University, 1967.

"Genetic studies were conducted in an isolate of Old Order Amish located in Holmes County, Ohio. Selected demographic characteristics were studied, and an attempt was made to ascertain and characterize all cases of hereditary neurologic disorders. The frequency of cervical cancer in Amish women was compared to that in non-Amish women living in the same area. An estimate was made of the size of the genetic load carried by this population." Some of the findings of this study are: there is no evidence that the Amish are attempting to curtail their high birth rate which is second only to the Hutterite ratio; age-standardized nuptial birth rates are nearly similar for Amish and Hutterite women up to the fourth decade, but Hutterite rates are nearly double the Amish rates in later years; the frequency of cervical cancer was lower in Amish than non-Amish women; and the size of the Amish genetic load is similar to that in other populations.

EGELAND, JANICE A.
"Belief and Behavior as Related to Illness: A Community Case Study of the Old Order Amish." Unpublished Ph.D. dissertation, Yale University, 1967.

This is a six-year ethnographic study of health beliefs and behavior in the Old Order Amish community of Lancaster County, Pennsylvania. The first few chapters center on discussions of the

Amish social system, the components of the Amish health belief systems, the viability of primitive medical beliefs, the pattern and prominence of folk medical beliefs, and the official position of the church regarding health and healing. A major section of the study seeks to explain the reason for preference of folk versus orthodox treatment procedure. Hypotheses are tested to determine whether the type of etiological belief, the nature of the illness, or selected factors such as age, sex, and degree of conservatism explain this preference of medical care. It was found that "family culture, seen in terms of kinship lines, appears to be the most important determining factor." The last chapter attempts to answer the question: "How are cultural values related to health beliefs and behavior?" In this chapter, the nature and direction of change processes is indicated and the values related to health and sickness are shown.

FLAUGHER, RALPH

"Comparison of the Rorschach Protocols of First Grade Amish Children with Those of Non-Amish Children from the same Rural Schools." Unpublished M.A. thesis, University of Pittsburgh, 1951.

It is assumed that the Rorschach test produces responses that are reflections of basic personality attributes. This study compares "the Rorschach performances of two groups of individuals whose perceptual experiences have much in common in that they speak the same language, live in the same community, and attend the same schools, yet, who in spite of these shared experiences, constitute objectively distinct cultural groups." The hypothesis of this study is that differences will be found between the Rorschach productions of Amish-Mennonites and non-Amish individuals of the same rural area. More specifically it is hypothesized that the Amish records will show a significantly higher percentage of form responses "as evidence of constriction and lack of spontaneity."

FREY, KENNETH D.

"Comparative Occupational Aspirations of Old Order Mennonite and Non-Old Order Mennonite Farm Youth." Unpublished M.Sc. thesis, University of Guelph, 1971.

Using solid empirical data, Frey proves that the Ontario Old Order Mennonite youth have significantly different occupational aspirations than non-Old Order Mennonites. All Old Order Mennonites, for example, plan to farm while the mainstream groups aspired to a broader range of vocations. Other differences were in relation to government controls, availability of capital, family influence, and manual versus intellectual labor.

The study is particularly important for those students of Mennonite culture who do not yet understand the differences among the wide range of Mennonites.

FRIESEN, ABRAHAM
"Emigration in Mennonite History with Special Reference to the
Conservative Mennonite Emigration from Canada to Mexico and
South America after World War I." Unpublished M.A. thesis, Uni-
versity of Manitoba, 1962.

The first part of this dissertation deals with the background of
emigration in Mennonite history. The second part uses original
material on the Conservative Mennonite Emigration to Mexico
and South America. The author divides the Mennonites into
three distinct groups: the liberal group, the middle way between
liberalism and extreme conservatism.

HIEBERT, CLARENCE
"The Holdeman People: A Study of the Church of God in Christ,
Mennonite, 1848-1969." Unpublished Ph.D. dissertation, Case
Western Reserve University, 1971.

The Holdemans, officially known as the Church of God in
Christ, Mennonite, number around 8,000 in North America.
Under John Holdeman's leadership some conservative,
German-speaking, revivalistically-inclined Mennonites from
three groups merged. Two migrant groups from Russia, relocat-
ing in Kansas and Manitoba continue to be the largest nucleus of
the Holdemans. "This study is an attempt to identify the factors
which merged to bring this movement into existence: environment, history, social aspects, religious situation, and political aspects. The converging forces of religious lethargy and discon-
tent in an era of revivalism and a frontier setting provided the
ripe moment for John Holdeman to share his frustrations and
convictions with other like-minded seekers." Some accommodation to changing times have given the movement sufficient balance, stability, and momentum to grow. Since only "ordained"
leaders make decisions and since members are rigidly disciplined, they have maintained effective resistance to worldly accommodation. But, the author states, there are some indications
that this may not be easy in the future.

HOHMANN, RUPERT K.
"The Church Music of the Old Order Amish of the United States."
Unpublished Ph.D. dissertation, Northwestern University, 1959.

This study has two main purposes: 1) to determine the original
source of the music employed today in the hymn-singing of the
Old Order Amish, and 2) to give a detailed analysis of the musical study of Amish music. The Amish were chosen for this study
because of their extreme isolation, their use of unharmonized,
unaccompanied hymn tunes in worship, and their ornamental
vocal style. A portion of the paper is given to the history of the
Anabaptist movement, the relationship of the Amish to other re-

ligious groups of the Reformation period in Germany, and to the settlement of the Amish in North America. It was found that the origins of Amish hymns depend upon secular and sacred folk song tunes of the fifteenth, sixteenth, and seventeenth centuries. These tunes of an untutored simple folk developed into highly ornamented tunes because of the refusal of the Amish to notate their music. Great variations were also found in the singing practices of various Amish communities due to the lack of social interchange among them.

JANTZEN, CARL R.
"Boundary Maintenance and Personality Score Differences Between Old Order Amish and Non-Amish Children." Unpublished M.A. thesis, Michigan State University, 1959.

"This study of the Old Order Amish social system is an investigation of the way in which Amish children score on standardized tests of personality and interpersonal relations. Boundary maintenance and systematic linkage are used as conceptual tools in the descriptive analysis. Dividing the Old Order Amish into those who own or do not own certain items, facilitates comparisons of Amish test scores with non-Amish test scores and may illustrate both boundary maintenance and systemic linkage." The findings indicate that differences in personality between Amish and non-Amish children seem to exist, that Amish children coming from families who are adopting proscribed practices are also adopting orientations which are closer to non-Amish orientations than those orientations of the Amish children whose families have not adopted these practices, that the adoption of these practices seems to have no particular influence on choice of friends, and that school experience has a great effect in linking the Amish and non-Amish social systems.

JENTSCH, THEODORE WERNER
"Mennonite Americans: A Study of a Religious Subculture from a Sociological Perspective." Unpublished Ph.D. dissertation, University of South Africa, 1973. (Available from the author, Sociology Dept., Kutztown State College, Kutztown, Pa. 19530.)

This is the best study to date of the Old Order Mennonites who are easily confused with the Amish because they drive buggies instead of cars. Upon closer examination it is obvious their men do not wear beards; and that their worship services are held in meeting houses instead of homes.

There are 540 Old Order families in Ontario and 658 in Pennsylvania with small settlements in Virginia, Missouri and Indiana. The Old Order group emerged in 1893 in Pennsylvania when objections arose to the installation of a pulpit in a Mennonite church. Cars were officially banned in the 1920's.

Testing Nisbet's concept of social change and K. Davis' theory of religion and stability, Jentsch made a sociographic study of the Old Order people near Kutztown, Pa., employing an interview-participant observer method. The theoretical constructs of Nisbet and Davis were substantiated by the data.

Jentsch's study is applicable to the Ontario Old Order Mennonites. His work makes more urgent the completion of Fretz's research in Waterloo County, Ontario.

LANNING, JAMES WALTER
"The Old Colony Mennonites of Bolivia: A Case Study." Unpublished M.A. thesis, Texas A and M University, 1971.

The purpose of this study is to provide a base for Mennonite scholars and sociologists interested in studying the Old Colony pioneer experience. For the most part, the thesis focuses on the institutions and beliefs of the Old Colony Mennonites in Bolivia. But one chapter centers on their Manitoba heritage. Here they developed a sense of corporate identity, which was recognized by 1890 as a separate Mennonite group. The reasons for their migration from Canada to Mexico are also discussed.

MELTON, JAMES JOE
"Old Order Amish Awareness and Understanding of Mental Retardation: A Religious Subcultural Approach to the Phenomenon." Unpublished Ph.D. dissertation, Ohio State University, 1970.

This study is based on the premise that mental health is best understood when studied as a social and cultural phenomenon. It begins by introducing the Old Order Amish in a historical sketch as a religious-separatist closed culture and also makes a survey of contemporary research dealing with language development, education conflicts, and genetics. The study employs two methods from which conclusions are drawn. The first is an extensive review of Amish literature with reference to mental retardation, and the second is an eight-month field study of an Amish settlement in Ohio. These two methods revealed the following findings: an awareness of hereditary abnormalities leading to the birth of retarded children and support for proper medical diets and treatment, the ill effects of long-term institutionalization, and the futility of seeking non-medical aid; the belief that an abnormal child is part of God's will; and an increasing awareness of the appropriateness of institutions for severely retarded children, but a willingness to go outside for help in training the Amish retardate.

MILLER, D. PAUL
"Amish Acculturation." Unpublished M.A. thesis, University of Nebraska, 1950.

The purpose of this study is to describe the process of acculturation in a religio-cultural situation. It is felt that the Old Order
Amish clearly exemplify this process since they have maintained
specific traditions, since they have contributed to the outside
community, and since they have taken on a limited amount of
non-Amish practices. Of primary interest, the author wishes to
consider to what extent the acculturation of the group has led to
secularization or assimilation, and to test the hypothesis that the
group which most strictly holds to its traditional customs will
most likely preserve its group identity. This is done by considering the Old Order Amish, the Old Mennonites, and the Conservative Amish in their religious customs, social and family life,
economic life, and by considering their views and activities in
education and politics. The study includes an account of Amish
origins, of their split from the Mennonite Church in the seventeenth century, of their emigrations from Europe to North
America, and of their migrations westward.

MILLER, WAYNE E.
"A Study of Amish Academic Achievement." Unpublished Ph.D.
dissertation, University of Michigan, 1969.

The purpose of this study is to determine whether Amish pupils
do as well as, better than, or less well than non-Amish pupils in
integrated and non-integrated schools and also whether extroverted Amish pupils do better or more poorly than introverted
Amish pupils. Intelligence and personality tests were given to
schools located in Indiana, Iowa, Michigan, Ohio, and Ontario.
Findings indicated that integration with non-Amish is not a positive factor in relationship with the achievement of Amish children. Also extroverted Amish pupils, when compared with
Amish introverted pupils, generally do better in all achievement
areas but the differences are not great. Author concludes that
Amish pupils do well in areas tested and possess the basic skills for
their way of life. He, therefore, suggests that Amish teachers
need less professional training than would be necessary for teaching pupils without Amish background, that an area vocational
school for the Amish would teach skills acceptable in Amish
vocations, and that flexibility should be exercised toward Amish
educational objectives and methods.

VAN DYKE, EDWARD W.
"Blumenort: A Study of Persistence in a Sect." Unpublished Ph.D.
dissertation, U. of Alberta, Anthropology, 1972.

An anthropological field study of the Blumenort Old Colony
Mennonite community located near Fort Vermillion, Alberta.
This colony underwent sectarian division in 1969 with one seg-
ment opting to remain in Canada while the other group migrated

to Bolivia. In the Spring of 1970 over half of the migrants returned to Canada.

The data are distinctive in that they indicate a significant amount of factionalism, schism and conflict in the Old Colony community. The study utilizes the dissonance theory of Leon Festinger to interpret the data. A theoretical model is also used to explain socio-cultural persistence of this sect by way of a cyclical sequence of revitalization, encroachment, dissonance, division, isolation and again revitalization. Van Dyke appends an essay describing his own struggles, actions and responses to the community as he carried out his work.

WALHOUSE, FREDA
"The Influence of Minority Ethnic Groups on the Cultural Geography of Vancouver." Unpublished M.A. thesis, University of British Columbia, 1961.

This is a study of the relationship between the various ethnic groups of Vancouver and the spatial differentiation of the city. A section is devoted to the Mennonites. Pages 179-185 reveals how the early attempt by Mennonites at close settlement in an urban area is revealed in today's pattern. For example, there is a marked concentration of Mennonites in Southern Vancouver. This study also outlines three distinctive characteristics of the Mennonite population of the Lower Fraser Valley: 1) excess of females over males; 2) ratio of religious groups is approximately two-fifths General Conference to three-fifths Mennonite Brethren; and 3) a pronounced urban movement, particularly to Vancouver. It is also emphasized that changes in Mennonite settlement patterns have led to economic reorientations, a more progressive outlook, and the disappearance of features pronounced in Mennonite rural life.

C. Articles

THE AMBASSADOR OF PEACE
Aylmer, Ontario: Pathway Publishers.

A monthly periodical for Amish young people that promotes Christian living and a consistent peace witness. It contains short stories, letters concerning previous articles, and a question and answer column called "Let's Talk It Over."

BALDWIN, SIOUX
"Amish Plain Costume: A Matter of Choice." *Pennsylvania Folklife*, XIX (Summer, 1970), pp. 10-17.

This article takes the form of a discussion with an Amish family as a means of presenting the use of folk costume among Amish and Mennonite groups in Pennsylvania. Through description and the use of diagrams, the author illustrates the "plain" bonnet styles from the Cape Bonnet to the Turban and also the varieties in "plain" suits. Modernizations in the dress are noticed such as the use of buttons, zippers, and caps with very little rim. But despite these changes, the author feels that the Old Order Amish are still very conservative and not any closer to joining the "World."

BARCLAY, HAROLD B.
"The Protestant Ethic and the Spirit of Capitalism." *Review of Religious Research*, X (Spring, 1969), pp. 151-158.

Barclay is typical of a growing number of scholars in the Prairie universities who are doing field studies in the economics of Hutterites and Mennonites. In this analysis of the Church of God in Christ, Mennonite, popularly known as the Holdeman Mennonites, in Linden, Alberta, he shows that Max Weber's insights shed light on the complex manner in which the Holdemans have capitalistic drives under severe restraints. A dialectical relationship between capitalism and mutual aid exists in an agrarian setting with a distrust of the city, undue expansion, and conspicuous consumption. At some point the Holdeman businessman who is successful must either restrain his business or leave the church. Thus, the capitalistic outlook has a ceiling of restraint. Further studies are needed to test this Weberian view with the less strict Mennonite groups who have no restraining force other than the gifts from surpluses to church institutions.

BENDER, HAROLD S.
"Sommerfeld Mennonites." *ME*, IV, pp. 576-578.

A very conservative body of Manitoba Mennonites of Russian background who originated as a separate group in 1890 when the Bergthal Mennonite Church divided into a minority progressive wing and a majority conservative wing. Of special interest is a discussion on the statement that the Sommerfelder culture has remained practically unchanged. Author feels their outward forms of social organization have remained the same but this has led to deterioration in spiritual life and alienation of the young people. Author also explains that the loosely organized Sommerfeld Church has led to the formation of three groups that are different in attitude: orthodox, liberal, and diaspora or scattered.

BLACKBOARD BULLETIN, THE
Aylmer, Ontario: Pathway Publishing Corporation.

A monthly periodical founded in 1957 in the interest of Amish schools and homes. It includes tips for teachers, educational methods, news from various schools in North America and letters showing the interests of parents and teachers.

CROSS, HAROLD E. and McKUSICK, VICTOR A.
"Amish Demography." *Social Biology*, XVII (1970), pp. 83-101.

Restriction of birth control by the Amish and high standards of living and mental care are two characteristics which make the Amish especially useful for population studies. This particular demographic study is based on the Amish of Holmes County, Ohio. The data collected in 1964 was used to determine age and sex distribution, sex ratios, occupations, marital patterns, pre-marital conceptions, sterility, twinning, fertility, and birth intervals.

DRIEDGER, LEO
"Saskatchewan Old Colony Mennonites." *ML*, XIII (April, 1958), pp. 63-66.

The community-oriented life of the Old Colony Mennonites is described in this article. Evidence of this is seen in the hog slaughtering bees, building bees, and Freundschaft gatherings. Other factors leading to disintegration or preservation of the brotherhood are discussed. Of interest is a discussion of the Schulze, the administrator of the Old Colony village. A map is included to indicate the Mennonite settlements in the Osler-Hague-Rosthern area.

ENGLE, T. L.
"An Analysis of Themes on the Subject of War as Written by the Amish and non-Amish Children." *The Journal of Educational Psychology*, XXXV (May, 1944), pp. 267-73.

An analysis of themes written by Amish and non-Amish children on the subject, "How war affects me." It was found that the mentioning of rationing and shortage of merchandise was the outstanding characteristic of themes written on this subject. Themes written by Amish children indicated much less desire to help in winning the war than did the themes written by non-Amish children.

ENGLE, T. L.
"Attitudes Toward War as Expressed by Amish and Non-Amish Children." *The Journal of Educational Psychology*, XXXV (April, 1944), pp. 211-219.

A comparison of attitudes toward war of Amish children with non-Amish children. Attitudes were measured by two methods: free expression in a written theme and a standardized attitude-toward-war scale. In general Amish children were found to indicate less favorable attitudes toward war than non-Amish children and indicated less acceptance than non-Amish children of the statements that war has some value and that war is necessary to maintain justice. Both groups agreed that war was not glorious and that there can be progress without war.

ENGLE, T. L.
"Personality Adjustment of Children Belonging to Two Minority Groups." *The Journal of Educational Psychology*, XXXVI (December, 1945), pp. 543-560.

In this study the author compares the personality adjustments of a group of young Negro children and a group of Amish children with a control group of non-Amish children. The California Test of Personality was given to students in the second and third grades of public school. There is evidence to suggest that membership in a minority group is associated with feelings of personal insecurity, and with a less satisfactory balance between self and social adjustment than is the case for children belonging to a majority group. But, the author states, this does not hold true at all when Amish and control boys are compared and, in fact, Amish boys may be better adjusted within their social group than either Negro or control boys within their social groups.

ENGLE, T. L. and ENGLE, ELEANOR
"Attitude Differences Between Amish and Non-Amish Children Attending the Same Schools." *The Journal of Educational Psychology*, XXXIV (April, 1943), pp. 206-214.

This study is an attempt to measure certain aspects of personality by means of an inventory presented to Amish school children and to compare the results with those of non-Amish children attending the same schools. The term Amish refers only to children wearing the distinctive dress. The subjects were children in grades V through VIII in three rural schools in Indiana. The results did not find great differences in personality patterns and, although there is some tendency for Amish children to be more submissive and introverted, Amish children seemed to be as well adjusted emotionally as non-Amish children.

FAMILY LIFE
Aylmer, Ontario: Pathway Publishing Corporation.

A monthly periodical, founded January, 1968, concerned with the promotion of Christian living among the Amish, with emphasis on the appreciation of their heritage. It contains a number of short stories which present Christian views and values, a section on Bible stories for children, letters, and a column which relates news from the other Amish settlements. Frequently there is also a short article on the historical or social organization of some Amish settlement.

FREY, J. WILLIAM
"Amish Hymns as Folk Music." *Pennsylvania Songs and Legends*. Edited by George Korson. Philadelphia: University of Pennsylvania Press, 1949.

The hymns of the Old Order Amish "constitute a unique and fascinating study in both American and European folklore." This article presents some of the outstanding features of the history, content, and music of Amish hymns. It begins by providing a description of Amish background, dress, customs, work, religion, and speech. This is followed by a description of the tunes, rhythm, and pitch of the Amish hymns. Author states that the hymns of the Amish differ greatly from the worship songs of Luther in that they are not odes or lyrics; nor are many of them hymns of praise. Rather they are martyr hymns that originally were poems or epics relating the story of the tortures endured by the Amish forefathers. These were adapted to folk tunes, Gregorian chants, or other melodies current in the early sixteenth century.

GEHMAN, RICHARD
"Amish Folk." *National Geographic*, CXXVIII (August, 1965), pp. 226-253.

This popular, pictorial account of the Amish in Lancaster County, Pennsylvania outlines the Amish skill in farming, the reasons for some schisms within the Amish Church, their self-sufficiency, Amish barn raisings, weddings and hymn singings, conflicts with the state, and the problem of tourism for the Amish.

GINGERICH, ORLAND
"Early Amish Settlements and Their Development." Waterloo: Mennonite Historical Society, 1966.

This is a detailed summary of the origins, early beginnings, and later developments of the Amish in Ontario. A brief sketch of the current fourteen congregations in the Western Ontario Conference is also given.

HAMILTON, O.
"The Amish Settlements in the Township of Wilmot in the County of Waterloo." *Waterloo Historical Society*, XXXII (1944), pp. 15-21.

A brief historical account of the Amish Mennonites in Waterloo County, with a list of congregations and some distinguishing features of the Amish Mennonites such as industry, frugality, and common sense.

HARK, ANN
"Amish Christmas." *The American-German Review*, XXVI (December, 1959/January, 1960), pp. 4-6.

A popular account of the Amish Christmas, mentioning the din-
ner, the lack of decorations, and the Amish custom in the matter
of exchanging gifts.

HILDEBRAND, MENNO
"The Sommerfeld Mennonites of Manitoba." *ML*, XXV (July,
1970), pp. 99-107.

The Sommerfeld Mennonites established themselves on the East
and West Reserve separated by the Red River in Manitoba. Their
life and customs are discussed with a special reference to their
church life.

HILLER, HARRY H.
"The Sleeping Preachers: An Historical Study of the Role of
Charisma in Amish Society." *Pennsylvania Folklife*, XVII (Winter,
1968-1969), pp. 19-31.

Sleeping preachers, "under the guise of divine empowerment,
rendered scintillating sermons to large hosts of people while in an
unconscious state." This paper seeks to formulate an accurate
description of the sleeping preachers through historical analysis.
The first section of the article provides the biographical base,
centering on Noah Troyer and J. D. Kauffman, from which perspective can be gained for psycho-social analysis. The second section
deals with the role the sleeping preachers assumed in the Amish
community and the status ascribed to them by their
peers. Max Weber's theory of charisma is applied which enables
the reader "to understand the genesis of reaction and response of
the community to them and their message." The last section
attempts a psychological explanation of the causation of these
unique experiences.

HOPPLE, C. LEE
"Spatial Development of the Southeastern Pennsylvania Plain Dutch
Community to 1970: Part I." *Pennsylvania Folklife*, XXI (Winter,
1971-72), pp. 18-40; Part II (Spring, 1972), pp. 36-45.

The spatial development of the Amish, Mennonites, Dunkards,
and Schwenkfelder is traced from the arrival of each group in
Pennsylvania to 1970. Although specifically on Pennsylvanian
communities, this study provides a new dimension in the study of
Mennonites and Amish since it is concerned with the direction of
territorial adjustments and internal spatial reorganizations caused
by social, cultural and economic changes. In fact, the patterns of
spatial development which emerged as distinctively religiously
controlled spatial systems, and which reveal the development of
clusters of sectarian rural farm residences, the organization of
these clusters into congregational districts, and the emergence of
these congregational districts as multi-bonded symbolic, self-

governing communities, are directly applicable to some Mennonite and Amish groups in Canada. Religion, the extended family,
and mutual aid are three factors which could account for these
clusters.

HOSTETLER, JOHN A.
"Evidences of Cultural Change Among the Amish." *Conference on
Mennonite Educational and Cultural Problems*, VIII (June, 1951), pp.
87-96.

Past and current cultural changes of the Amish are discussed to
determine the extent and direction of Amish acculturation. Data
from the Amish in Mifflin County, Pennsylvania is given to indicate changing religious affiliation. Shortage of land, questioning
of old customs by the young, and conflict with the public school
system are discussed as reasons for loss of church members.

HOSTETLER, JOHN A.
"Old World Extinction and New World Survival of the Amish." *Rural
Sociology*, XX (September-December, 1955), pp. 212-219.

"This article discusses the Swiss and German origins of the
Amish-Mennonites, the early history of the sect, its dissolution in
Europe, and its survival in America. Survival in the New World is
attributed to the perpetual sectarian conflict between the parental group and the subject, the emergence of a consciousness of
difference from the world—expressed in costume and other traditions, and community association and proximity never realized
on the Continent on account of differing landholding systems."

HOSTETLER, JOHN A.
"Amish Costume: Its European Origins." *The American-German
Review*, XXII (August-September, 1956), pp. 11-14.

"Amish dress is more striking and probably more integrated with
a total way of life than that of the other surviving Reformation
sects." But research indicates that dress styles were not originally
instituted as part of the Amish religion. This article seeks to
discover where the Amish got their costume in the first place and
traces some of the current styles of the Amish to their European
sources. These styles include the beard and hair, hook and eyes,
trousers, white caps, halsduch (kerchief or cape), the lepple (bus-
tle), and the scoop straw hat. It is concluded that the Amish
became conscious of a distinctive uniform dress for the first time
in America.

HOSTETLER, JOHN A.
"The Amish Citizens of Heaven and America." *Pennsylvania Folklife*,
X (Spring, 1959), pp. 32-37.

A look at some of the differences between the Amish and American lifestyles. The Amish life is centered around three major possessions: the Bible, the soil, and the gemeinschaft relationships. While the American way is to let the government look after the needy families, the Amish take these responsibilities upon themselves. Hostetler concludes that there is a need for more understanding and appreciation of fundamental differences.

HOSTETLER, JOHN A.
"Amish Family Life—A Sociologist's Analysis." *Pennsylvania Folklife*, XII (Fall, 1961), pp. 28-39.

A sociological examination of one of the most important aspects of Amish life. This article is an excerpt from the author's M.S. thesis, "The Amish Family in Mifflin County, Pennsylvania." It deals with the following topics: patterns of authority, relationships between married mates, parent-child relationships, sibling relationships, and differences between families.

HOSTETLER, JOHN A.
"Old Order Amish." *ME*, IV, pp. 43-47.

A general account of the history, nonconformist attitudes, worship experience, and the rural way of life of the Amish. Their settlements in North America are also described. Author discusses general findings from sociological research such as the ability of the Amish to maintain certain features of stability through isolation and ingroup loyalty and the gradual infiltration of Amish culture by outside patterns which bring about disintegration of old values. Author also examines the reasons for the ability of the Amish to survive in North America as a group with a distinct and separate culture.

HOSTETLER, JOHN A.
"Folk and Scientific Medicine in Amish Society." *Human Organization*, XXII (Winter, 1963-64), pp. 269-275.

"The exploration into Amish medical behavior suggests that both folk and scientific concepts prevail in the same culture." This study of the medical behavior of the Old Order Amish seeks to discover how these two forms of medical knowledge exist in the same society, and to learn how they are integrated. The topics of discussion include "The Sick Role," "Folk Knowledge and Illness," and "Physician-Patient Relations." A chart is included which indicates a long list of ailments and the method of treatment (professional or folk). An analysis of the content of this chart reveals that the Amish are health-conscious and that the scientific concepts of healing do not conflict with Amish values. The author believes that this acceptance of scientific treatment may be one of the most vulnerable inroads to change into a folk culture. Two conclusions are made: 1) in the Amish case, changes occur selectively; and 2) the practice of folk medicine persists in a culture that places a premium on isolation.

HOSTETLER, JOHN A.
"The World's War Against the Amish." *The Johns Hopkins Magazine*, XV (February, 1964), pp. 4-11.

A discussion of Amish nonconformity to the world and their self-sufficiency, and the problems for the Amish in maintaining this position. Topics of discussion include mutual aid which promotes self-sufficiency, conflicts with the state which only increase Amish separatism, and the use of the ban and shunning as a means for maintaining conformity of attitudes among the Amish. Hostetler believes the Amish have maintained a stable existence but also points to evidence of Amish disintegration. He views defections, deviation in attitudes, and suicide as forms of adjustment for individuals who cannot find fulfillment in the Amish community. Other changes in this society can be seen in the acceptance of certain modern conveniences, in the cleavages among the Amish, and in the loss of control of the family and church over the young. It is concluded that no society can maintain complete isolation or completely avoid change and that the "Amish society will thrive or perish to the degree that it can provide community and personal fulfillment for its members."

HOSTETLER, JOHN A.
"The Amish Use of Symbols and Their Function in Bounding the Community." *Royal Anthropological Institute of Great Britain and Ireland*, XIV (January-June, 1964), pp. 11-22.

"The ability of the Amish to withstand the pressures of the American scene, urbanism and technology, suggests that they use effective ways for maintaining group consciousness." One means is the use of visual symbolism in maintaining psychological boundaries. This article discusses the symbols of Amish life as manifest in dress since, as the author states, in Amish life, dress becomes highly symbolic of one's attachment to the group and of one's place within the society. The article deals with Amish grooming and dressing in some detail, noting especially its symbolic and sociological function in bounding the community. It also throws some light on the origin of Amish styles of dress "as diffusion phenomena of past cultures." Hostetler concludes that it is interesting "that a society which places emphasis on personal trustworthiness and religious devoutness should inadvertently centre its symbols in styles of clothing."

HOSTETLER, JOHN A.
"Persistence and Change Patterns in Amish Society." *Ethnology*, III (April, 1964), pp. 185-198.

Consistency of "charter," or consistency in "the system of values for the pursuit of which human beings organize," is often noted as characteristic of Amish society. This has often led to the misconception that Amish society is free from stress and personal conflicts. This paper develops five elements in the Amish charter which demonstrate a high degree of consistency. They are formulated from observation in contemporary communities, from the original documents, and from personal experience as a participating member of the culture. Also evidence is presented for sustained personal conflicts "in this seemingly remarkably compatible culture" which reveals stress patterns such as thwarted motivations for higher education, the practice of marginal occupations, the presence of suicidal behavior, and rowdyism. Finally the study shows how "persons with unresolved conflicts make meaningful contacts with outgroups by means of acculturation agents."

HOSTETLER, JOHN A.
"The Amish: Rural Communities of Love." *Fellowship*, XXXI (January, 1965), pp. 19-21.

The Amish believe they must separate from the world in order to attain eternal life. This article looks at the Amish life-style and both the external and internal pressures that attempt to change this life-style. The author concludes that "Amish society will thrive or perish to the degree that it can provide community and individual fulfillment for its members."

HOSTETLER, JOHN A.
"Amish and Hutterite Socialization: Social Structure and Contrasting Modes of Adaptation to Public Schooling." *Report on the Conference of Child Socialization*. Washington, D.C.: Health, Education and Welfare, 1969. (See annotation under Hutterite section.)

HOSTETLER, JOHN A.
"Old Order Amish Child Rearing and Schooling Practices: A Summary Report." *MQR*, XLIV (April, 1970), pp. 181-191.

The purpose of this study is to understand the life participation level of Amish schooling in the context of their own culture by examining such questions as: How do Amish children perform in the light of their own cultural goals and values? In what ways do they differ from other children in their capabilities and learning patterns? The author discards the assumption that public school children are better achievers on standardized tests than Amish children in private schools. He aslo says that Amish children are not deprived of meaningful aspirations and participation in the goals of culture. By private education the Amish have been able to stop, at least temporarily, the loss of their own identity.

HOSTETLER, JOHN A. and McKUSICK, VICTOR A.
"Genetic Studies of the Amish, a Summary and Bibliography."
MQR, XXXIX (July, 1965), pp. 223-226.

"Knowledge of hereditary conditions of which the genetic features are little known may be advanced through a study of isolated populations." The Amish are useful for certain genetic studies because they are a closed population, their origins are well known, genealogical records of them are extensive, and medical care is high. Methods of this study include several disciplines: sociology, epidemiology, genetics, and medicine. Article also presents several genetic disorders which have been discovered.

HOSTETLER, JOHN A. and MOOK, MAURICE A.
"The Amish and Their Land." *Landscape*, VI (Spring, 1957), pp. 21-29.

It is the intention of this article to present the Amish "as realistically as possible, and to treat their farming practices and manner of living matter-of-factly as another variant of modern rural America." Although the study is specifically on a group of Old Order Amish in Pennsylvania, it provides important general information on the Amish religious beliefs which permeate their economic and social life, and above all on their farming activities. It is felt that the Amish aims of "order, sufficiency, and peace" have been accomplished in their farms and homes. Their cooperation and mutual aid activities are stressed in this article as an essential aspect of the Amish effort to make their rural life as self-sufficient as possible. Also discussed are the features which distinguish the rural Amish material culture from the non-Amish such as their Swiss "bank barns," the large size of their houses, and the plainness in their house furnishings.

KRAHN, CORNELIUS
"Alte Kolonie (Old Colony)." *ME*, I, p. 76.

In 1874-80 the Mennonites from Chortitza and Fürstenland settlements established homes on the West Reserve in Manitoba. They were referred to as Altkolonier (Old Colonists). Their official name is Reinland Mennonite Church but are generally known as the Old Colony Mennonite Church. This group can be found in Manitoba, Saskatchewan, and Mexico and represents the most conservative wing of the Russo-German Mennonites.

LANDING, JAMES E.
"Geographic Models of Old Order Amish Settlements." *The Professional Geographer*, XXI (July, 1969), pp. 238-243.

The author introduces several areas of geographic study such as the structure of the Amish settlements and interaction models of

Amish settlement. There are three well defined cultural zones based on family response to change: the Zone of Innovation, the Zone of Tradition, and the Zone of Acceptance.

McKUSICK, VICTOR A.; HOSTETLER, JOHN A.; and EGELAND, JANICE A.
"Genetic Studies of the Amish: Background and Potentialities." *Bulletin of the Johns Hopkins Hospital*, CXV (September, 1964), pp. 203-222.

After a description of pertinent features such as Amish origins, growth in North America, age distribution, and Old Order Amish family names, the article discusses the usefulness of the Old Order Amish groups of the United States and Canada for some types of genetic studies. For historical reasons and because of differences in family names, partial genetic distinctiveness for the Amish is suggested.

McKUSICK, VICTOR A.; ELDRIDGE, ROSWELL; HOSTETLER, JOHN A.; RUANGWIT, UTAI; and EGELAND, JANICE A.
"Dwarfism in the Amish." *Bulletin of the Johns Hopkins Hospital*, CXVI (May, 1965), pp. 285-300.

"In the course of a study of dwarfism in the Old Order Amish two relatively frequent types were found. The Ellis-van Creveld syndrome is the most frequent 'cause' of severe dwarfism in the Amish of Lancaster County, Pennsylvania, but has not been observed in Amish living elsewhere. A second frequent type of dwarfism has been observed in Amish throughout the United States and Canada and is called 'cartilage-hair hypoplasia.' Dwarfism was selected for study because it was reported to be frequent in the Amish and because it was expected that almost complete ascertainment of cases could be achieved. By contacts with many Amish laymen and with physicians practising in Amish communities, an attempt was made to identify all cases of dwarfism in the Old Order Amish of the United States and Canada."

MESSERSCHMIDT, H. EDGAR
"Working with the Amish." *The American-German Review*, XII (August, 1946), pp. 22-24.

A simple description of the author's personal experiences working in a ring the Amish had formed for filling silos. He noted such things as a strong religious spirit manifested in their irreproachable behavior in overcoming obstacles, a genuine friendliness, and a great deal of tolerance.

NETTL, BRUNO
"The Hymns of the Amish: An Example of Marginal Survival."
Journal of American Folklore, LXX (October-December, 1957), pp.
322-328.

It is the assumption of folklore theory that members of a cultural
group who have become isolated from the greater portion of that
group often preserve certain traits of culture which have been lost
in the original habitat. The Amish serve as a useful example of
this theory of marginal survival. This article provides a brief
discussion of the style of Amish slow tunes and an analysis of the
recorded material with comparison to the published transcrip-
tions. Author interprets the Amish style as one of style which was
common in European folk hymnody in some locations and which
was abandoned in North America.

PETERS, HERBERT
"Martensville: Half-way House to Urbanization." *ML*, XXIII (October, 1968), pp. 164-168.

Martensville, Saskatchewan is a conservative society which serves
as a half-way house for those who suffered from cultural shock.
Its prevailing values are typical to that of a pioneer existence. An
Old Colony settlement which is one of four social patterns used by
Old Colony people.

REDEKOP, CALVIN
"Decision Making in a Sect." *Review of Religious Research*, II (Fall,
1960), pp. 79-86.

This paper reports on the decision-making process in a "typical
sect," the Old Colony Mennonite Church. To orient the reader,
author discusses the chief elements of a sect and the basic elements of decision-making. From the data collected through personal interviews with Old Colony Mennonites, Redekop comes up
with four dimensions of the decision-making process in sectarian
groups: principle of shock insulation; principle of efficiency;
principle of the Camel's Nose in the Tent; and the principle of
perpetuation. It is concluded that there are two assumptions
upon which the decision-making theory is based. The first is the
development of a dichotomy—"a black-and-white world"—and
the second is the emergence and transformation of the sect.

REDEKOP, CALVIN
"The Old Colony: An Analysis of Group Survival." *MQR*, XL (July,
1966), pp. 190-211.

Article briefly presents the basic traits of the Old Colony Mennonites and their problems of survival. These Mennonites represent
the most conservative element of Russian Mennonitism and are
shown to be an ethnic minority which has been, throughout
its history, a self-contained entity. This entity consists of a relatively homogeneous genetic collective, a geographically isolated
society, and sub-society which is culturally unique.

REDEKOP, CALVIN and LOOMIS, CHARLES P.
"The Development of Status-Roles in the Systematic Linkage Process." *Journal of Human Relations*, VIII (April, 1960), pp. 276-283.

Following migration from Canada, the emergence of new status-
roles has allowed the Old Colony Mennonite sect in Chihuahua,
Mexico to maintain its unique way of life, while permitting a
certain amount of systematic linkage with the Mexican society.
Eleven of these status-roles are examined in this article. Most of
these linkages relate to the economic and other external patterns
of the two social systems. The Old Colony group feels that any
amount of contact with Mexican citizens will mean changes in and
loss of beliefs and other practices. The emerging linkages via
special-status-roles seem to regulate both the nature and the
amount of interaction between people of both systems. The Old
Colony Mennonites in the Municipio of Cuauhtemoc, Chihuahua, Mexico, offer rich material for studying the articulation of
two social systems. This paper attempts to illustrate the concept
"systemic linkage," in the relations between the native Mexican
social system and the Old Colony social system. One element of
the social system "status-role," has been chosen to present the
case.

SAUDER, DOROTHY
"Sesquicentennial of Amish Settlement in Ontario." *ML*, XXVII
(September, 1972), pp. 91-92.

A brief outline of the history, settlements, and present state of the
Amish in Ontario. Author indicated how the more progressive
Mennonite conference has made many contributions to community development while a small number of Old Order Amish, who
have survived because of their isolationism, still adhere to sixteenth century tradition and shun all modernity. She also states
that a few divisions over the years "give credence to the
Amishman's reputation for individualism."

SAWATZKY, LEONARD
"Colony Leaders Must Realize that Present Trends Lead to Disaster." *The Canadian Mennonite*, XIV (March 29, 1966), pp. 20-21 and
23.

Main interest in this article is the Canadian farmers in Mexico
who represent three branches of the Mennonite faith—the Alt-

kolonier, Sommerfelder, and Kleine Gemeinde. Author describes their motivations for leaving Canada and their adaptation to their new environment. The survival of the colonies is seen as revolving around a reversal of the processes of cultural and resource attrition.

SCHREIBER, WILLIAM I.
"Amish Wedding Days." *Journal of American Folklife*, LXXIII (January-March, 1960), pp. 12-17.

This article is an explanation of the rigid adherence by the Amish to the practice of holding weddings only in the fall and winter and only on Tuesdays and Thursdays. Although practicality explains why weddings are most advantageous in fall and winter, this is not necessarily the complete explanation for the strict adherence to only two possible days. In fact, the writer states, the Amish, by adhering to this wedding tradition, have preserved ancient pagan cults which predate the Christian era.

SCHREIBER, WILLIAM I.
"The Hymns of the Amish Ausbund in Philological and Literary Perspective." *MQR*, XXXCI (January, 1962), pp. 36-60.

This article is an analysis of the Amish Ausbund, the standard hymnbook used in the Old Order Amish services. Author states that "the Amish are the only Anabaptist group which adheres faithfully to these songs written during the centuries of their greatest struggle for existence." In the final analysis of the various hymns, the author concludes that, although the Ausbund has preserved the sixteenth-century language better than any other Anabaptist texts in use in the twentieth century, it is also a remarkable admixture of Amish dialect and High German.

SHANER, RICHARD H.
"The Amish Barn Dance." *Pennsylvania Folklife*, XIII (Winter, 1962-1963), pp. 24-26.

A description of a social event considered by the Amish to be the major social activity of the youth. Author considers the problems faced by the host of the barn dance, and examines the type of dancing which takes place at these events.

STAEBLER, EDNA
"Why the Amish Want No Part of Progress." *Macleans Magazine*, September 27, 1958, pp. 20-21, 50-56.

This is a popular, descriptive account of the Old Order Amish in Ontario's Waterloo and Perth Counties who, the writer states, are primarily concerned with "their faith, their family, and their prosperous farms." Brief descriptions are made of their style of clothing, the Amish church service, the hymns of martyrdom in the Ausbund, courtship, brotherhood, and the persecution that the Amish of the past suffered. It is felt that despite the rigid austerity of these Old Order Amish, they enjoy fun and games.

STOLL, JOSEPH (ED.)
The Challenge of the Child; Selections from "The Blackboard Bulletin," 1957-1966. Aylmer, Ontario: Pathway Publishing Corporation, 1967, 272 pp.

The growing number of Amish schools has made some means of communication necessary between the teacher and the home. This series of articles presents a look at the reasons for church schools, the influence of the home on the child, and the teacher's role towards the child and the parent. The Amish today see such things as language, government, and church taking on worldwide proportions and they view this as a threat to their isolated way of life. In order to protect their children from worldly corruption, and to teach them to resist evil, the Amish have provided church schools.

THOMAS, BILL
"Among the Amish, Yesterday is Today." *TWA Ambassador*, III (October, 1970), pp. 8-12.

Article gives a summary of the Amish life-style and beliefs. They are presented as a very simple, frugal, and nonconformist group of people. Author also sees them in constant conflict with the surrounding culture.

TORTORA, VINCENT R.
"Amish at Play." *The Pennsylvania Dutchman*, VIII (Summer-Fall, 1957), pp. 14-34.

To the outsider the Amish often appear to be a very somber people because of their dress, surroundings, and living conditions. Tortora shows the reader another side of Amish life, their social relationships. He describes many of the games and activities which are common among the Amish, such as botching, "morsch balle," "blumstock," and singings.

TORTORA, VINCENT R.
"Courtship and Wedding Practices of the Old Order Amish." *Pennsylvania Folklife*, IX (Spring, 1958), pp. 12-21.

A descriptive, pictorial account of a "typical" Old Order Amish wedding, to which the author was invited. The Amish courtship, honeymoon, and collection of wedding gifts are described.

TORTORA, VINCENT R.
"The Get-Togethers of the Young Amish Folk." *Pennsylvania Folklife*, IX (Spring, 1960), pp. 17-21.

A simple description of a Sunday evening "singing," a time when the Amish youth get together for an evening of singing and courting.

TORTORA, VINCENT R.

"The Amish in Their One-Room Schoolhouses." *Pennsylvania Folklife*, XI (Fall, 1960), pp. 42-46.

A pictorial account of an average one-room schoolhouse and a typical school day. Author also touches briefly on the Amish views of education and of teachers, as well as the role the school plays in young Amish life.

TORTORA, VINCENT R.

"Amish Funerals." *Pennsylvania Folklife*, XII (Summer, 1961), pp. 8-13.

A pictorial description of present day Amish funeral practices which have been derived from half a millennium of tradition and custom. Author examines the impact on the Amish community when one of its members dies. The activities of each day, from the time of death until the time of burial, are also described.

TORTORA, VINCENT R.

"Amish Barn Raisings." *Pennsylvania Folklife*, XII (Fall, 1961), pp. 14-19.

A pictorial account of an Amish barn raising. Reasons for maintaining this custom are discussed. For example, the author states that it seems to embody in its essence much of what these pious people believe about religion and ethics especially mutual aid in a Christian brotherhood.

UMBLE, JOHN

"The Old Order Amish, Their Hymns and Hymn Tunes." *Journal of American Folklore*, LII (January-March, 1939), pp. 82-95.

This study of the hymns and hymn tunes of the Old Order Amish begins with a description of Old Order Amish church services. The major section of the article deals with the Amish hymnal, the Ausbund, and considers the origins, pattern, and subject matter of the hymns in the Ausbund. The interest of the folklorist in the Amish is particularly emphasized. This is for several reasons: the Amish have preserved a simple sixteenth century German peasant tradition; they use the sixteenth century German hymnal, containing hymns composed by their martyr forefathers in the best sixteenth century German folk-poetry tradition; and they still sing those hymns to the same tunes to which their Swiss Brethren forebears sang them over four centuries ago.

WENGER, J. C.
"Old Order Mennonites." *ME*, IV, pp. 47-49.

Account of a conservative Mennonite group who maintain the "Old Order" customs of worship and church life. The schisms which divided the Mennonites are mentioned in detail. Old Order Mennonites are strongest in Waterloo County, Ontario.

WITTMER, JOE
"Homogeneity of Personality Characteristics: A Comparison of Old Order Amish and Non-Amish." *American Anthropologist*, LXXII (October, 1970), pp. 1063-1068.

"The purpose of this study was to compare the variability of measured personality characteristics of twenty-five Amish and twenty-five non-Amish male youth between the ages of eighteen and twenty-one, from the same community. This study assumed that the homogeneous nature of the Amish culture would predetermine greater similarity of personality among the Amish youth. The findings indicate that the aspect of personality similarity was significantly greater for the Amish group on nine of sixteen measures of personality. The findings are discussed in light of Amish culture."

WITTMER, JOE
"The Amish Schools Today." *School and Society*, XCIX (April, 1971), pp. 227-230.

This article is concerned with the threatening nature of modern education upon the Old Order Amish sect's values and way of life. It outlines the reasons for Amish opposition to the public school system and explains that only recently have the Amish grown opposed to the elementary schools. Attempts to develop their own schools ran into conflict with the state because of the Amish desire to employ their eighth grade graduate teachers. One Amish school system which has been accepted in Indiana by the state educational authorities is described in detail. Agreement was reached on a test to qualify teachers and on a vocational division for those passing grade eight but not sixteen. Author favours this type of school since it helps the Amish maintain their integrity and uniqueness as a minority group.

D. Unpublished Sources

GINGERICH, ORLAND
"The Difference Between Drift and Change." Unpublished paper.
Amish Mennonite Western Ontario Conference, 1961 (Conrad
Grebel College Archives.)

The church has always been affected by the environment and,
therefore, change. Author outlines several changes that have
occurred among Amish Mennonites such as the change from the
German to English language, from church in homes to large
church buildings, from horse and buggy to luxurious automobiles, etc. Author then attempts to distinguish between simple changes and drift. Drift is defined not only as changing with
each current fashion, but also with following the fashions of a past
generation. For example some Old Order Brethren are nonconformist in appearance but not in attitude. Author says that the
Mennonite Church in general is very drift-conscious and suggests
this can be avoided by not being afraid of change: and by distinguishing between principle and application.

HUNTINGTON, GERTRUDE ENDERS
"Age Grading and Socialization Patterns in the Traditional Amish
Culture." Unpublished paper delivered at the Conference on Child
Socialization, Philadelphia: Temple University, 1969.

A discussion of socialization patterns in the traditional Amish
community. Author begins by making some generalizations
about the Amish and by comparing the traditional and emergent
Amish families. She states that "socialization cannot be divorced
from the religious concepts that structure the Amish view of
human nature." The second part of the paper describes the six
socialization stages of the Amish which does not stop at adulthood
but which continues throughout the life of the individual. Huntington concludes that "in spite of pressures from the outside
world, the Amish have continued to show remarkable success in
socializing their children. The Amish have reacted vigorously
and imaginatively when the outside world threatened the true
education of their children."

LEWIS, RUSSELL
See annotation of article in Hutterite unpublished sources.

STOLL, JOSEPH
"Recent Amish Immigration to Ontario." Unpublished manuscript
(available in the Archives at Conrad Grebel College), October, 1966.

In 1964 the Ontario Amish had a population of 1,000 with 141
families. This article describes the seven new Amish settlements

in Ontario, their background, reasons for coming to Canada, and family names. These seven churches, which have much in common, represent the larger group of Amish found in the U.S.A. An appendix follows which presents the statistics for each individual settlement.

YODER, MARVIN
"A Study of Family Characteristics of Old Order Amish, Conservative, and Mennonite Families." Unpublished paper, Goshen College, 1961.

"The problem of the study is whether variations in certain aspects of family inter-personal relations and socialization processes are associated with variations in religious conservatism, that is between Old Order Amish, Conservative Mennonites and 'Progressive Mennonite Families.'" The problem is considered by testing the following: the quality of the marital relationship; the quality of the child-parent relationship; the quality of the child-peer relationship; and the personality traits of the child. Some of the hypotheses tested are: the Old Order Amish are more traditional in family type than the conservatives; the quality of the child-parent relationships is better in the progressive group than in the other two; the success with which the child relates to his peers is greater in progressive families than in conservative families, and both of these groups evidence greater success than the Old Order Amish; and the quality of the husband-wife relationship is greater in the conservative families and lower in the Old Order Amish.

Index

Name Index

Subject Index

Erratum

On p. viii the grant that made publication of this book possible was credited to the Humanities Research Council of Canada, using funds provided by the Canada Council, whereas the grant was made by the Social Science Federation of Canada, using funds provided by the Canada Council.